One Green Hill
Journeys through Irish Songs

John McLaughlin

First published 2003
by
Beyond the Pale
BTP Publications Ltd
Unit 2.1.2 Conway Mill
5-7 Conway Street
Belfast BT13 2DE

Tel: +44 (0)28 90 438630
Fax: +44 (0)28 90 439707
E-mail: office@btpale.com
Website: http://www.btpale.com

British Library Cataloguing-in-Publication Data.
A catalogue record for this book is available from the British Library.

ISBN 1-900960-21-4

Printed in Dublin by Colour Books Ltd.

Cover illustration: Eamonn O'Doherty's sculpture near the Three Rocks, Forth
Mountain, Co. Wexford. Photo: Avril Green.

Cover map: reproduced by permission of the Ordnance Survey of Northern
Ireland © Crown copyright 2003. Permit no 30035.

Portrait of Henry Joy McCracken (p.76) by Sarah Cecilia Harrison (1863-1914)
reproduced with the kind permission of the Trustees of the National Museums and
Galeries of Northern Ireland.

Photograph of Florence Wilson (p.108) reproduced with the kind permission of
Fred Heatley and of the Trustees of the National Museums and Galeries of
Northern Ireland.

Photograph of 'Hackler at work' (p.158) reproduced with the kind permission of
the Green Collection and the Trustees of the National Museums and Galeries of
Northern Ireland.

Dedicated to the memories of
Robert McCormack
and
Eddie McLaughlin

'Blame not the bard'
Thomas Moore
Irish Melodies (1808)

'To thoroughly appreciate the history of this or any country it is
necessary to sympathise with all parties.'
A.G. Richey
A Short History of the Irish People (1869)

Acknowledgments

I would like to record my appreciation to everyone who helped in the production of this book, especially those who have provided information. In particular I wish to thank, in alphabetical order, the following librarians for their patience, persistence and professionalism: Pat Browne (Friends' School Lisburn), Eileen Burgess (Letterkenny), Rory Gallagher (Letterkenny), Linda Greenwood (Belfast City), Gerry Healy (Belfast Linen Hall), Mike Maguire (Limerick), Frances O'Gorman (Clare), Noreen O'Neill (Limerick) and Noreen O'Sullivan (Cahersiveen). Thanks also to the staffs of Ballymena Library, Ballynahinch Library, Queen's University Library, Belfast, the National Library of Ireland, Dublin, the Mitchell Library, Glasgow and the Irish Traditional Music Association, Dublin.

I would also like to record my gratitude to Fionnuala Williams at the Institute of Irish Studies, Queen's University: for exchanging with me the information relating to Florence Wilson. To Helen Meehan of Mountcharles: for generously sharing the results of her research on Ethna Carbery and Seumas MacManus. To Anthony McGinley of Donegal: for recounting to me his memories of *The Drumboe Martyrs*. To John Moylan of Ardrahan: for detailed local history of his part of Galway. Thanks also to Bobby Eaglesham and Tom Hickland for their recollections of Five Hand Reel's recording of *The Man From God Knows Where*.

Major thanks to Bill Rolston at Beyond the Pale Publications: for advice in general, for editorial hints, for patience, courtesy and for having faith in the project since the early days.

Special personal thanks to my family: to my brothers Brian and Daniel in Donegal, for keeping me in touch with Irish ways and Irish laws. To my brother Eddie in Paisley, who sadly died before publication, for sharing his love of the songs with me and for his spirited renditions of them. To my two girls Carol and Gillian for ever-loyal, if at times somewhat bemused encouragement. Finally, inestimable thanks to my very Scottish wife Jan Douglas, for putting up with me during the last five years of my obsessive involvement in All-Things-Irish and for putting up with me for thirty 'normal' years before that.

Table of Contents

Contexts:
From Green Hill to Green Hollow

The legends and songs of Ireland have been imprinted on me for as long as I can remember. I was born on a Donegal hillside and to soak up the atmosphere had only to stand at the front door, look around me and listen to the old people talking. As a young child, stories from Irish history became part of me. I scanned Lough Foyle, fearful of the marauding Vikings that I'd heard about. Later I discovered they had bequeathed my family name of *Lochlainn* to Donegal more than a thousand years ago. In 812 AD they sailed up the Lough for the first time and burned Derry. They sacked the monastery, massacred the monks and plundered their treasures. Eight hundred years on came new invaders, the English, who later became the British. Unlike the Vikings they stayed; they were stronger and they became rulers of Donegal and more. They didn't burn Derry; instead they built walls round it, gave it a new name and the consequences are still with us.

The written story of these events fills libraries and keeps historians busy. Often though it has been the songs that have kept the stories alive. Though fiercely partisan and usually downright biased they are nevertheless the repositories and touchstones of tradition, both reflecting and influencing politics and history. I have tried to get at what Thomas Davis called the 'gem-like history' contained in the songs: respecting the traditions, but weeding out much of the bias, trying to separate the real story from legend, myth and propaganda.

The simple solutions suggested in the songs – on the one hand 'drive the British into the sea', on the other 'croppies lie down' – are no longer viable. The old songs though won't simply be abandoned for they are too integral a part of both Catholic and Protestant history and culture, etched into our being in the cradle and in the cradles of our ancestors. However by looking at them afresh, in context and appreciating that the participants on both sides were mere victims of the chance and circumstance of history, it's my hope, however vain, that both traditions may be able to view the other with just a little more tolerance and appreciation. After four hundred years of rivalry, conflict and misunderstanding it will be a long, slow and difficult road.

I was born in the Inishowen Peninsula, overlooking Lough Foyle, about ten miles north of Derry. On the other side of the Lough was County Derry, which I discovered was in the 'black North'. Both Derry City and Magilligan Point at the mouth of the Foyle, later to be used as a political prison, were visible from our cottage on Crockglass, 'green hill'. At that time I couldn't understand why the land a couple of miles across the water was in a foreign country. I do now, though I have never quite managed to square the circle of looking south from 'southern' Ireland towards Northern Ireland.

At the age of eight my family moved to Glasgow, coincidentally derived from the Gaelic, *Glaschu*, 'green hollow'. The 'Scotch Boat' had transported us a mere hundred miles as the crow flies but socially and culturally we had come a long way. From a primitive rural cottage, without electricity or running water, in an 'old fashioned', conservative, Catholic country to a city tenement block with electricity, cold *and* hot water, in a 'modern', Protestant country. For the first couple of years I was a bit of an innocent abroad but gradually I learned the necessary lessons.

One day Sandra, the girl next-door, asked me, 'Who do you support?' I was stumped; Scottish sophistication had again triumphed over Irish ignorance! 'Whit dae ye mean?' I shamefacedly replied, though secretly pleased that at least I was making inroads with the Glasgow accent. 'What football team do you support, Rangers or Celtic?' I knew nothing about that kind of football, soccer, or about 'supporting' and could only lamely reply 'I don't know'. 'You're a Catholic, so you must support Celtic,' said Sandra. Thus did I learn the most fundamental lesson of working class Glasgow culture. I became a Celtic supporter, because I was a Catholic.

It was 1953 and by the time I started secondary school, high school, four years later, I had lost my Irish accent, forgotten any Gaelic that I had learned and had become an enthusiastic soccer player. I had also become a regular in the Celtic End at 'Parkhead', Celtic Park, the home of Celtic Football Club, the greatest team in the world, ever! The team was going through a bad spell at the time, not having won a trophy for years, but to me that didn't really matter, I was just happy to be with 'my own kind'. I accepted the identity thrust upon me by historical and cultural forces beyond my ken and found it very consoling to stand on the terracing and sing *A Soldier's Song*, the first time that I had heard the *Irish National Anthem*. Then came *Sean South of Garryowen*, *The Merry Ploughboy*, even *Faith of Our Fathers* and *Hail Glorious Saint Patrick*, for in those days Celtic supporters went to Mass on Sundays. The greatest excitement came in matches against 'the enemy', Rangers, the Protestant team. On a Saturday afternoon their supporters became members of a contemptible sub-species of 'Orange bastards', 'animals' and 'Huns', to use some of the milder terms of endearment. Of course they cursed us in equal measure with similar epithets, with the adjective 'Fenian' often thrown in for good measure. Ironically it was the first time that I had heard of the Fenians. After giving vent to their inherited mutual hatreds, often to the accompaniment of glasses, bottles and urine-laden beer cans hurtling in the direction of the 'enemy', on Monday mornings the supporters of both teams went back to working quite amicably beside each other in the offices, shops, factories and shipyards of the West of Scotland.

And so the education of the Irish boy in Glasgow continued. After completion of secondary school I started work as a librarian at the Mitchell Library, Glasgow's central public reference library. On the staff were a few beatniks and folkniks who played in the folk group Clutha (Clyde) and they introduced me to the joys of traditional music. I began to devour the big folksong books in the Music Department. I learned about Professor Francis Child and the classic Scottish and English ballads, Gavin Greig and the folksongs of the northeast, John Ord and the bothy ballads of the 'ploughboy laddies'. The books also carried me across the Atlantic where I discovered American songs of protest: the Wobblies, Joe Hill, Pete Seeger, Ramblin Jack Elliott, Cisco Houston and Woody Guthrie.

All the while, though, I was still listening to Irish music, especially rebel songs. I acquired my first record player in 1960 and learned most of the standard rebel songs from the recordings of people like Willie Brady, Teresa Duffy, Josh McCrae and Enoch Kent. The first single I bought was *Kevin Barry* sung by Lonnie Donegan. I came across it by accident in a music shop in Maryhill Road and hurried it home under plain cover before one of the 'enemy' spotted it! The song almost reduced me to tears of rage but the 'B' side had equal impact; it was called *My Lagan Love*. I was fourteen years old and although it was all a bit above my head, too adult and mysterious, there was something about the song that stirred my youthful imagination. I had no idea where the Lagan was and I assumed that the song was centuries old rather than written by a man who had died just one year before I was born. I could never have imagined that one day I might follow in the author's footsteps by the banks of the Lagan itself. If I still didn't have that old record, on the Pye label, sitting in my attic to this day I would probably think that I had imagined the whole thing.

By now however I was also coming into contact with the unionist and Orange songs of the majority population. I had Protestant friends who would go along to the football on a Saturday afternoon, cheer on their team and sing their people's songs, like *Derry's Walls*, etc. I would go along and cheer on my team, and sing my people's songs, like *Sean South of Garryowen*, etc. In the evening we would meet up in the Avalon Bar or the Ritz at Charing Cross. After Old Firm games (Celtic versus Rangers), discussion of football and the singing of 'sectarian' songs were strictly off the agenda. After a few pints we might enjoy a few choruses but it would be the unifying songs of Bob Dylan, like *Blowin in the Wind* or *Chimes of Freedom*. Sometimes at parties, where both Catholics and Protestants knew each other well, we might safely fit in a couple of controversial songs and if I got the chance I enjoyed nothing better than singing *Derry's Walls* and *The Green Grassy Slopes of the Boyne*, often to the annoyance of my 'co-religionists'. To me these were essentially Irish folksongs, with deep roots and strong foundations. This book is dedicated to the memory of one of those Protestant friends.

Following a fortuitously early retirement I finally had the opportunity to pursue and to purge my musical obsessions. Over the years I had travelled on four continents but I knew little about Ireland other than the little corner of Donegal where I was born and regularly revisited. Now I began to study the map of the old country and was amazed at how many of the place names just jumped off the page at me. Although I knew very little about them, I recognised most of them by a line from one song or another. I started listening to the old songs again, more closely now; I started to look at the travel guides for information on the places and I started to look at the history books for the story behind the songs. Initially I had well over a hundred songs, covering every corner of the country, and at this stage the project was as much about geography as history. Gradually the history began to take over and slowly the idea developed of choosing songs that would contribute towards a very basic outline history of Ireland that might encourage the reader or listener to delve deeper. The geographical element has survived in my fascination with the origins of Irish place names and I have attempted to give a translation and meaning for every place name mentioned in each of the main songs featured. I have also tried to give the precise locations of all of the smaller place names for those who may want to visit the sites.

Gradually I covered the distance: geographical, historical, political, cultural and emotional, from the Peace Line in Belfast to the birthplace and the death place of Sean South. From atop Cave Hill to Dolly's Brae, from Derry's Walls to Tipperary so far away. From the site of the Portadown massacre in 1641 to the scene of ruthless political executions in Killaloe and Drumboe two hundred and eighty years later. From a famine graveyard at Carndonagh where I was born, to the graves of Archibald Warwick, Florence Wilson and Thomas Russell. From a famine graveyard at Drumshanbo in lovely Leitrim to the final resting places of Wolfe Tone, Henry Joy McCracken, John Kelly and Father John Murphy. From Toome on the Bann to Boolavogue and Killanne, to The Harrow, Enniscorthy and Slaney's red waves.

After half a dozen trips, about three and a half thousand miles on the clock, thirty counties under my seatbelt, Kerry and Mayo being the exceptions, I felt that I understood my homeland a little better. My belated journeys in time and space around the country where I was born were always illuminating and enriching, often pleasurable but far too often painful. The songs that led me there had haunted me for more than forty years. Finally I was able to lay their ghosts to rest.

Sir John Temple's propaganda on the 1641 rising

1.

Outlaw Rapparee

My spurs are rusted, my coat is rent, my plume is dank with rain
And the thistledown and the barley beard are thick on my horse's mane,
But my rifle's as bright as my sweetheart's eye, my arm is strong and free
So what care have I for your King and laws, I'm an outlaw rapparee.

Chorus
Lift your glasses, friends with mine and give your hand to me.
I'm Ireland's friend, I'm England's foe, I'm an outlaw rapparee,
I'm an outlaw rapparee.

The mountain cavern is my home, high up in the crystal air,
My bed the limestone, iron-ribbed and the brown heath scented fair.
Let George or William boldly send his troops to burn and loot,
We'll meet them upon the equal ground and fight till we drive them out.

[Chorus]

Hunted from out of our fathers' home, pursued with steel and shot,
Swift is the warfare we must wage or the gibbet be our lot.
Hurrah! The war is welcome work, for the hunted outlaw knows
He steps up to his country's cause o'er the corpses of her foes

[Chorus]

Outlaw Rapparee
The Plantation of Ulster, the First Rebels, Oliver Cromwell

This introductory song may not be numbered with Ireland's greatest but it illustrates well enough the conflicting historical traditions that have been central to Irish life for the past four centuries. On the one hand is the displaced Gaelic-speaking Catholic native, always resentful and often rebellious. On the other hand is the powerful newcomer, the suspicious and guarded English-speaking Protestant settler, often from lowland Scotland and the Borders.

Outlaw Rapparee, a traditional song of uncertain origin, makes no concessions to the subtleties and complexities of Irish history. Nevertheless it can serve as a useful starting point in attempting to untangle the complex web of historical circumstances that have resulted in centuries of discord and in almost four thousand people being killed during the most recent 'Troubles'. The story behind this sorry statistic has in essence been a timeless rivalry revolving around territory, religion, language, conflicting cultures and intolerance.

The chief Ulster planter was Arthur Chichester (1563-1625), a commoner from Devon. He became ruler of Belfast and owner of Donegal's entire Inishowen Peninsula. By the 18th century his now titled family, the Donegalls, were the biggest landowners in Ireland. The cautious Chichester had advocated a gradualist approach but after the defeat of Cahir O'Doherty's revolt in Donegal in 1608, the policies of Sir James Ley and Sir John Davies prevailed and rapid, large-scale plantation was well under way by 1609.

The motives of King James I were many and varied but included political aggrandisement, economic opportunity, and the elimination of Ireland as a base for an invasion of England by rival foreign powers. Coincidentally, it also allowed for the introduction of the 'true' religion and 'culture' to a 'superstitious' and 'barbarian' people. The concept of 'different but equal' lay several centuries in the future. The settlers quickly built fortified towns, Derry being the best example, and bawns, bulwarked enclosures, from the Irish *badhun*, to protect their homes from the displaced Catholic natives, some ten thousand of whom now became outlaws or rapparees, derived from the Irish *rapaire*, a short rapier or pike. The name came into vogue towards the end of the Williamite Wars (1691), earlier names for these rebels being kerne (*ceithearn*) 'trooper', and tory (*tórai*) 'raider'. (In England, 'Tory' was applied disparagingly to what later became the Conservative Party.)

These outlaws never posed a military threat at national level but locally they caused considerable disruption as they hit back at their conquerors and evictors with all the savage fury of desperation. For around a hundred years they provided the main resistance to colonisation, confiscation, expulsion and to the subjugation of Catholicism and Gaelic culture. In the 18th century they evolved through the Whiteboys into the Defenders and Ribbonmen, the forerunners of modern republican organisations.

Despite the threat posed by the rapparees, the Protestant settlers had invested too much in their Irish venture to be deterred. They were determined to hold on to their newly acquired assets, as a land agent's letter to London in 1615 makes clear:

> There were never soe many kernes out in the woodes as now... so that men can travel no way neare anie woodes without great danger... divers robberies and some murders have been committed... on tuisdaye last a companie of rebels entered into an Englishman's home six miles on the side of Derry... they wounded the man verie sorre... and took eight pound in money and all the rest of the goods that were worth carrying... these mischiefes and miseries cause us to continually stand upon our guard... send over some more armes... musketts, powder and bullets.

The Englishman above was in fact fortunate to have escaped with his life, it being the normal rapparee custom to mutilate and then decapitate their victims. Equally no one raised an eyebrow, let alone asked questions in parliament, if government forces burned Catholic homes and massacred the inhabitants as they routinely did.

The names of some individual rapparees have survived in fact and legend. The best known is the displaced County Down 'nobleman' Redmond O'Hanlon (1640-81) from Aghanttaraghan, near Poyntzpass. For five or six years O'Hanlon led a 'pack of insolent bloudy outlaws' so powerful that they exercised 'a kind of separate sovereignty in three or four counties'. This however was government language and O'Hanlon, though undoubtedly ruthless and motivated more by self-preservation than patriotism, would have had plenty of sympathisers among the Catholic natives.

After his men murdered Henry St John, who lived on the O'Hanlon's confiscated property at Tandragee, O'Hanlon's existence became precarious and in desperation he sued for peace. In a letter to the Bishop of Clogher in 1680 he offered to surrender and in return for mercy offered 'to banish and apprehend and behead all other tories within them counties [Down and Monaghan]'. By now, however, Redmond was in no position to bargain. The offer was ignored and on 25 April 1681 he was murdered by his foster brother Art O'Hanlon, who claimed the reward of £200. He is buried in Relicarn Graveyard at Balinabeck near Tandragee. The only commemorative song traced is P.J. McCall's *Ballad of Redmond O'Hanlon* (1899).

> A shepherd that lived on Slieve Gullion
> Came down to the County Tyrone
> And told us how Redmond O'Hanlon
> Won't leave the rich Saxon alone.
> He rides over moorland and mountain
> By night, till a stranger is found,
> Saying, 'Take your own choice to be lodging
> Right over or under the ground!'

Possibly the most genuine of all the rapparees was Dudley Costello (c. 1620-67), 'the Scourge of Mayo'. His ancestral lands lay in the Barony of Costello, bordering in the north with Sligo and in the east with Roscommon. He had fought under Owen Roe O'Neill at Benburb in 1646 and, after a last stand on Inishbofin Island, had been forced to flee to Spain during the Cromwellian suppression. After the Restoration in 1660, he returned to Ireland in the vain hope of recovering his title and lands. Disappointed, he turned instead to raiding the new British landowners in five or six counties before being finally killed in a skirmish on the River Moy. His severed head was taken all the way to Dublin, a backhanded compliment, and displayed on St James's Gate, facing west towards Mayo. He is commemorated in *Lament for Dudley Costello*, the first verse of which is:

> On the sweet Moy's banks at Tumgesh Ford
> Where wild free garlands grow
> A lonely oak still guards the spot
> Where they shot brave Costello.
> As he approached the river wide,
> Framed in the setting sun,
> By a ball laid low so long ago
> From Captain Dillon's gun.

Another verifiable rapparee was Eamonn Ó Riain, Edmund Ryan, (1670-1724) from Atshanbohy, near Upperchurch in County Tipperary. A 'failed priest' and accomplished poet, he is immortalised as *Eamonnn a Chnoic (Ned of the Hill)*.

> I am long outside in snow and frost,
> Not daring to approach my home.
> My horse team still tied,
> My fallow field unsown,
> I no longer have them all,
> Nor friends, alas, to harbour me,
> I have no kindred and must go over the sea.

His family had been dispossessed following the second Desmond rebellion (1579-83) and a hundred years later resentment still ran deep. Ryan became a rapparee after shooting a tax collector dead during a quarrel over the confiscation of a poor woman's only cow. He was prominent in the Ballyneety Raid in 1690 and also fought at the Siege of Limerick and at the Battle of Aughrim the following year. He was never to make it 'over the sea' as he was murdered by a relative, beheaded while asleep, like Redmond O'Hanlon for 'blood money', a reward of £200. A memorial marks the spot where he is buried at Curraheen, near Hollyford, Tipperary.

The most successful rapparees, both in terms of financial gain and physical survival, were the Brennan brothers, James and Patrick, from the townland of Croghtenclogh in Kilkenny. After amassing a fortune, millionaires by present-day standards, with the 'tory hunters' closing in on them, they fled to Chester in Lancashire. After only a few months they were recognised, captured and incarcerated in Chester Gaol. However they managed to escape almost immediately and make it back to Ireland, using their wealth to smooth and bribe the way. In 1687 they finally accepted terms, turning over a proportion of their plunder and joining the ranks of the Jacobite rebels.

Others well-known rapparees included: 'Big' Charles Caragher (South Armagh), Shane Crossagh ('The Derry Outlaw'), William Crotty (Waterford), James Freney (Kilkenny), Jeremiah Grant (Tipperary), 'Galloping' Dan Hogan (Tipperary), Richard Power (Cork) and of course 'young Willie Brennan' of north Cork, hanged in 1812 and immortalised as *Brennan on the Moor*. By this time the rapparees had descended into common criminality though some still enjoyed a Robin Hood image, an attitude well illustrated by a verse from *Brennan on the Moor*:

> A brace of loaded pistols he carried night and day
> But he never robbed an honest man upon the King's highway.

> What he'd taken from the rich, like Turpin on Black Bess,
> He always did divide it with the poor folk in distress.

After the Ulster Plantation Catholics in general lived in much reduced circumstances as well as in fear and suspicion of an increasingly fundamentalist, puritan English parliament. In 1641 therefore the Catholics of Ulster staged a revolt led by Gaelic gentry such as Sir Phelim O'Neill (1605-53) and Owen Roe O'Neill (1582-1649). The revolt was about Catholic grievances, not independence, and the rebels always declared their loyalty to the King of England.

In the early stages Catholic attacks were of a strategic nature, but as the Protestant settlers banded together in resistance, atrocities, sectarian by definition, became commonplace. Also in the initial stages the rebels distinguished between the Scottish and the English settlers, with the Scots, although Presbyterian, regarded as brother Gaels.

However the distinction didn't last for long and many Protestant settlers, including the Scots, were killed or thrown off the land. Eventually the struggle developed into the Confederate Wars, with the whole country involved, plus the Pope through his representative Rinuccini. Although the rebels proclaimed their loyalty to Charles I, what had begun as a controlled political coup soon became a 'holy war'. The leaders of the rising lost control of their peasant followers as the resentments and rivalries of the previous thirty years boiled over and the Rising degenerated into bloodlust. The truth about the various massacres is now probably beyond even the most objective and determined of historians. However the coincidence of evidence contained in the 'Depositions', some thirty-four volumes of sworn statements taken from Protestant survivors in an effort to settle compensation claims for lost land and property, is often seen as convincing that massacres by Catholics took place on a considerable scale.

Of course no one bothered to record Catholic grievances and as ever in politics, exaggeration and propaganda were exerted to the full. One such early work, dated 1642, and attributed to 'G.S. — Minister of God's Word in Ireland' was entitled,

> Declaration of the barbarous and inhumane dealings of the Northerne Irish rebels and many others in severall counties uprising against the English that dwelt both lovingly and securely among them. Written to excite the English nation, to relieve our poore wives and children that have escaped the rebels savage cruelties, and that shall arrive safe among them in England; And in exchange to send aid of men and meanes forthwith to quell their boundlesse insolencies with certaine encouragements to the work.

An illustration from the above, showing babies being pitchforked into the water, was captioned,

> Companys of the rebells meeting with the English flying for their lives, falling downe before them cryinge for mercy, thrust their pitchforks into their childrens bellyes & threw them into the water.

Sir John Temple's book *True Impartial History of the Irish Rebellion* (1644) is now generally accepted as being crude propaganda, with many illustrations of supposed Catholic atrocities being taken straight from a similar book on the Thirty Years War in Europe. Another key piece of virulent anti-Catholic propaganda was the *Remonstrance* of Henry Jones (1605-82), the Anglican Bishop of Clogher. At the time of writing, such works received much credence, with Oliver Cromwell who was deeply religious, probably accepting them as fact. He was determined to redress the balance, to ensure that it never happened again, leading to the introduction of anti-Catholic policies that were later to develop into the Penal Laws.

The best remembered atrocity is the massacre of Protestants at Portadown in November 1641 when between eighty and three hundred and eighty from the area around Loughall and Kilmore were forced into the River Bann and drowned. To this day, members of Portadown Loyal Orange Lodge No. 273 still carry banners depicting the massacre in their town. This is very unusual as most LOLs mainly celebrate the later triumphs at Derry, Enniskillen, the Boyne and Aughrim. This can therefore be safely taken as an indication of the impact of the Portadown massacre on the Protestant psyche.

Inevitably though the atrocities were a two-way process. In 1601 Arthur Chichester wrote, 'I burned all along the Lough [Neagh] within four miles of Dungannon and killed 100 people, sparing none, of age, or sex soever, besides many burned to death. We killed man, woman, and child, horse, beast and whatever we could find'. During the 1641 rebellion at least thirty Catholics were murdered at Islandmagee, with further massacres at Lisnagarvey (Lisburn) and at Ballydavy, near Bangor, where seventy-three men, women and children were killed. As respected historian, Charles Dickson, has written, 'this lamentable business continued on both sides... the massacres were merely incidents in that murdering time'.

The Portadown atrocity is commemorated in a long loyalist ballad, *Portadown (The Drowning of the Protestants From the Bridge Over the Bann)*, probably written in the 19th century.

> In sixteen hundred and forty-one, those Fenians formed a plan
> To massacre us Protestants down by the River Bann,

To massacre us Protestants and not to spare a man
But to drive us like a herd of swine into the bloody Bann.

Brave Porter fell a victim because he did intend
To help his brother Protestants, their lives for to defend,
The blood did stain the waters red, their bones lay all around
As they drove them down into the Bann that flows through Portadown.

A lady living in Loughall and with her children five,
She begged for the sake of them, to let her be alive
That she might go to England, her husband there to see
And to live in peace and unity and far from Popery.

And after having tortured her to a pain she could not stand,
Down through the streets of Portadown they dragged her to the Bann.
They said, 'You are a heretic, the Pope you do defy
And it's on this bridge in Portadown this day your fate to die'.

At least ten hundred faithful souls in Portadown were slain,
All were the deeds of Popery, their evil ends to gain,
But God sent us brave Cromwell, our deliverer to be,
To put down Popery in this land and set all Protestants free.

King William soon came after him and planted at the Boyne
An Orange tree there that we should bear in mind
That Popery did murder us, Protestants did drown,
The bones of some can still be seen this day in Portadown.

However the Protestant, loyalist tradition is probably best represented in song by the classic, historical *Lilliburlero*, written around 1687. Viewed objectively, it is a blatant piece of satirical propaganda, but it is also an authentic insight into the political thinking of the period. It is set to a terrific melody, innocently used to this day as a signature tune by the BBC World Service.

Ho! Brother Teague, dost hear de decree?
Lilliburlero bullen a la,
Dat we shall have a new Debittie,
Lilliburlero bullen a la.
Ho! By my soul it is Talbot,
Lilliburlero bullen a la,
And he will cut all the Englishmen's throat,
Lilliburlero bullen a la.

And the good Talbot is made a Lord,
Lilliburlero bullen a la,

And he with his brave lads is coming aboard,
Lilliburlero bullen a la.

Ah but why does King James stay behind?
Lilliburlero bullen a la,
Ho! by my soul 'tis a Protestant wind!
Lilliburlero bullen a la.

And he dat will not go to de Mass,
Lilliburlero bullen a la,
Shall be turned out and look like an ass,
Lilliburlero bullen a la.

And now this prophecy has come to pass,
Lilliburlero bullen a la,
For James is the dog and Tyrconnell's the ass,
Lilliburlero bullen a la.

The lyrics are a derogatory parody of Catholic hopes that they would regain the ascendancy as they celebrate the appointment of a Catholic, Richard Talbot (Earl of Tyrconnell), as King James II's Deputy, 'Debittie', in Ireland. They are usually attributed to Lord Thomas Wharton (1648-1715), a leading English Whig politician, one of those who had welcomed William of Orange to England in 1688. The great melody, which gives the song its real impact, is usually said to be by the English composer Henry Purcell (c. 1658-95) although it is also sometimes attributed to his brother Daniel (c. 1660-1717). Another authority traces the tune back to an old psalm published in Antwerp in 1540.

'Teague' (from the Irish name *Mac Tadhg*), represents the native Irish and as 'Taig' is still used by unreconstructed loyalists as a derogatory term for Catholics. It is also still used as an Irish first name, as in the song *The Bold Thady Quill*. The 'Protestant wind' is a reference to favourable gales in the English Channel in 1688, which helped William during his invasion of England, meaning either that the lyrics couldn't have been written in 1687 or that this line is a later addition. *Lilliburlero bullen a la* is sometimes said to be a corruption of the Irish *An lile ba leir e ba linn an lá* (the lily has triumphed and we won the day). The Orange Lily was of course adopted as a symbol by William's Irish followers but this explanation must be wrong if the song was indeed written in the 1680s, as the triumph of the Orange Lily did not come until the Battle of the Boyne in 1690. (Confusingly, the Easter Lily is an important republican symbol!) A more probable explanation is that the term is a parody of a Catholic password from the 1641 Rebellion, *Buallaidh ár lá*. Today a variant of this, *Tiocfaidh ár lá*, 'our day will come', is a well-know republican slogan.

After the Rising of 1641 the next individual to make a significant contribution to Irish history, for better or worse depending on your prejudices, was the English Lord Protector Oliver Cromwell (1599-1658). Cromwell believed that he was divinely inspired and that he was therefore merely carrying out 'God's will'. However he was not doing it for want of material reward, demanding and receiving a personal salary of £13,000 per month, more than the present Prime Minister receives 350 years later. His invasion in 1649 was based on the assumption that England was the legitimate ruler of Ireland and that he had therefore a duty to discharge. However just as the massacre at Portadown has remained such an influence on loyalist thinking, Cromwell's actions, whether propagandised out of all proportion or not, have had a similar searing effect on the Catholic psyche. His major victories and massacres at Drogheda and Wexford left 5,000 people dead, many of whom were defenceless civilians. Cromwell attempted to justify this by references to Catholic massacres in 1641. He also instigated the subsequent clampdown on Catholicism and any hint of opposition and Catholic civil rights were not restored until 1829. Whether or not Cromwell's actions were within the normal rules of war of the period is still a controversial historical subject.

To loyalists Cromwell is 'our deliverer'; to the English he is 'Our Chief of Men', the champion of the common people against the Divine Right of Kings and seldom connected with Ireland; to nationalists he is 'that man of demon guilt'. The latter perspective is exemplified in an emotive ballad *The Wexford Massacre*, written in 1843 by Michael Joseph Barry, a prominent Protestant Young Irelander.

They knelt around the cross divine, the matron and the maid,
They bowed before redemption's sign, and fervently they prayed;
Three hundred fair and helpless ones, whose crime was this alone,
Their valiant husbands, sires and sons, had battled for their own.

Had battled bravely but in vain, the Saxon won the fight;
The Irish corpses strewed the plain, where Valour slept with Right;
And now that man of demon guilt, to fated Wexford flew,
The red blood reeking on his hilt, of hearts to Erin true.
He found them there, the young, the old, the maiden and the wife,
Their guardians brave in death were cold, who dared for them the
    strife;
They prayed for mercy 'God on high', before thy cross they prayed,
But ruthless Cromwell bade them die, to glut the Saxon blade.

Three hundred fell, the stifled prayer was quenched in woman's blood,
Nor youth, nor age could move to spare from slaughter's crimson
    flood,

But nations keep a stern account of deeds that tyrants do,
And guiltless blood in Heaven will mount, and Heaven avenge it too.

By May 1650 Cromwell was back in England. By 1653 the War was over. Catholic lands were confiscated wholesale to pay Cromwellian soldiers wages, to punish Catholics and to terrorise them into future 'good affection'. Under the *Act for the Settling of Ireland* (1652) and the *Act of Satisfaction* (1653) approximately half the land of Ireland was confiscated and ownership transferred from native Catholic hands to British Protestant investors or 'adventurers'. It would be over three hundred years before this process began to be reversed by Land League agitation. In addition, 35,000 Irish soldiers fled to Europe. Thousands more ordinary Catholics, including many who had played no part in the Rebellion, were 'transplanted' to poorer quality land in the western counties of Clare, Galway, Mayo and Roscommon. Additional thousands were executed or starved and 50,000 were shipped to slavery or servitude in Barbados, a virtual death sentence. The overall population was reduced by a third, from one and a half million to under a million.

Ireland was subdued for the time being, and Catholic resistance had been reduced to desultory raiding by the few remaining outlaw *rapparees*.

The Reverend George Walker and the Siege of Derry

2.

Derry's Walls

The time has scarce gone round boys, 200 years ago,
When rebels on old Derry's Walls, their faces dared not show,
When James and all his rebel band came up to Bishop's Gate
With heart and hand and sword and shield we caused them to retreat.

Chorus
Then fight and don't surrender but come when duty calls,
With heart and hand and sword and shield we'll guard old Derry's Walls.

For blood did flow in crimson streams for many a winter's night
They knew the Lord was on their side to help them in the fight;
They nobly stood upon the walls determined for to die
To fight and gain the victory and raise the Crimson high.

[Chorus]

At last, at last, with one broadside can't help but send them aid,
The boom across the Foyle was broke and James he was dismayed.
The banner boys, that floated was run aloft with joy.
God bless the hands that broke the boom and saved the 'Prentice boys.

[Chorus]

Derry's Walls
The Siege of Derry, George Walker, Adam Murray, Lundy the Traitor

This loyalist anthem celebrates the determined and successful resistance of Ulster Protestants against the mainly Catholic army of James II in Derry in 1689. The siege was set against the background of the larger power struggle between Britain and France and their various allies for dominance in Europe. In Ireland however the wars were the latest round in the continuing struggle between rapparee and ruler. It wasn't about Irish independence, though some Catholics may have entertained hopes that James could become King of a separate Ireland, but about the religion of the monarch and Catholic hopes, and Protestant fears, of a restoration of Catholic land ownership.

The political background to the siege was fraught with the uncertainty of the dispute for the throne between James and William of Orange. At local level the situation had been complicated by the circulation of a fake document in late 1688, the *Comber Letter*, which revived Protestant fears of the Catholic rebellion of 1641. The letter appeared anonymously in Comber, County Down addressed to a 'Protestant gentleman' [Hugh Montgomery, Lord Mount Alexander] and stated ' all our Irish men is sworn… to fall on to kill and murder [Protestant] man, wife and child'. The *Letter* was copied and circulated throughout much of Ireland. A copy reached Derry on 7 December, the day before a regiment of Lord Antrim's Catholic glensmen and Scottish highlanders, the 'Redshanks', reached the town. Derry's Protestant inhabitants therefore believed that if they opened the city gates they would all be put to the sword.

The Protestants also felt badly treated by Richard Talbot (1630-91), James' Deputy in Ireland, the Catholic Earl of Tyrconnell ('lying Dick' in loyalist mythology). Talbot's views were no doubt strongly influenced by his experience at Drogheda in 1649 where he had been fortunate to survive the Cromwellian massacre. His personal mission was to revive the political and economic status of Catholics and he quickly set about this by appointing Catholic privy councillors, judges and sheriffs and issuing new town charters, which provided for Catholic governing majorities. He also catholicised the army, although James had instructed him to afford Protestants equality of treatment. Tyrconnell's policy proved to be shortsighted and by 1689 he, and more importantly the King, had lost Protestant trust. Many of the purged Protestant officers and men went straight over to the Williamite army.

James arrived at the city walls on 18 April, exactly a week after William of Orange had been crowned at Westminster Abbey. He was ignorant of the local situation on the ground and was expecting to be welcomed by loyal subjects. He was unaware that the Comber Letter had poisoned the atmosphere and also that one of his local commanders had already held surrender negotiations with the defenders. As an interim measure agreement had been reached that no royalist troops would come within four miles of the city gates. When James therefore blithely rode up to the walls he was, not surprisingly, fired on for breaking the agreement although he had no knowledge of it. An aide de camp was shot dead, James retreated in surprise and the siege was on, though the king himself moved back to Dublin.

The city could probably have been taken on 18 April if James had decided to attack there and then but he delayed, giving the defenders time to re-group and strengthen the defences. Ironically Derry may have owed its survival to Robert Lundy, the Scot who was Governor of the City, and who had organised its defences before switching sides. Lundy had seen military service in North Africa and had been present at the siege of Tangiers where he gained valuable knowledge of siege tactics. His biggest single contribution to the defences was the construction of a ravelin, a protruding triangular fortification, at the Bishop's Gate. To this day loyalists still burn effigies of Lundy the Traitor.

The siege is usually counted as lasting a hundred and five days, from mid April to early August. James's forces had enjoyed earlier successes and Williamite loyalists from all over north Ulster poured into the relative security of the walled city on the River Foyle. The walls had been erected during the early plantation period, between 1613 and 1618, when the planters had to fortify their homes and towns for protection from the displaced natives.

The basic position was that the city at the time was virtually impregnable due to its stout walls, its well-armed defenders and the inadequacy of the Jacobite firepower. The walls stretch for about a mile, being twenty-four feet high and up to thirty feet wide. In 1689 an army of 7,000 men and some twenty strategically mounted cannons defended them. These included one on the flat roof of St Columb's Protestant Cathedral, which afforded a clear view to the river. A defiant bloody flag was also flown from the tower of the Cathedral, inspiring the reference in Derry's Walls to 'raise the Crimson high'. Commemorative crimson flags are still carried at loyalist parades to this day.

The besieging army, camped to the west on the hill that is now the Creggan Estate and on the east just above the Waterside, didn't have sufficiently heavy weaponry to penetrate the walls so as long as the defenders had enough food, they could hold out indefinitely. Due to the niggardliness of Louis XIV of France (the 'Sun King'), to whom the Irish campaign was a mere sideshow, James' army was poorly equipped, with only ten per cent having serviceable firearms. They even lacked sufficient shovels to dig proper trenches. The spring of 1689 saw unusually heavy rainfall, uniforms quickly became ragged and rotten and the usual plague of dysentery from contaminated drinking water set in. Armies of the period marched on small beer (low alcohol) and if supplies ran low, as on protracted campaigns they usually did, water from local rivers, which doubled as sewers, had to be drunk. Basically many of the men were fighting tired, sick, hungry, damp and far from home, 'their backsides hanging out of their trousers'.

Relief ships waited at nearby Culmore on Lough Foyle (the river broadens out into the Lough of the same name just north of the city). However they couldn't sail up as the attackers had erected a wooden barricade, a boom, at almost exactly the spot where the modern road bridge now crosses the river. Today the area is dotted with commemorative names such as Boom Hall, Boomhall Light, King James Well, and Mountjoy Light (the *Mountjoy* being the first relief ship to break through the boom).

As the weeks became months, the plight of the defenders became more desperate; food supplies dwindled and they were reduced to eating almost anything they could lay their hands on including horse, dog, cat and rat. The narrow streets were extremely dangerous, with shells exploding and ricocheting in all directions and most people spent long periods confined to the cellars. It is estimated that the Williamites lost about 3,000 dead and the Jacobites (from 'Jacobus', Latin for James) around 8,000, the majority being victims of disease and exposure. Within the walls however the cry was still 'No surrender'.

Then on the evening of 28 July the *Mountjoy*, driven by desperation and a strong tide crashed into the boom, snapping its restraining chains and by 1 August the siege was over. The Captain of the *Mountjoy* Michael Browning, himself a Derry man, was killed in his moment of triumph by a fusillade from the shore. Today he is commemorated with a plaque on the walls near Shipquay Gate.

> Near this spot landed the body of Michael Browning, Master of the ship Mountjoy, Of Londonderry, killed in action at the breaking of the boom July 28th 1689 while leading the van of the relieving squadron against the forces of King James II & Louis XIV
>
> 'He died the most enviable of all deaths in sight of the City which was his birthplace, which was his home and which he had just saved by his bravery and self-devotion from the most frightful form of destruction' — Macauley

Technically the siege is probably more accurately described as a blockade. However, interesting as this may be to military historians, it is a purely semantic distinction. The defenders saw it as a siege and the bottom line is that the city didn't fall to the Jacobites. For months the Scottish Jacobite leader, Sir John Graham of Claverhouse (Bonnie Dundee), had been urging James to send his troops to Scotland. Another option was that, had Dundee not been killed during his army's victory at the ferocious Battle of Killiecrankie in Perthshire on 27 July 1689, when about 3,000 men from both sides were killed in around five minutes fighting, he could have brought his army to Ireland. This would have had serious implications for the conduct and possible outcome of the Williamite Wars. However the protracted siege of Derry tied down valuable resources and the Jacobite cause in Scotland and England faltered as a result.

The song commemorating the siege is, I think, another example of how a good song is more than just words on a piece of paper. Although not strong on poetic imagery, apart from the great chorus, it is set to a terrifically stirring tune and is usually performed with gusto and bravado, making it a highly effective rallying call. Like many nationalist songs it was written long after the events described and is, like them, essentially good propaganda. The first line would indicate that it is already over one hundred years old and it is still as popular today as it ever was. It will probably still be sung in another hundred years.

The song is derived from an old broadside ballad called *The Siege of Derry* set to the tune of *God Bless the Prince of Wales* ('Among our ancient mountains and among our lonely vales, Oh let the prayer re-echo, God bless the Prince of Wales').

> Full many a long winter's night and sultry summer's day
> Are past and gone since James took flight from Derry's walls away.
> Cold are the hands that closed the gates against the wily foe
> But still till time's remotest date their spirit still shall glow.
> And here's a health to all good men, now fearless men are few
> But when we close the gates again, we'll then be all True Blue.
>
> Lord Auuntrim's [sic] men came down yon glen with the fife and drum
>   so gay,
> The 'prentice boys soon heard the noise and then prepared to play.
> While some opposed, the gates they closed, and joining hand to hand
> Before the war they resolved to fall or for their freedom stand.
> When honour calls to Derry's walls, the noble and the brave,
> He that in the battle falls must find a hero's grave.
>
> Then came the hot and deadly fray with many a mortal wound
> While thousands in wild war's array stood marshalled all around.

Each hill and plain was strewn with slain, the Foil [Foyle] ran red with
  blood,
But all was vain the town to gain, there William's standard stood.
Here's to those who met their foes as men and heroes should,
Then let each slave steal to his grave who fears to shed his blood.

The matchless deeds of those who here defied the tyrant's frown
On history's bright rolls appear emblazoned in renown.
Here deathless Walker's faithful word sent hosts against the foe
And gallant Murray's bloody sword the Galic [sic] chief laid low.
Then here's to those heroes dead, their glorious memory,
May we who stand here in their stead, as wise and valiant be.

Given their huge mythological status, it is surprising that both songs
make only passing reference to the thirteen apprentice boys who locked
the city gates against the besiegers in December 1688 and who are credited
with having inspired the determined and defiant tone of the resistance.
The apprentice boys' youthful impetuousness didn't have the full support
of the more conservative Town Council. As *The Siege of Derry* correctly
asserts, 'while some opposed, the gates they closed'. When the 'youthood
by a strange impulse ran in one body and shut the gates', James was still,
arguably, the legal King for William wasn't formally offered the crown until
13 February 1689. The apprentice boys could therefore be seen, in some
quarters at least, as rebel traitors! The modern loyalist brotherhood, the
Apprentice Boys of Derry, founded in 1814, is of course named after them.

The Siege of Derry pays tribute to the best-known loyalist heroes of the
siege, the Rev. George Walker (c. 1646-1690), who had assumed joint
governorship of the city with Major Henry Baker after the desertion of
Lundy and Adam Murray, a local farmer from Faughanvale. Walker's
reputation is somewhat disputed, even among loyalists, as for the most
part it is based on his own book, *True Account of the Siege of Londonderry*,
published just after the events in 1689. Walker's main critic was one of his
own regimental chaplains, the Rev. John McKenzie (c. 1648-1696) who in
1690 published *A Narrative of the Siege of Londonderry or the late Memorable
Transaction of that City, Faithfully Represented to Rectify the Mistakes and
Supply the Omissions of Mr. Walker's account.* However although Walker's
book is undoubtedly selective in his own favour, he was indisputably a
courageous and committed leader. Sadly he didn't live long to savour his
triumph as he was killed fighting at the Boyne the following year.

The reputation of Captain Adam Murray is unblemished. Before the
siege began he had fought bravely, until he ran out of ammunition, at the
loyalist defeat of Cladyford. Later he confronted Lundy, accusing him of
treason. He led a successful sortie against the Jacobites at Pennyburn, just

north of the city on the road to Culmore. As the loyalists retreated on the arrival of enemy reinforcements, which left them hopelessly outnumbered, they then successfully ambushed the pursuing Jacobites, killing 'a great number' and leaving 'not one man or horse uninjured'. Murray is said to have personally killed the French Jacobite leader Lieutenant-General Maumont, the 'Galic chief' of the ballad. Just a few days later Murray led a second successful sortie to Pennyburn and again the Jacobite commander, Pusignan, died of his wounds. Murray refused to buckle even after the Jacobites captured and threatened to kill his father. Eventually the old man was freed unharmed. Supposedly Maumont's 'bloody sword' remained in the Murray family for over a hundred years. Surprisingly not a street in the City is named after either Walker or Murray.

Observant readers will no doubt have noticed that I never use the name 'Londonderry' unless in quotation marks. This is a difficult one for use of 'Derry' or 'Londonderry', in public at least, almost always implies or betrays political or cultural bias. All I can say is that I was born within ten miles of the place and never heard it called anything other than 'Derry' for about the first ten years of my life. The 'Lough Swilly' buses that passed our front door were all going to or from 'Derry' and every Friday the only newspaper that ever came into the house was the 'Derry Journal'. For me therefore to use any name other than 'Derry' would be completely artificial. However the official name of the city is 'Londonderry' and, like so many symbolic things in Northern Ireland, remains a bone of contention. A reasonable compromise, recognising the legitimacy of the two traditions, could be to refer to the City of 'Derry', which outside of politics everyone does anyway, and to the County of 'Londonderry'. A compromise is required and (London)derry, or 'Londonderry/Derry', 'Stroke City', is not a very good one.

The place name of Derry is derived from the Irish *doire* 'oak-wood'. St Columcille founded a monastery there in 546 A.D., though there was a settlement on the site even before that, *Doire Chalgaig*, Calgagh's oak-wood. The prefix 'London' was added in 1613 when James I granted a charter for the 'settlement', or alternatively, the 'expropriation' of the town by merchants from London. At the same time, County Coleraine was renamed County Londonderry. The name is an extremely common one throughout Ireland and in south Antrim alone we find Derryloughan, Derrylee, Derrytransa, Derryadd, Derrylileagh Lough, Derrycor, Derrykeevan, Derryvan, Derrymeen, Derryash, Derrycrow plus Ballinderry. The name also occurs in two hundred and twenty-nine townland names in Northern Ireland. There must have been an awful lot of oak trees here at one time!

Today the 'Maiden City' that repulsed all invaders is again enjoying relative peace. However the city is divided by the River Foyle, and it is also divided by religion and politics. The west bank, the Bogside and the Creggan, is mostly Catholic while the east, the Waterside and surrounding area, is predominantly Protestant. However considering all that has happened since 1689 hopeful signs are emerging from the gloom. Cross-cultural bridges are being built and efforts are being made to organise the city council on an equitable basis with the mayorship being shared between the two communities. People of good will on both sides are bending over backwards, at least in public, to walk a mile in the other man's shoes.

In June 2000 this new spirit of mutual recognition and tolerance was put to the test with the election of a Sinn Féin and former IRA 'blanket protest' man, Cathal Crumley, to the mayorship. Crumley was elected by twenty-one city council votes to eight, figures that reflect approximately the sectarian divide. Wearing the green *saoirse* (freedom) symbol, he declared, 'Today is a very powerful chapter in the history of Ireland. The failed politics of exclusion ends tonight. I can assure you during my term of office no one will be denied their rights. I will be open, impartial and pragmatic. During my election as the first Sinn Féin Mayor of Derry I will represent every deserving citizen of Derry. I offer my hand of friendship to the unionist community and trust that they will have the maturity to react in reciprocal fashion for the benefit of the city.' However Assembly member Gregory Campbell of the Democratic Unionist Party argued: 'There have been three nationalist Mayors in a four year term. We do not accept that and we want to work towards some sense of equality and balance.' In June 2001, Mildred Garfield of the DUP was unanimously elected with cross-party support, including from Sinn Féin. In June 2002 it was the turn of the SDLP.

Although the city, like most places, has its share of social problems, possibly a little more than its fair share, it is a place that I always find stimulating and exciting to visit. Without wishing to be too dewy eyed about it, what makes Derry special for me is its people: the ordinary people who have had to put up with so much from war, unemployment, poverty and emigration but have never lost their spirit. The place definitely has a buzz to it, an energy and vitality that can be felt after five minutes in the Diamond (the central area within the walls). Once more the walls are accessible and the walk around the top of them is spectacular and free.

In 'lovely Derry on the banks of the Foyle' it seems to me, being almost a native of the city, and where my own name is so common, that even the buskers play a superior brand of music. Unfortunately though the political and social climate still requires a good deal of further progress before it is regarded as quite acceptable to give a public rendition of *Derry's Walls*.

3.

The Green Grassy Slopes of the Boyne

Some folks sing about glens and valleys
Where the wild flowers abundantly grow
And some sing of the waves crystal billows
That dash 'neath the waters below.
But I'm going to sing of a river
And I hope in the chorus you'll join,
Of the deeds that were done by King William
On the green grassy slopes of the Boyne.

Chorus
On the green grassy slopes of the Boyne
Where the Orangemen with William did join
And fought for a glorious deliverance,
On the green grassy slopes of the Boyne.

On the banks of that beautiful river
Where the bones of our forefathers lie,
Awaiting the sound of the trumpet
To call them to glory on high.
In our hearts we will cherish their memories
And we all like true brethren will join
And praise God for sending us King William
On the green grassy slopes of the Boyne.

[Chorus]

Orangemen will be loyal and steady
For no matter what e'er may betide
We will still mind our war cry "No Surrender"
As long as we've God on our side,
And if ever our service is needed
Then we all like true brethren will join
And fight like good valiant King William
On the green grassy slopes of the Boyne.

King William of Orange

The Green Grassy Slopes of the Boyne

The Battle of the Boyne, Patrick Sarsfield and the Flight of the Wild Geese

This rousing celebration of the Protestant victory at the Battle of the Boyne in 1690 first impacted on my consciousness in the late fifties on the old Ardrossan to Belfast ferry crossing between Scotland and Ireland. It was during the week before 12 July and many Scots Orangemen were heading over for the celebrations. Despite my 'southern' Catholic background there was something in the music that I found was getting through to me. I was aged about fourteen and had not yet started to frequent the folk clubs of Glasgow. Apart from a few rebel songs picked up at Celtic Football Ground this was my first taste of what was in essence folk music. The rhythms made me want to get up and join in the frolics but I knew that I was excluded because I belonged to the other tribe. Although well aware that the politics behind the music were opposed to everything in my own experience, I was still fascinated. The pride in cultural heritage on display was very similar to that in much of my own people's music. I won't pretend that I immediately wanted to rush and join the Orange Order but I began to realise that the music had similar roots to my own.

The Battle of the Boyne took place on 1 July 1690, though it really started on the evening of 30 June when men on both sides were killed during a five-hour artillery exchange. However King William was very superstitious and delayed the battle proper until the following day, a Tuesday, because he believed it to be unlucky to fight on a Monday. In the end his luck held. That evening, the Williamite army lit their bonfires, the origin of the loyalist bonfires that are still lit on the eve of ' The Twelfth '. An additional difficulty also surrounds the dating of the Battle. A new calendar had been introduced in 1752 and using this, the equivalent modern date would be 11 July. The discrepancy goes back to the introduction of the Gregorian calendar in Catholic southern Europe by Pope Gregory XIII in 1582, replacing the Julian because it was inexorably getting out of astronomical kilter. However it was not introduced in Protestant northern Europe for another hundred and seventy years until it was absolutely certain that it was not yet another Popish Plot! At this point the chronology becomes even more complex. The year 1700 was a leap year under the Julian calendar but not under the Gregorian and somehow the confusion led to an extra day being added to the date of the Boyne, making it 'The Twelfth '. Republicans may question the logical thought processes of loyalists but the shrewd loyalist places the blame firmly where it belongs, on the Pope of Rome!

The anniversary of the Boyne and the iconic status of William of Orange as the all-conquering, fearless Protestant soldier and slayer of Catholic 'hereticks', Croppies, Fenians and Taigs has been taken up by the Orangemen and invested with the utmost symbolic significance. The image of 'King Billy' on his white horse trampling over enemy territory and theology remains one of the most resonant in Irish history. However although it was a crucial victory, giving William control of Dublin, Leinster, much of Munster and leaving the Jacobites isolated west of the Shannon, it was a battle won and not a war. The final decision in the historic struggle between Protestantism in Britain and Ireland, as represented by King William III (1650-1702) and Catholicism, as represented by King James II (1633-1701) came the following year with the Williamite triumphs at Aughrim and Limerick.

William first set foot in Ireland at Carrickfergus on 14 June 1690 and met up with his leading general, the German Duke Frederick Herman Schomberg (1615-90) who had landed the previous year and who was destined to lose his life at the Boyne. His army had suffered a terrible winter of wet and cold, losing around seven thousand men to dysentery and fever. Schomberg had spent much of his military career in the service of the Catholic King of France, Louis XIV, but switched allegiance when Louis revoked the Edict of Nantes and deprived French Protestants of their civil and religious liberties. As a result over 100,000 French Huguenots left France for more friendly environments. Many came to the Lisburn area where they made an important contribution to the development of the linen industry. Today a street in the town, Huguenot Avenue, commemorates this link.

James had landed in the far south, at Kinsale in County Cork, on 12 March 1689. He marched north as William headed south and the two met on opposite sides of the River Boyne just outside Drogheda about twenty five miles north of Dublin. (James had been as far North as Derry in April 1689 but had made his HQ in Dublin.) With an army of 36,000 at their disposal the Williamites outnumbered the Jacobites by about 11,000. The Williamite army also benefited from a significant artillery advantage. The Battle was a very international affair as the Irish dimension was interwoven with a major European power struggle. Various treaties resulted in Irish, English, French, German and Dutch troops on the Jacobite side and Irish,

English, Dutch, Germans, Danes, French, Swiss, Italians, Norwegians and Poles in the Williamite ranks. Pope Innocent XI, alarmed by Louis' expansionist ambitions, supported William, though apparently he did not, as is sometimes said, immediately rush and say a thanksgiving Mass when news of William's victory reached Rome! Another myth is that William's men wore orange; in fact they wore green identifying sprigs!

The decisive phase of the Battle began when Schomberg's son Meinherd led a force of about 12,000 men three miles upriver and forced a crossing at the ford of Rosnaree at low tide. James overreacted to this by deploying 16,000 men upstream, which left only about 9,000 to oppose 24,000 Williamite soldiers down river at Oldbridge. As the tide of battle began to go against him, James feared becoming encircled and having lost both his will and his nerve, decided to order the retreat. A few days later he was back in France bringing, like Johnny Cope, 'the news of his own defeat, so early in the morning'. Many troops on both sides were only marginally engaged (especially the 7,000 French Jacobites, who had been ordered by Louis XIV's war minister Louvois to join in only if James looked like winning). Although there had been some fierce close-range fighting, casualties were relatively light with about 1,000 dead on the Jacobite side to around 500 Williamites.

The two Kings had commanded their armies personally but while James had stayed on the edge of the battlefield, William was at the centre of the action throughout and had almost been killed by a cannonball that grazed his shoulder before the fighting began in earnest. However with admirable self-possession he shrugged, 'It is nothing, but the ball came very near'. Later, in the confusion of battle, he was almost shot at point blank range by one of his own men but is said to have defused the situation by asking, 'Would you kill a friend?' James on the other hand did not cover himself in military glory and is certainly thought to have ordered the retreat far too soon, although he probably knew that he was never going to win, despite insisting on fighting against the advice of his generals.

Afterwards William did not pursue James, for the relationship between the two men was complicated by the fact that James was William's father-in-law. Until the summer of 1688 William had supported James in the hope of eventually securing the throne for his wife, James' daughter, Queen Mary (1662-94) who was a Protestant. However in June of 1688 James, at the age of fifty-five, fathered a son by his second wife, Mary of Modena, thus relegating Mary in the order of succession. A group of powerful English noblemen, 'The Immortal Seven', alarmed at James' increasing autocracy and pro-Catholic policies, proposed to William that he depose James and that he and Mary become joint monarchs of Britain and Ireland. William accepted the offer and the first step had been taken on the road to the Boyne. The infant son, James Edward Stuart (1688-1766), was to become known to history as the Old Pretender who led the Jacobite revolt of 1715. His son Charles Edward Stuart (1720-88), 'Bonnie Prince Charlie' was destined to lead the final Jacobite uprising, which ended at Culloden in Scotland in 1746.

Queen Mary had, naturally enough, a 'great tenderness' for her father. William was well aware of this, saying, 'I cannot help feeling for the poor queen… the path of duty is hard on my wife that her father and I must be opposed to each other in the field, God send that no harm may happen to him'.

William died on 8 March 1702, largely unmourned by the English who regarded him as a bit of an overly serious, sober and dour Dutchman. To the Protestants of Ireland though he was, and remains, the Great Deliverer. In Ireland news of his death was received with shock and incredulity. Already in failing health his death was hastened by a fall from his horse in Richmond Park in London. The horse had stumbled on a molehill and for some time afterwards Jacobites supposedly referred to the mole as 'The Little Gentleman in Velvet'! Perhaps appropriately, an Irishman, the Poet Laureate Nahum Tate (1652-1715), who was a Presbyterian, wrote William's official epitaph.

> William the Third lies here, the Almighty's friend,
> A scourge to France, a check to Imperious Rome,
> Who did our rights and liberties defend,
> And rescued England from its threatened doom.
> Heaven snatched him from us, whom our hearts caressed,
> And now he's King in Heaven among the blest.
> Grief stops my pen, reader pray weep the rest.

Not surprisingly there was no Williamite cult in the 'South' where a fine, equestrian lead statue of him erected in College Green, Dublin in 1701, had a chequered history. It was defaced on a number of occasions from 1710 onwards and was blown up in 1836. Repaired and replaced on its pedestal it stood relatively unmolested until destroyed by a bomb in 1928 and was finally removed for safety reasons by Dublin Corporation the following year. Intriguingly the head of the statue is said to have surfaced again in London in the late 1980s and to have changed hands for £7,000.

After the Jacobite disaster at Aughrim in 1691 (see *The West's Awake*) the remaining Jacobite forces retreated west of the Shannon to the port, and possible escape route, of Limerick. With the Marquis de Saint Ruth killed at Aughrim, control of the Jacobite army finally passed to the ambitious Irishman, Patrick Sarsfield (1655-93). The first Williamite Siege of Limerick in 1690, just a few weeks after the Battle of the Boyne, can be seen as a Jacobite success as the city managed to hold out and Jacobite hopes were renewed. It was at this time that Sarsfield carried out his now legendary raid on the Williamite siege train and food supply at Ballyneety, a few miles south east of Limerick. A number of cannons and a hundred wagons of equipment, including 12,000 pounds of powder, were destroyed. Sarsfield's six hundred dragoons were also intent on capturing or killing William's chief siege engineer, Willem Meesters, but the Dutchman is said to have eluded them by hiding in a nettlebed. Sarsfield's guide on the raid was the rapparee Galloping Dan Hogan. The raid gained the Jacobites valuable time and is celebrated in the rousing ballad *Ballyneety's Walls*.

The night fell dark round Limerick and everything was still
As for our foe in ambush we lay beside the hill,
Like lions bold we waited, to dash upon our prey
As we rode with Sarsfield at our head at the dawning of the day.

From Dublin came the foemen, with guns and warlike store
To take the town of Limerick, they wanted ten times more
But little was their dreaming, that we would be their doom
As we rode with Sarsfield at our head, right down from wild Slieve
    Bloom.

At the lonely hour of midnight, each man leapt on his steed
And through the town of *Cuilleann* [Cullen] we dashed with lightning
    speed
And o'er the hills we thundered to Ballyneety's walls
Where lay the foe securely, with guns and arms and all.

They asked us for our password and 'Sarsfield' was the man
And 'here I am' our General cried, as down on them we ran.
Then God! he cleared the firmament, to the moon and stars gave light
And for the Battle of the Boyne, we had revenge that night.

When the convoy it was scattered we took their mighty store,
Pontoons and carts and powder casks and cannons by the score,
Then hastily with eager hands we piled them all on high,
Laid down the fuse, applied the match and blew them to the sky.

Loud laughed our gallant General, as fast he rode away
And many's the health we drank to him in Limerick town next day.
Here's another health to Sarsfield who led us one and all
When we blew up the royal artillery at Ballyneety's Walls.

Sarsfield died fighting for the French from wounds received at the Battle of Landen in Flanders in 1693. Legend has it that his dying words were 'Oh that this blood had been shed for Ireland'. He is the first real hero in the popular nationalist imagination and is celebrated in numerous songs and poems and hundreds of children of patriotic parents have been given the unlikely first or middle name of Sarsfield. However some historians now question whether or not he may have surrendered Limerick too soon in 1691. Was he too keen to get out, to join the French army and acquire his Marshal's baton? A French force of 12,000 men was only two days away and if Sarsfield had delayed, William who by now was thoroughly fed up with Ireland, would probably have settled on more favourable terms. As it was, Limerick surrendered, the articles of surrender promising 'said Roman Catholics such farther security in that particular as may preserve them from any disturbance on account of their said religion' were later revoked. Limerick became 'the City of Broken Promises', further stoking historical Irish resentment. Thousands of Irish soldiers fled to Europe in the 'Flight of the Wild Geese' and the Penal Laws, severely limiting Catholic civil rights, were introduced. The Wild Geese planned to return but they never did.

Jacobitism in Ireland was all but dead, as were hundreds of thousands of people, the victims of war, famine and plague during the Cromwellian and Williamite campaigns. The vast majority of these were Catholics. Many survivors had been shipped off to slavery in the West Indies. The 17th century had seen the country ravaged, savaged and exhausted. It was to remain quiet and subdued for a hundred years though even a century was not to prove long enough for a rapprochement between ruler and rapparee.

Today the River Boyne (*An Bhoinn*), ['river of the] cow white [goddess] *Boand*', continues to flow, ancient, majestic and quite oblivious of its significance to human beings. Long before it acquired its modern political symbolism it already occupied a special place in ancient Irish mythology. The name is derived from a pre-Christian goddess *Boand* (or *Boinn*) and it's thought that two of Ireland's other well known rivers, the Bann in Ulster and the Bann in Leinster, itself a tributary of the Boyne, have the same derivation. The name is an example of a river being named after the supernatural being once believed to inhabit its waters.

Rising near the village of Carbury in Kildare, the Boyne meanders west by Edenderry, forming the county boundary with Offaly for a few miles before turning northeast, now forming the boundary with Westmeath, and is crossed by the Royal Canal near Longwood. Continuing on through the sylvan countryside of 'Royal' Meath, near some of the most important archaeological sites in Ireland, it passes through Trim, Navan and Slane before entering the sea at Drogheda. Saint Patrick is said to have begun his ministry by lighting the pascal fire at the nearby Hill of Slane, a theological challenge to pagan Tara, symbolically bringing the light of

Christianity to Ireland. Important early monastic ruins can be found at Monasterboice and at Mellifont Abbey (where the Williamite army had camped the night before the Battle).

Apart from a few viewing points and notice boards, there is little on the Boyne today to indicate that the most important battle in modern Irish history took place here. One monument, a hundred-foot obelisk, erected in 1736 at the supposed spot where William was almost killed, was destroyed by a bomb at 3 am one morning in 1923. The site is nevertheless still well worth visiting because of its historical and symbolic significance. Not as many northern loyalists and Orangemen as might be imagined make the trip south. One Orangeman I spoke to in Armagh had never visited the site despite the fact that he had lived all his life less than fifty miles from it. However local *Bord Fáilte* officials assured me that the warmth of their reception usually pleasantly surprises those who do make the effort.

Just a few weeks after I visited the Boyne in October 1999 the government announced plans to buy the site and turn it into a heritage centre with improved visitor access, facilities and information. After consultations with unionists, including the Orange Order, Taoiseach Bertie Ahern stated, 'We must dedicate ourselves to promoting mutual respect and reconciliation. I believe that if the site is presented sensitively, the divisions of the 17th century can be explained in a way that will help foster reconciliation in the 21st'.

Although at present there may not be much to see regarding the Battle itself, three of the most important historical sites in Ireland are within a short drive. These are the Hill of Tara, the 'Mecca' of Ireland, the awe-inspiring prehistoric complex of the ancient High Kings, which for many is a symbol of Ireland itself. The other major attraction in the area of national significance is *Brú na Bóinne*, 'the bend of the Boyne', known in English as Newgrange, an ancient passage-grave, the oldest in Ireland and contemporaneous with the pyramids of Egypt. Here on the shortest day of the year the winter sun penetrates the dark recesses of the tomb for seventeen minutes, once indicating to the area's ancient inhabitants that new life would follow in the spring. A few miles south, on the road between Slane and Naas, is the grave of Wolfe Tone at Bodenstown. So whether you are a student of ancient Ireland, an Orangeman intent on procuring a bottle of 'holy' Boyne water or a republican wishing to gaze on the 'sacred' grave of Wolfe Tone this area, all within thirty miles of Dublin, has it all.

The old ferry service between Belfast and Ardrossan has long ceased to run. However if you care to take a trip on one of the modern routes that have replaced it, during the week before 12 July, you still stand a very good chance of hearing a live rendition of *The Green Grassy Slopes of the Boyne*.

Turlough O'Carolan, the blind harper (1670 - 1738)

4.
The Bard of Armagh

Oh list' to the lay of a bold Irish harper
And scorn not the strength of his old withered hand,
Remember his fingers once could move sharper
To raise the merry strains of his own native land.

When I was a young man King Jamie did flourish,
Before Erin was crushed beneath the lion's paw
And all the fair *cailíns* [colleens] from Wexford to Durrish
Called me bold Phelim Brady, the bard of Armagh.

At a *pátrún*, wake or fair I could twist my shillelagh
Or trip through a jig, my brogues bound with straw.
I was called by the *cailins* around me assembled,
The bold Phelim Brady. the bard of Armagh.

Ah! I love to muse on the days of my boyhood
Though four score and three years have flitted since then,
Still it gives sweet reflection as every young joy should
For the merry-hearted boys make the best of old men.

In truth I have wandered this wide world all over
But Erin's my home and a parent to me
And oh let the turf that my old bones shall cover
Be cut from a sod that is trod by the free.

So when sergeant death in his cold arms shall embrace me,
Low me to sleep with sweet *Erin-go-Bragh*,
By the side of my Cathleen, my dear pride oh place me
Then forget Phelim Brady, the bard of Armagh.

Note: In verse three *'pátrún'* is often rendered in English as 'pattern'. The derivation is from a patron saint's day or holy day.

The Bard of Armagh
Poets, Priests and the Penal Laws

This old favourite has much of the ring of the authentic folk song about it, although it seems that it wasn't written until the 19th century, at least a hundred years after its subject 'Phelim Brady' had died. It's an effectively atmospheric song in its own right, but is there more to it than meets the eye? Who was 'Phelim Brady', a real person, or just a figment of the poet's imagination? Paradoxically, the least likely candidate for the bardship of Armagh is 'Phelim Brady' himself for this is almost certainly an alias for a man whose identity had to be kept secret.

It is now generally accepted that the real 'Phelim Brady' was in fact Patrick Donnelly (c. 1650-1716), born near Cookstown in Tyrone, who became the Catholic Bishop of Dromore in County Armagh. He had been deposed under the Penal Laws, introduced between 1695 and 1728, with the express purpose of limiting Catholic influence and activity. Doctor Donnelly had been ordained as a priest by Saint Oliver Plunkett (1625-81) who was appointed Bishop of Armagh in 1669 and who was later executed for his supposed part in the so-called Popish Plot, to assassinate Charles II, of 1678-81.

The use of the term *cailín*, ('colleen'), 'girl or girlfriend', raises the question of how literally the ballad should be taken to represent the life of a Bishop. The same applies to the use of 'wife' or 'pride' in the final verse though this may be merely a symbol, with the bard being 'married to Ireland' (see below). Though it's probable that the song is loosely based on Patrick Donnelly's life, it has become so encrusted in myth that it is virtually worthless in terms of biographical detail. The tune has been used on many other occasions, for example in *Bold Robert Emmet*, and further afield, in *The Streets of Laredo* and *St James Infirmary Blues*.

Patrick Donnelly had spent some time in Paris before returning to Ireland in 1690 when he was made Vicar General of Armagh before becoming Bishop of Dromore on 22 July 1697, just as the Penal Laws were being introduced. That year the unambiguously entitled, *Bishops' Banishment Act* became law, requiring all bishops and regular clergy, such as Jesuits, but not ordinary priests, to 'leave the Kingdom' by 1 May 1698. The regular clergy often travelled in Catholic Europe and were suspected, with probable justification, of acting as couriers for Britain's enemies.

Bishop Donnelly evidently refused the government's invitation 'to leave the Kingdom' for he was arrested and imprisoned in 1706. However, no doubt aided by the local peasantry, he managed to escape and take up outlaw refuge on the slopes of Slieve Gullion, which at an altitude of 1893 feet dominates the landscape of South Armagh. For disguise he adopted the persona of 'Phelim Brady' and the role of the poor, itinerant harper. He is thought to have continued his ministry as best he could from a primitive mountain hut near Lislea where a townland is still called the Doctor's Quarters.

According to Nancy Calthorpe 'when the Bishop died in 1716 the people of South Armagh, under cover of darkness, carried his coffin back to Tyrone'. After his death the See of Dromore remained vacant until 1747 when Bishop Anthony O'Garvey was appointed. Since then the position had been filled consecutively right down to modern times.

In 1710 came a further attempt to undermine Catholic influence when an Oath of Abjuration, to abjure or denounce the authority of the Pope, was introduced. However only some thirty priests throughout Ireland complied. Catholics were now forbidden to hold weapons and were banned from education at home or abroad, thus providing the basis for the future myth of the 'thick Paddy'.

In 1702, just months after the death of William of Orange, the London Parliament introduced an *Act for the Relief of the Protestant Purhasers of the Forfeited Estates in Ireland*. This is a fairly typical example of the general language, content and tone of most of the Penal Laws. The *Act* stated:

> None of the said purchased premises may ever descend or come to any Papist... but shall remain to be held and enjoyed by Protestants for the strengthening and supporting of the English interest and the Protestant religion in Ireland... And it is further enacted that every such Papist or person making profession of the Popish religion shall be disabled and is hereby made incapable to purchase... any of the lands, tenements or hereditaments or premises aforesaid... all leases shall be made to such persons only as are of the Protestant religion and to none other'.

In 1704 another plainly named piece of legislation, *The Act to Prevent the Further Growth of Popery*, was crucial in that it strengthened the ban on Catholics from owning land. The result was that by the end of the 18th century they owned only about 14 per cent of the land of Ireland. The figure is sometimes given as low as 5 per cent but this is usually taken to mean cultivable land only. The bottom line however was that Catholics, who comprised about 80 per cent of the population, now owned very little of their native soil and most of what they did manage to retain was of poor quality: hill, moor and bog. In 1728 a further law excluded them from the legal profession, the civil service and local government, jury service, membership of the armed forces or of parliament.

In the wake of the wars of the 17th century the English government and the Irish Protestant establishment decided, not unreasonably after two major revolts, that Catholics couldn't be trusted to co-operate with the state. Given half a chance they would rebel in an attempt to reclaim their ancestral lands and to reinstate the Stuart dynasty. They had therefore to be kept ignorant and excluded from politics and society. Many members of the Protestant establishment also had a personal antipathy towards Catholicism on theological grounds, seeing it as superstitious and controlled by a foreigner, the Pope. However first and foremost they were practical politicians and the Penal Laws were essentially political rather than theological in character, though they were enacted during an age when it was still believed that one Christian sect could and should try to 'win' over another. Although the Laws were aimed mainly at propertied Catholics, they were also, on the ground at peasant level, instrumental in creating and maintaining the divisions that are still endemic in the North to the present day.

The long-term result of the Penal Laws was an almost indelible, apartheid-like, mark on the Catholic psyche, one which is only now being finally erased. For although Catholic Emancipation was introduced in 1829 and long before that many of the Laws hadn't been rigidly enforced, their long-lingering legacy was to leave the vast majority of Irish people disadvantaged, disenfranchised and dispossessed. Well into the 20th century Catholics were still borrowing money to buy back land confiscated from their ancestors in the 17th. This legislated marginalisation and underachievement of Irish Catholics is only now finally reaching the end of its historical process with the emergence of a new, self-confident, educated and affluent society. The words of Thomas Davis, written in the 1840s, still rang true many years later:

> Oh! Weep those days, those penal days,
> Their memory still on Ireland weighs.

By the time 'Phelim Brady' began his itinerant life in South Armagh the traditional role of the bard in Old Irish Gaelic society was almost over. For more than four hundred years they had enjoyed an exalted and respected position in society for they were more than just the singer/songwriters of their day. Effectively they were the chroniclers and interpreters of Irish society who used verse to express much more than love and emotion. The word *bard* is a Gaelic term meaning 'poet', though the status gradations of the bards was part of a complex social system. In Old Irish society the bardic caste belonged to the *áes dána* or 'men of art', a high status group that included the professions, trades, arts and crafts. Highest ranked of the poets or *fili* were the *ollamh* whose period of study lasted for twelve years as they had to master some 350 long and complex stories dealing with traditional knowledge and legend. The *fili* were also regarded as seers with the gift of divination, the ability to foresee the future. Such a gift would obviously have been highly sought after and from the 12th century until the demise of Gaelic Ireland under English rule the bards enjoyed great prestige and influence, often travelling around the country accompanied by a retinue of twenty-four servants.

Bard and harper were separate, though sometimes complementary, professions, as Douglas Hyde has forcefully pointed out:

> Most people, owing to their comparative neglect of Irish history, seem to be of the opinion that the bards were harpers, or at least musicians of some sort. But they were nothing of the kind. The popular conception of the bard with the long white beard and the big harp is grotesquely wrong. The bards were verse-makers, pure and simple, and they were no more musicians than the poet laureate of England... when they wrote a eulogy or panegyric on a patron, and brought it to him, they introduced along with themselves a harper and possibly a singer to whom they had taught their poem, and in the presence of their patron to the sound of the harp, the only instrument allowed to be touched on such occasions, the poem was solemnly recited or sung. The real name of the musician was not 'bard' – the bard was a verse-maker – but 'oirfideadh' [errh-fid-ya] and the musicians, though a numerous and honourable class, were absolutely distinct from the bards and 'files'. It was only after the complete break-up of the Gaelic polity, after the wars of Cromwell and of William, that the verse maker merges in the musician, and the harper and the bard become fused in one as was the case with Carolan, commonly called the last of the bards, but whom his patron, O'Conor of Belanagare, calls in his obituary of him, not a 'bard' but an 'oirfideadh'.

Together, the bards and the harpers were the court poets and musicians of the Gaelic aristocracy on whom they were largely dependent for a living. Each great family had its own bard and consequently much of their composition would sing the praises of their patrons while denigrating and satirising their enemies. Hyde summarised their subject matter as consisting of tribal genealogy, religious meditations, personal eulogies, clan history and elegies for the dead.

If the image of Phelim Brady carrying a large concert harp on his back while on the run in the hills of South Armagh seems unrealistic it should be remembered that the harp at that time was much smaller than now, played held on the knee. Today's larger harp only evolved in the 19th century to meet the acoustic demands of the concert hall stage. Ireland must surely be unique in having a musical instrument as a national symbol, appearing as it does almost everywhere, on coins, the Irish passport and even on police uniforms, both north and south. This political significance goes back a long way, with Elizabeth I decreeing 'hang the harpers wherever found' and the United Irishmen adopting the harp along with the slogan: 'Equality - It Is New-Strung and Shall be Heard'. The bards too were the subject of punitive Elizabethan legislation, Hyde noting that 'the severest acts were passed against them over and over again'. One *Act* stated 'those rhymours by their ditties and rhymes...[in] praise of extortion, rebellion, ravin, rape, and other injustice, encourage lords and gentlemen to follow those vices rather than to leave them... for so heinous an abuse orders are taken.'

The harpist, then as now, produced a sound that could both arouse and soothe the emotions but which was above all enchanting, mysterious and magical. Adjectives commonly associated with harp music include beauty, harmony, order, balance, glamour, nobility and dignity. Some of the best-known classic harpists include the following:

Ruadhri Dall O'Cathain: 'Rory Dall', Blind Rory Kane (c. 1590-c.1650). He was certainly from Ulster, probably north Antrim. He spent much of his career travelling in Scotland, meeting and playing for the King, James VI (of Scotland) (1566-1625), a Presbyterian, who became the first Stuart king of England and Ireland and who instigated the Ulster Plantation. Today Rory Dall is best remembered as the composer of the beautiful air *Tabhair dom do lámh* ('Give me your hand'). He is also sometimes credited with having composed another classic, *The Londonderry Air* ('Danny Boy').

Tuirdhealbhach O Cearbhallain: Turlough O'Carolan, (1670-1738), born in Meath but associated with Mohill and Keadue in County Roscommon where he spent most of his life. He also wrote poetry and composed original melodies, especially 'planxties' or dance tunes, including *Gracey Nugent*, *Mabel O'Kelly* and his best-known work, *Carolan's Farewell to Music*. He is said to have 'liked a good drink' and his own wake lasted four days. He is buried in Kilronan Churchyard, just south of Ballaghaderreen in Roscommon.

Denis O'Hempson (or O'Hempsy) from Craigmore, near Garvagh, in County Derry. This redoubtable troubadour, who was born in 1695 and who did not die until 1808, led a remarkable life. He travelled all over the country and even visited Edinburgh in 1745 where he played for Bonnie Prince Charlie, a grandson of 'King Jamie', at the time of the final Scottish Jacobite rebellion. A biography from 1821 included the following: 'At the age of eighty-six [he] married a woman from Innishowen [sic]... "I can't tell", quoth Hampson (O'Hempson), "if it was not the devil buckled us together; she being lame and I blind". By this wife he had one daughter, married to a cooper, who has several children and maintains them all'. He seems like an excellent model for Phelim Brady!

Arthur O'Neill (1734-1818), from Drumnastrade, Dungannon, County Tyrone. As well as being a harpist of distinction, he was also renowned as a teacher and master of the Irish Harp Society. His *Memoirs* are an important musical and social document, containing much biographical information about other harpists as well as fascinating detail about the musical life of the period. In his old age O'Neill lived on an annual pension of £30 paid to him by William Drennan.

By the time of Arthur O'Neill's death the traditional role of the bard-harpist had diminished almost to extinction. The famous Belfast Harp Festival of 1792, organised by the town's leading citizens, including the McCrackens, was both an attempt to recapture the past and to preserve something for the future. It is widely regarded as seminal in the revival of traditional Gaelic music and literature. The event involved an assembly of a dozen or so harpists playing over a three-day period, with prizes being awarded at the finale. The Festival inspired Edward Bunting (1773-1843) to devote the rest of his life to the pioneering work of collecting and publishing traditional melodies and lyrics and of course Bunting's works provided rich pickings for Thomas Moore (1779-1852), widely regarded as Ireland's greatest known songwriter.

Moore's songs, though Big House friendly and, for some tastes, saccharine sweet, have done more to enshrine the harp and the bard as symbols of Irish identity than anything else. These songs are still very popular today and provide an evolutionary link with a musical tradition that stretches back for nigh on a thousand years. Songs like *The Harp That Once Through Tara's Halls, Dear Harp of My Country*, and most famously, *The Minstrel Boy*, are ingrained in the Irish consciousness.

> The minstrel boy to the war is gone,
> In the ranks of death you'll find him.

His father's sword he has girded on
And his wild harp slung behind him.
'Land of Song' said the warrior-bard
'Tho' all the world betrays thee,
One sword at least thy right shall guard,
One faithful harp shall praise thee'.

The bards of old have also bequeathed us a rich legacy of poetry, though this is now almost exclusively an intellectual and academic preserve. Paradoxically as Gaelic power declined there was a final flourishing of poetry as the bards reacted in fear, outrage and despair to the collapse of a social system that had been in place for centuries. Many of their poems were in the form of *aislings*, vision poems or dreams, with Ireland depicted in numerous distressed female forms. These symbols include *Ériu* (Eire), from whence *Éirinn* or *Erin*, her sisters *Banba* (Ireland in the heroic sense) and *Fodla* (Fola – Ireland in the intellectual sense), *Cathleen Ní Houlihan*, *Síle Ní Ghadhra* (*Siúil a Grá* or *Siúil Aroon* - 'farewell my love'), *Gráinne Mhaol* or *Granuaile* (Grace O'Malley) and *Róisín Dubh* (Dark Rosaleen). To fully appreciate these poems it would be necessary to be fluent in the Irish language for, as Sir Walter Scott, writing of Scottish Gaelic said, 'it is difficult if not impossible to render the exquisite felicity of the original'. Nevertheless even in translation we can grasp a certain amount of the expressiveness and musicality of the original, giving us at least an insight into the poet's mind and 'soul'. Some very, very freely adapted translations include:

Daibhi Ó Bruadhair (c. 1625-98), of County Cork. He was so disgusted at the cultural revolution taking place that he swore he would compose no more verse.

For Cuchonnacht Ó Dalaigh's Family

The high poets are gone, and I mourn the world's waning,
The sons of those learned masters are no more responding.

Aodhagán Ó Rathaille (1670-1729) of County Kerry. He bemoaned the confiscation of the lands of his patron Sir Nicholas Browne (De Brun), a Catholic Jacobite.

Last Lines

Now I shall cease, death comes and I cannot delay
By Laune and Laine and Lee, [rivers in the south west] diminished of
    their pride
I shall follow the heroes into the clay;
My fathers followed theirs, before Christ was crucified.

Fear Flata Ó Gnimh (c. 1540 -c.1630), *ollamh* to the O'Neills of Ulster. He
accompanied Shane O'Neill, Shane the Proud, (*Seán an Diomais*) to
the court of Queen Elizabeth in London in 1562.

After the Flight of the Earls

The race of Murrough and O'More,
Bravely fought with sword in hand
But scarce one of that noble seed
Now holds a sod in his native land.

Pádraigín Haicead, Pat Hackett, (c. 1600-1654), a Dominican priest from
Cashel, Tipperary, associated with the Butlers of fabled Kilcash. These
lines were written following the Cromwellian suppression.

On Learning That the Friars Are To Make No more Songs

I will say no word about their mean complaining,
I will stitch up my mouth with a twisted thong,
I will scorn and condemn those petty censors,
O God they have stifled my people and song.

The place name of Armagh (*Ard Mhacha*), 'Macha's height', is derived
from *Mhacha* a pre-Christian queen who had built a fort on the main hill
of the site. Saint Patrick arrived here around the middle of the 5th century
and gradually Armagh developed into the main centre of Christianity in
Ireland. Today the city, population 14,000, has two Saint Patrick's
Cathedrals, one Anglican, one Catholic, with the former containing 'the
ashes of Brian Boru' the king who supposedly 'drove the Danes' from
Ireland at the Battle of Clontarf in 1014.

In recent years the city has not been able to fully benefit from its ancient
origins and ecclesiastical importance for the Troubles have had a severe
social and economic effect. When I visited the town I found that the
shutters went up at six o'clock in the evening. After wandering around the
town centre looking in vain for a place to eat, I eventually plucked up the
courage to enquire of a group of teenagers. They regarded me quizzically,
decided that I was a genuine foreigner, and then directed me to the local
chip shop! Eventually I found a pub, proclaiming itself a 'Drugs Free Zone'.
However it was also food free. After supping a pint of Guinness, I decided
to settle for the chip shop after all and then retired early to my hotel room.

Today South Armagh is seen either as 'bandit country', from a speech by
the British Secretary of State Merlyn Rees in 1975 (not Margaret
Thatcher), or as 'gerrymandered undemocratic country'. The area, with
its large nationalist majority, is widely regarded as the most flagrant
breach of the spirit of the Treaty of 1922, which should never have been

included in the North at partition. My main impression of the area was of a people glad to be at peace again, to be almost free of the army helicopters circling overhead, the constant surveillance and the restrictions on movement. Here however were a people who identify with Gaelic history and culture, especially regarding music and sport, and who see themselves as Irish not British.

Around Crossmaglen, the quintessential republican village, 'capital' of South Armagh, the roads are still festooned with Irish flags and 'road signs' such as 'Beware, Sniper at Work', more recently, 'Disband the RUC', and more recently still 'De-militarise – Brits Out'. After a look around the area it's not difficult to see why the nationalist tradition is so strong. It's impossible to walk more than a couple of hundred yards without stumbling across the symbols of history. An ancient *ráth* (ring fort), the site of the *crannóg* on Lough Ross where the 1641 rebellion was planned, the much resented border along the Fane River and the defiant republican sculpture which now dominates Crossmaglen's town square.

> Glory to all you praised and humble heroes
> Who have willingly suffered
> For your unselfish and passionate love of Ireland

As I sat reading about Bishop Donnelly in the *Tí Chulainn* Cultural Activity Centre in Mullaghbawn my mind wandered back to the 17th century and my eyes were drawn to the slopes of Slieve Gullion, 'a home and a refuge' for bold 'Phelim Brady', *The Bard of Armagh*.

5.
The Boys of Mullaghbawn

On a Monday morning early, as my wandering steps did take me
Down by a farmer's station, his meadows and green lawns,
I heard great lamentations, the wee birds they were making,
Saying 'We'll have no more engagements with the boys of Mullaghbawn'.

I beg your pardon lady, and ask you this one favour,
I hope it is not treason, on you I now must call.
I'm condoling late and early, my heart is nigh on breaking
All for a noble lady that lives near Mullaghbawn.

Squire Jackson he's unequalled for honour or for reason,
He never turned a traitor nor betrayed the rights of man,
But now we are in danger from a vile deceiving stranger
Who has ordered transportation for the boys of Mullaghbawn.

As those heroes crossed the ocean, I'm told the ship in motion
Would stand in wild commotion as if the seas ran dry.
The trout and salmon gaping, as the Cuckoo left her station
Saying 'Fare thee well Killeavy and the hills of Mullaghbawn'.

And to end my lamentation, we're all in consternation
None dares for recreation until the day does dawn
For without hesitation, we are charged with 'combination'
And sent for transportation from the hills of Mullaghbawn.

Courtesy Linenhall Library

Peep O' Day Boys looking for weapons

The Boys of Mullaghbawn

Secret Societies in South Armagh,
Banishment to Australia

This two hundred-year-old broadside ballad, probably written by an anonymous hedge schoolteacher, makes it very clear that something terrible once happened in the hilly countryside of South Armagh and that the full force of the law was brought to bear against the perpetrators. From the beginning the language used is consistently dramatic and powerful, creating an atmosphere of calamity and brooding mystery. However we are not given the names of the participants and very little information about the crimes that caused them to be sentenced to transportation, bonded servitude halfway around the world.

To the modern mind the charge of 'combination' seems innocuous enough. However during the period in which the ballad is set it would have struck terror into the hearts of the accused, who would have been well aware of the likely consequences. Perhaps this is reflected in the line, 'I ask you this one favour, I hope it is not treason'. The charge referred to membership of an illegal organisation, either one of the numerous agrarian secret societies or to an embryonic trade union. They were strictly forbidden under the Combination Acts of 1719 and 1743 and often operated as underground cells or in the guise of friendly or benevolent societies. Landlords and other employers resisted these 'combinations' with all the force of the draconian legislation then available.

In the case of *The Boys of Mullaghbawn* the charge of 'combination' related to the activities of the Defenders, the generic term for the many Catholic secret societies that had grown up during the worst of the Penal period after the Williamite Wars. The peasant members of these organisations were concerned only with basic localised agrarian grievances such as rents and security of tenure. They had no ambitions of challenging government and were indeed loyalist, swearing to be 'true to his majesty King George'.

On the Catholic side were the Blackfeet, Rightboys, Rockites, Terry Alts, Tommy Downshires, Whitefeet and Carders, who used their weavers carding combs to mutilate their enemies. Groupings on the Protestant side were less numerous though no less determined. The main ones were the Hearts of Steel and the Peep O' Day Boys, who often carried out their depredations at first light.

The term Defender is said to have originated in an area called Bunker's Hill at Edenknappagh, about a mile south of Jonesborough. If this is indeed the case, it would mean that the name did not come into use until after 1775, as the place name commemorates the Battle of Bunker Hill during the American War of Independence. A local Catholic 'fleet' adopted the name Bunker's Hill Defenders after clashes with the rival Protestant Edenknappagh Fleet, Peep O' Day Boys. By 1790 the Defender movement had spread throughout most of Ulster and south into Louth and Meath and was beginning to assume nationalist political aspirations through contacts with the Presbyterian United Irishmen. In the 19th century many of these localised groupings coalesced into the umbrella organisation known as the Ribbonmen. Most of the groupings, on both sides, were of a similar general nature and operated by way of binding oaths, disguises and acts of violence of varying degree, including murder. Lesser crimes included threats against landlords, beatings, damage and destruction of property and the mutilation of farm animals.

The incident that inspired *The Boys of Mullaghbawn* took place in South Armagh in January 1791, when the culmination of a local sectarian feud ended in murder, execution and transportation. As the Penal Laws began to be less rigorously applied, Catholics began to bid for farm tenancies, in the process often undercutting better-off Protestants. This exacerbated traditional tensions and Catholics and Protestants often came into conflict. Although Catholics were the more discriminated against, Presbyterians often shared their hardships, especially regarding high rents and the payment of tithes for the support of the established Anglican Church. In 1772 one Protestant complained 'betwixt landlord and rector the very marrow is squeezed out of our bones'.

Mullaghbawn was part of the Forkhill Estate and the landlord Richard Jackson (c. 1722-1787) had made provision in his will for the establishment of a school in the area. In his lifetime Jackson had been a popular landlord with a reputation for treating all of his tenants fairly. For some reason though his will favoured his Protestant tenants. One clause stated that when the leases of Catholic tenants expired they should be offered to Protestants only. However what upset Catholics most was another clause that bequeathed a school to the area. Again this favoured Protestants for although the school was thought to be inter-denominational, it was seen as a threat. Lessons were to be in English only and it was also planned to move English-speaking Protestants into the largely Catholic and Irish-speaking area.

Squire Jackson had died without issue and the running of the Estate now passed to the Reverend Edward Hudson and his bailiff and tithe proctor James Dawson, both perceived as having little sympathy for the majority Catholic tenants. When the school was established, Dawson's first act was to replace a popular local teacher, a bilingual Protestant, with his brother-in-law Alexander Barclay who spoke no Irish. The implication of this was that if Catholics wanted to get an education they would have to sacrifice their native language. Tensions rose and the Reverend Hudson was the victim of a murder attempt when his horse was shot from under him. Then on Christmas Day 1790 the local parish priest, Father Cullen, was attacked by Peep O' Day Boys and badly beaten, his chalice and vestments destroyed. The Catholics blamed Barclay for the attack and retaliated by marching on his home.

The assault, thought to have been led by a Defender called Terence Byrne, resulted in the mutilation, 'violation' and later death of Mrs. Barclay and the mutilation of her husband and brother. In court the victims, who had their tongues cut out during the attack, could only identify their assailants by nods of the head. One account of the Barclay attack stated that the assailants had made no attempt to hide their identity, which could be interpreted as an indication that they had intended to murder the whole family. The fate of the attackers after their arrest is uncertain, though it is known that at least one Defender, a man called Peter Murphy, was hanged in May 1791. An account of the trial names another of those executed as Donnelly, whom Hudson swore had stabbed Alexander Barclay. Of those transported the only name to have survived is that of a man called Bennett. Terence Byrne is thought to have avoided arrest by hiding in the hills before being eventually spirited out of the country. Hudson also had to leave the area for his own safety. The 'Armagh Outrages' culminated in the flight of 7,000 Catholics to Connacht in 1795-96.

Although full details of what actually happened in Mullaghbawn all those years ago are sketchy and sometimes conflicting, it is certain that there was a long-running feud, a number of violent assaults, a murder, at least two executions and a number of men transported. However the legacy of the episode was the composition of a very fine and atmosperic ballad, one that provides a fascinating insight into a way of life that has long since vanished. If that weren't enough, the lyrics are then set to a melody that stuns the senses with its subtle beauty and shows no sign of diminishing with the passage of time.

The ballad's general tenor is straightforward enough but a number of questions are raised. Is there a hint of ambiguity concerning the role of the 'noble lady' for whom 'my heart is nigh on breaking'? Could she be the wife or daughter of some local man of high status that one of the peasants had become involved with? Who was 'the vile deceiving stranger' and could he have brought some grudge to bear concerning the 'noble lady'? The law of the period delegated great discretionary powers to local magistrates, who were government political appointees with no legal qualifications, always Protestant and usually ultra-loyalist. They could introduce curfews and martial law and suspend trial by jury almost on a whim. It's possible that 'the vile deceiving stranger' was one of these terrorising magistrates or simply the hated Hudson who had sworn the 'boys' into virtual slavery.

In later versions of the song the local place name of Killeavy (*Cill Shléibhe*, 'Church of the mountain') has been replaced by 'Erin'. While this is understandable it does remove an important pointer to the origins of the song. Killeavy is an area on the other side of Slieve Gullion from Mullaghbawn and the reference to it could be an indication that the homes of the 'boys' were located on the mountain's northern slopes. Is the 'rights of man' a reference to the publication of the same name by Thomas Paine (1737-1809), the English political theorist, who had published his radical work in two parts over 1791-92? This advocated far-reaching political, economic and social reforms, including freedom of thought and action. The ruthless totalitarian attitude of the government towards such ideas is evident, for Paine had to flee to France to escape arrest and in his absence was convicted of 'treason'.

Is the 'cuckoo' mentioned in verse four simply a bird and just another example of the stupefaction of nature at the 'crime'? Or is it a symbol of daybreak or of spring, when the 'boys' were parted from their loved ones for the final time? Could it be *The Cuckoo*, the name of the ship that carried the victims to their fate? The latter is how it is given in Colm O'Lochlainn's book, *More Irish Street Ballads*, in 1965. However in an article by Sean O'Boyle in *Ulster Folk Life* in 1959, to which O'Lochlainn refers, it is simply given as 'cuckoo' with a small 'c'. The most likely explanation however is that it is slang term for a female informer. Local tradition strongly asserts that the boys of Mullaghbawn were betrayed by a woman named Betty O'Neial, the wife of Sean O'Neial who was a United Irish commander in 1798, a man 'well known for his seditious activities in these parts'. On the evening of 21 June 1798 Lieutenant John Duff of the Killeavy Yeomanry reported: 'at this hour Slieve Gullion was ablaze and there was much horn blowing... but there was no sight of rebels'. Would it be stretching credulity too far to consider the possibility that Betty O'Neial may also have been the 'noble lady'? After all the term 'cuckold' for the husband of an adulterous wife is also derived from the cuckoo, the bird that lays its eggs in the nest of another.

Statistics relating to transportation are scarce but it is generally agreed that the number ran to many thousands especially during the first thirty years of the 19th century. The total figure is estimated to be in the region of 400,000, consisting of about 320,000 'common criminals', 80,000 'agrarian outrage' or 'social rebels' and about 600 political rebels. Thus very few were political prisoners though many of the 'agrarian outrages' could ultimately be traced back to political root causes. The policy of transportation was not of course a uniquely Irish one with many social and political undesirables being transported from all over Britain. The best known case of transportation in England was that of the 'Tolpuddle Martyrs', six farm workers from Dorset, in 1833. They had founded the Friendly Society of Agricultural Labourers and were framed on a charge of administering illegal oaths. Today they are regarded as the founders of English trade unionism. The most celebrated Scottish transportee was Thomas Muir of Huntershill, just north of Glasgow, who received a fourteen-year sentence in 1793 for publicly advocating parliamentary reform. In 1792 Muir, an advocate (barrister), had presented an address from the Dublin Society of United Irishmen, at the first meeting of the Scottish Friends of the People. He later escaped to America but was to die in his early thirties, broken by suffering and hardship.

Prior to the independence of the American colonies in 1776 deportees were often sent there or to the West Indies. Effectively this was a form of slavery, bonded servitude, for periods of seven years, fourteen years or for life. Part of the transportee's income from the compulsory labour for the duration of the sentence was used to defray the costs involved in the transportation process. Sentences were often handed down without benefit of trial and vagrants and the politically non-compliant were at particular risk. Most transportees though were those who had committed petty crimes, the theft of everyday items such as a saddle, a yard of cloth, a pair of shoes or a loaf of bread.

With the independence of the American colonies Australia was designated as the next destination with Acts being passed in 1788 for Botany Bay (Sydney) and in 1803 for Van Diemen's Land (Tasmania). The first Irish transportees arrived in Sydney Harbour in January 1788. It would appear that the boys of Mullaghbawn were sent down under, a horrendous journey at the time, lasting almost six months and during which the conditions were inhumane and degrading. When John Mitchel, an exceptionally strong and resolute individual, was transported in 1848 he wrote, 'language was never meant to describe' his despair. Here Mitchel was referring to the greatest hardship: the forcible and often final separation from loved ones. Convicts were usually kept chained for long periods, suffered from scurvy, fever and unaccustomed tropical temperatures in the hold of the ship. It is little wonder that 'none dares for recreation until the day does dawn'. Ironically though transportees usually had the benefit of having a doctor on board and of being guaranteed basic rations: luxuries that many later 'voluntary' emigrants did not enjoy. On arrival at port they faced a life of unremitting hard labour, being assigned to chain gangs, work gangs or as farm labourers. Sooner or later about 20 per cent would be flogged or 'wear the red suit', a punishment that could cause permanent damage to the heart and lungs. Some would abscond to lead the precarious and usually fatal life of the bushranger. (Ned Kelly's father John, an agrarian activist, had been transported from Tipperary for the theft of two pigs). The majority however, who could not be classified as true criminals, gradually adapted to their new circumstances, with many going on to achieve considerable success and some even high office.

Another well-documented example of transportation deals with Hugh Larkin (1809-57) of East Galway who was sent to Australia in 1834. His was fairly typical of the experience of many 'agrarian outrage' tranportees. Larkin was a member of the Terry Alts, a Catholic secret society named after a Corofin shoemaker, who had been wrongly convicted of attacking a local land agent after being mistakenly identified. Hugh Larkin was a fiery young rebel from Lismany near Aughrim, who had been sacked by his local landlord, Simeon Seymour, for suspected membership of the Terry Alts. He also faced eviction from his tiny plot of land. The impulsive Larkin didn't take the punishment lying down. Instead he retaliated by threatening Seymour with 'an untimely fate' if he didn't raise wages and lower rents. Late one evening Larkin and his cohorts marched on the landlord's home, smashed down his door and threatened his wife, though no one was actually attacked or physically harmed in the incident. However Simeon Seymour, who had not been at home at the time of the attack, did not let the matter drop. Hugh Larkin was arrested, tried and 'sent for transportation' to Sydney. The twenty-four year old was never to see his young wife, his two children or his homeland again. Eventually, after serving most of his sentence, he remarried and raised a new family in the New World.

Hugh was to die in tragic circumstances before he reached fifty. Always a hard drinker, he took to the bottle seriously after the death of his wife in childbirth in 1854. In the two days before his final illness he is said to have consumed almost two gallons of home-made rum. However Hugh had somehow still managed to bequeath to Australia a decent family. The son born in 1854, also called Hugh, probably after one of his 'lost' half brothers in Galway, was to live to see out the Second World War, not dying until 1949 at the age of ninety-four. I find it quite amazing to think that I, born in 1945, was to share the earth for four years with the son of a Terry Alt transportee who had been born six years before the Battle of Waterloo.

Thomas Keneally tells the full story of the tragic life of Hugh Larkin in his outstanding book *The Great Shame*, published in 1998.

The last convict ship from Ireland was the *Hougoumont* on 12 October 1867, which arrived at Fremantle in Western Australia on 10 January the following year. The ship carried almost three hundred prisoners including some sixty-three recently convicted Fenians. The best known was John Boyle O'Reilly (1844-90) who escaped to America in 1869. There he went on to establish a considerable reputation as a literary figure and journalist. However he never fully recovered from his transportation experience and died relatively young after accidentally taking an overdose of medication prescribed to alleviate his chronic insomnia.

A fascinating record of the voyage was maintained by O'Reilly's friend Denis B. Cashman (1842-97), a clerk with a law firm in Dungarvan, found guilty of 'manufacturing rifle cartridges'. His diary, first published in 2001, shows that many of the Fenians were literate and literary men who distanced themselves from the 'ordinary' convicts on board, many of whom were thieves, rapists and murderers. Conditions, though strict, were not as punitive as might be imagined, with the Fenians being given a daily wine and tobacco allowance. When they had recovered from the initial shock of separation, and from months in solitary confinement, they whiled away the hours by writing poetry, publishing a newspaper and organising regular recitals and concerts, featuring both popular and nationalist songs. Their 'National Anthem' was Thomas Moore's *Let Erin Remember*. Cashman had been sentenced to 'only' seven years and was pardoned in 1869. He immediately set sail for America where he was reunited with his wife Catherine and his surviving son William. Two other sons, Denis and Arthur, died from measles while he was in Australia. In America the couple were to have another two children, daughters Mary and Kathleen. Over the next thirty years Cashman worked as a journalist, administrator and author, publishing a biography of Michael Davitt in 1881.

Less well-known Fenians on board the *Hougoumont* included John Sarsfield Casey from Cork, the original Galtee Mountain Boy, who was still in his teens and who also kept a diary of the voyage, published in 1988. Pardoned in 1870, he returned to Ireland and was astonished to find that he was accorded a hero's welcome. Also on board was John O'Neil Goulding (or Golden), one of those celebrated in *The Fenians of Cahirsiveen*. Goulding had joined the movement after the local landlord had shot his dog when it had barked at his coach on the road near Kells in County Kerry. He had been informed on by locals and was never to return home. Eventually he became a successful farmer, married and fathered seven children. He died at the early age of thirty-eight, though his widow

Ellen Feehan lived on until 1938. Today John Goulding's Fenian bones lie buried beneath a Celtic cross near Gerringong, eighty miles south of Sydney, on the coast of New South Wales.

Another *Hougoumont* veteran, James Kiely, or Keilley, of Clonmel died in 1918, aged 84. Separated from his wife and children, Kiely had attempted suicide in Dartmoor Prison in the 1860s. However at the time of the *Catalpa* rescue he was deliberately left behind, regarded as too 'trusty' towards the authorities, possibly to the point of having provided information. For many years he wandered western Australia half-destitute, living in a battered tent. In his old age he was rescued by the Celtic Club and lived on their charity for the remainder of his days. He too lies buried far from home, in Karrakatta Cemetery, Perth.

The *Combination Acts* were repealed in 1824 and transportation abolished in 1868. If the boys of Mullaghbawn survived their ordeal, their descendants would by this time be well into the third generation of Australian-born citizenship.

The place name of Mullaghbawn, often spelt 'Mullaghbane' on old maps, refers to both townland and village. It is more likely that the 'Boys of Mullaghbawn' lived on farms in the townland rather than in the village. The name is derived from the Irish, *An Mullach Bán*, meaning 'the white summit'. Mullaghbawn Mountain, standing at 805 feet, is just south west of the village which is located about eight miles north west of Dundalk, overlooking the western slopes of Slieve Gullion, off a minor road just north of Forkhill. Nearby is a small folk museum in the style of a traditional Irish farmhouse though it is probably far too cosily modern to bear much resemblance to the primitive cabins that would have been home to *The Boys of Mullaghbawn*.

6.

Boolavogue

At Boolavogue, as the sun was setting
O'er the bright May meadows of Shelmalier,
A rebel hand set the heather blazing
And brought the neighbours from far and near.
Then Father Murphy from old Kilcormick
Spurred up the rocks with a warning cry
'To arms!' he cried, 'for I've come to lead you
For Ireland's freedom we fight or die'.

He led us on against the coming soldiers
And the cowardly yeomen we put to flight.
'Twas at The Harrow the boys of Wexford
Showed Bookey's regiment how men could fight.
Look out for hirelings King George of England,
Search every kingdom where breathes a slave,
For Father Murphy of the County Wexford
Sweeps o'er the land like a might wave.

We took Camolin and Enniscorthy
And Wexford's storming drove out our foes.
'Twas at Slieve Coillte our pikes were reeking
With the crimson stream of the beaten yeos.
At Tubberneering and Ballyellis
Full many a Hessian lay in his gore.
Ah! Father Murphy, had aid come over,
The green flag floated from shore to shore.

At Vinegar Hill o'er the pleasant Slaney
Our heroes vainly stood back to back,
And the yeos at Tullow took Father Murphy
And burned his body upon the rack.
God grant you glory brave Father Murphy
And open heaven to all your men,
For the cause that called you may call tomorrow
In another fight for the green again.

Photo: John McLaughlin

Father Murphy memorial stone, Mullawn cemetery, Tullow

Boolavogue

The Epic Tragedy of Father John Murphy and the Wexford Rebellion

This most famous of all the rebel songs gives a passionate and comprehensive account of the 1798 Wexford Rebellion. For many today though it is more about heritage and identity than politics or rebellion. As Wexford singer Paddy Berry has written, 'its sound alerts Wexford men and women all over the world to the fact that they belong to one of Ireland's most historic counties, that they inherit a great tradition and that they are privileged and proud to sing a ballad that holds the essence of Wexford in its stirring words'.

Written by Patrick Joseph McCall, the ballad covers virtually all the action of the Uprising, from the opening skirmishes in late May to the critical rebel reversal at Vinegar Hill on 21 June. It first appeared in the *Irish Weekly Independent* on 18 June 1898 as *Father Murphy of the County Wexford*. P.J. McCall died in 1919, unaware of the huge success that his lyrics were to enjoy in the future. Originally the ballad had been set to a different melody and it was not until it was set to the air of *Youghal Harbour* in 1922 that it really took off. The revised song was popularised locally through the singing of Art Sinnott of Ferns who won his local *Feis Ceoil* with it in 1928. Afterwards it was picked up by national radio and the rest is history.

Father John Murphy (1753-98) was born in the townland of Tincurry, about three miles south west of Ferns, overlooking the River Slaney. Government forces burned his home to the ground in 1798 and since then it has been totally obliterated. He was the youngest of the six children born to tenant farmers Thomas and Johanna Murphy (nee Whitty). Thomas Murphy would have been born around 1715 and grown up under the full weight of the Penal Laws, as well as with stories of the loss of land in his grandparents' time. John Murphy was ordained to the priesthood in 1779 and then spent the next five years studying theology in Seville. Before that he had been in charge of the family horses and was an accomplished rider, a skill that would prove useful during his five weeks as a rebel. He often ventured on long hunting trips to the Blackstairs Mountains, staying with friends and relatives and was therefore very familiar with the terrain of north Wexford, east Kilkenny and south Carlow.

The Boolavogue area had for some time been a centre of United Irish activity and had been under martial law since November 1797. Until the very day before the rebellion Father Murphy had been a strong advocate of church policy, of surrendering arms in return for promises of protection. Many Boolavogue men took his advice and handed over their weapons. However in the prevailing anarchy, theoretical government guarantees couldn't protect local people and many of those who surrendered weapons were singled out for reprisals. Homes and crops were burned, pitch-capping militiamen roamed the countryside, suspects were shot or hanged on a whim, families slept out in hedges and rebel suspects were transported to Australia by the dozen.

In such circumstances John Murphy eventually sided with his own people and, ignoring the strictures of his ultra-conservative bishop James Caufield, was reluctantly sucked into the conflict, stating 'better to die like men than be butchered like dogs in the ditches'. There is no doubt that when he threw in his lot with the insurgents he became an inspiring, though imperfect leader, who played a major role in many of the decisive actions of the rebellion. He continued to say Mass in the open and held the rank of Captain with the rebels of his home Barony, Ballaghkeen North.

Although *Boolavogue*, the song, casts a giant shadow, the village of Boolavogue (*Baile Mhaodhóg*), 'Maodhog's homestead', named after a 6th century saint, is such a tiny hamlet that it appears only on large scale Ordnance Survey maps. The village is situated about five miles south east of Ferns near the tiny crossroads community of The Harrow (*An Bráca*). Take the left fork southeast and fabled Boolavogue is just over a mile further along this little county road. It was here that John Murphy, one of the best-known names thrown up by the rebellion, first emerged on the stage of history.

If approaching Ferns from Enniscorthy, the Father Murphy Centre (opened in 1998) is clearly signposted to the right. The Centre is an idealistic, not to say Disneyesque, reconstruction of the site in 1798. It consists of Father Murphy's House, the Pig Sty, the Lodge, the Cowhouse, the Barn and Stable and a Garden of Remembrance, which pays tribute to all of those who died in the conflict, including loyalists.

Kilcormick, (*Cill Cormac*) 'the church of Cormac', is the old parish name of the area around Boolavogue and includes The Harrow. Here on 26 May Father Murphy and his men, not yet rebels, killed Lieutenant Thomas Bookey and John Donovan of the Camolin Yeoman Cavalry when attacked by them after surrendering weapons to a local magistrate. It was hardly the great military victory implied by McCall's ballad but the lines are a good example of the author's imaginative style. After the deaths, there was no way back for men now classed as outlaws and rebels.

The attack was motivated as much by local personal jealousies as by political conviction. John Donovan, a convert to Protestantism, was well-known to the men of Boolavogue with whom he had a complicated and tempestuous relationship. He had been drinking with them in the inn at The Harrow just a couple of evenings previously when he was subjected to a good deal of ribald banter. The locals were well aware that Donovan's wife had become involved with a young farm hand called Boyne who was employed by his Catholic rival cousin Tom Donovan, a known United Irishman. Distracted by this, and an alcoholic binge, he instigated the vengeful cavalry attack at The Harrow, having earlier burned down the Boyne family home. Ironically he was killed by a shot from his first cousin, Tom Donovan. Lieutenant Bookey of nearby Rockspring met a savage death at the hands of the Boolavogue pikemen. Tom Donovan, still in shock, was himself killed the following day during the rebel success, the Battle of Oulart Hill a few miles to the south, where a hundred government soldiers died for the loss of six rebels.

Camolin (*Cam Eolaing*) 'Eolang's bend' is situated on the main road north of Ferns. Its military significance in the song is a trifle exaggerated. 'We took Camolin' is literally true but implies a great military victory when all that really happened was that the government troops garrisoned there made a strategic retreat to Enniscorthy, leaving it to the rebels.

The capture of the garrison town of Enniscorthy ('Island of Cortaidh') by an army of about six thousand men on 28 May was one of the major rebel successes of the whole campaign. The fighting was fierce and lasted some hours with heavy casualties on both sides before the government forces finally retreated south. During the fighting John Murphy is said to have shown great personal courage as well as leadership qualities. The captors then massacred many defenceless loyalist civilians. The rebels set up their main camp on Vinegar Hill just east of the town, much of which had been burned. Two days later they captured the abandoned Wexford Town, a name of Viking origin meaning 'sea washed'. They now controlled most of the County.

The rebels next set up camp on *Slieve Coillte*, 'wooded mountain', an eight hundred-foot hill south of New Ross. There were no military engagements here and the line 'at *Slieve Coillte* our pikes were reeking' is essentially triumphalist imagery. Tubberneering (*Toberanierin*), *tobar* meaning 'a well', a mile south of Clogh, was the scene of a fierce encounter on 4 June as the rebel column headed for Gorey. Each side suffered serious losses but the government soldiers came off worst and retreated in disarray. The Battle of Vinegar Hill took place on 21 June and was to prove the decisive rebel defeat. After about five hours of bombardment the insurgents were dislodged, though Father Murphy and many of his men managed to escape south by way of Drumgold. However his brother Patrick died in the Battle. The government army now took revenge for the rebel atrocities of three weeks previously and massacred many innocent non-combatant refugees. Today the modern housing estate at Vinegar Hill is called Father Murphy Park.

For the rebels the Wexford area was highly dangerous and, after a conference with Father Philip Roche, who had succeeded Harvey as United commander-in-chief, they immediately headed north through the Blackstairs Mountains. Philip Roche decided to throw himself on the mercy of the British. It was a forlorn hope and he was summarily and brutally executed as he rode into Wexford. The story of Father Murphy's three day, seventy mile meandering march with the remnants of his ragged and exhausted army through Wexford, Kilkenny, Carlow and Laois and of his fatal and short-lived alliance with the coal miners of Castlecomer is the stuff of epic historical dramas. En route the rebels contested two more victorious skirmishes, at Killedmond, three miles north east of Borris, and at Goresbridge, a few miles west on the River Barrow.

Ballyellis is a townland a couple of miles east of Carnew, near the Wicklow border. Here on 30 June the rebels, not Father Murphy's men, enjoyed one of their final successes when they ambushed a column of yeomen, killing over thirty of the hated and feared Welsh regiment, the 'Ancient Britons'. The 'Yeos', or Yeomen, were a defence force formed for internal security in 1796 when the threat of internal revolt and invasion by France were very real. They were mostly Protestant, often with strong Orange links. 'Hessians' was the local name given to the imported German mercenaries of the Hompesch Cavalry and 60th Jagers.

Tullow (*An Tulach*), 'the hill', is the small Carlow town on the banks of the Slaney where Father Murphy was taken after capture and where he was tortured and executed on 2 July. Ironically, John Murphy was fated to die overlooking the same river where he had been born. After the victory at Goresbridge, the rebels headed northwest to the coal mining village of Doonane in County Laois (then Queen's County). Here the miners had risen on 23 May but had been crushed by superior forces. In this area, on land confiscated from the O'Brennans, some of whom became well-known rapparees, coal had been mined since the 1630s.

Early on 24 June Father Murphy's men, allied with the miners, attacked and captured Castlecomer after a rebel emissary carrying a white flag had been shot dead. Although they lost about a hundred men dead, the success and fresh recruits to the cause gave the rebels renewed hope. The plan now was to march north to Athy where thousands more potential rebels were said to be rallying to the cause. The route taken was north east by

Monreenroe, crossing the River Dinin, and back into County Laois by Clonbrock to camp at Slatt Upper on the evening of 24 June. However it soon became apparent that local people were no longer flocking to join. Hardship and sacrifice had finally taken their toll on morale. Sensing the mood of hopelessness, some of the colliers now stole back to their homes. Aware that government forces had retaken Wexford Town a few days previously, the last hope for John Murphy and his diminishing band lay in seeking outlaw refuge in the mountains. The last incredible week in the life of the curate of Boolavogue was about to begin.

Rather surprisingly, McCall's ballad makes no reference to the Castlecomer campaign, though two verses are devoted to it in the older broadside ballad that had almost certainly originally inspired him.

> We marched to 'Comer and fought the soldiers,
> We travelled round through the Colliery.
> They stole our guns, leaving us disarmed.
> We lost our lives in Kilkenny.

> 'Twas by these means Father Murphy was taken
> On our retreat towards Castlemore.
> He was brought to Tullow and used severely.
> This blessed priest, they burned him sore.

Now the rebels were forced to head south again by way of Gorteen and Croghtenclogh, on through the high bogland of Baunreagh back to Goresbridge. Two miles further east Father Murphy spent his last night with the men who had followed him and fought by his side for exactly a month. The final rebel camp was at Kilcumney Hill on 25 June. As dawn broke on the 26th they awoke to the realisation that the miners had deserted, carrying off and sabotaging as many weapons as they could. Worse still, a formidable force of government soldiers had already surrounded the mist-shrouded camp. The position was now hopeless and it was every man for himself. In the confusion of hastily breaking camp under siege and disoriented by fog Father Murphy became separated from all of his men except his old friend and neighbour James Gallagher. Today the peak of Kilcumney Hill, only 430 feet high, is crowned with two monuments to John Murphy's last battle. The text of the older one, now in danger of obliteration by the weather, reads:

> Following the failure of their heroic campaign in the Midlands the rebel army, led by Fr. John Murphy and Miles Byrne, set up camp here for the final time late on the 25th of June 1798. On the early morning of June 26th the camp was besieged by the forces of

General Charles Asgill and Major George Matthews. Weary from months of marching and fighting and weakened by the desertion of the Midlands recruits the insurgents made one desperate stand before Fr. Murphy gave the order to retreat towards Scollagh Gap. Here the insurgent advance party overcame the cavalry of General Lake. However many of their exhausted comrades had become separated from the main party. The many nameless graves between Kilcumney and the Blackstairs bear testimony to their fate. In pursuit of the rebel army the forces of General Asgill wreaked vengeance on the area killing upwards of 140 innocent inhabitants. Kilcumney Hill was the final engagement of Fr. John Murphy's army. He was subsequently arrested and was executed in Tullow on the 2nd July 1798.

Eluding the government soldiers, the two rebels now crept eastwards towards the home of a family known to Father Murphy, the O'Connells of Killoughternane. Here they rested before pressing on, still eastwards, to the home of the priest's relatives, the Murphys of the Bawnogue, where they spent the next three nights, 26, 27, and 28 June. The plan now was to head for the Wicklow Hills via the Cromwell Gap, south of Tomduff Hill where they had made camp on 22 June, crossing the Slaney near Bunclody.

Now resting by day and travelling under cover of darkness the rebels next spent some time with a sympathetic farmer called Griffiths at Rossdellig. Then back to Killoughternane where they had their horses re-shod (backwards to confuse trackers but revealing if caught). The evening and early hours of 29 June were again spent at the safe haven of the O'Connell family. Now the fugitives veered some four miles northeast to Coolnasneachta where they spent the night of 30 June with the Jordan family. By now they were well north of the Cromwell Gap and had obviously been forced to change plan.

The next day, 1 July, was spent with the Nolan family about five miles further north near Fennagh. Until now Father Murphy, who knew the area fairly well, had always sought refuge with families known to him. Now, at Ballyveale, a mile north west of Ballon, he had to risk asking strangers for help, a Protestant family called Keppel. It would have been obvious that the unkempt strangers were rebels on the run, yet George and Anne Keppel placed their home, family and their very lives in jeopardy by offering them succour, a true act of Christian charity. The weary Catholic priest and rebel Captain told his story to the peaceful Protestant farmer and was offered a bed for as long as he wanted it. However, not wanting to place the family at any further risk, John Murphy turned the offer down. If he had elected to stay with the Keppels then he might just have survived. As it was this would be the day before he died.

The early hours of 2 July were passed in the open, travelling north towards Tullow through an area thick with government forces. At daybreak the weary rebels stumbled into the stables of the O'Toole family at Castlemore, just west of Tullow. Here the gods who had smiled on them through so many dangers now looked away.

The O'Tooles stabled their horses and allowed them to bed down in the hayloft. However as the family worked in the fields, a band of yeomen approached and demanded their team of horses for 'the service of the government'. Panic stricken, Mrs O'Toole blurted out that two strangers asleep in the stables had better horses. The yeomen entered the stables and discovered the telltale reverse-shod horse's hooves. John Murphy and James Gallagher were rudely awakened, triumphantly arrested and immediately dragged into Tullow.

There, openly in the Market Square, the two men were subjected to terrible torture but absolutely refused to reveal their identities. Witnesses maintain that both John Murphy and James Gallagher never uttered a word or a cry. Eventually his captors, still unaware of his true identity though they knew that he was a priest, grew bored and hanged Father Murphy. Afterwards, amid much hilarity, he was decapitated and his body burned in a barrel of pitch. Yeomen burst into the adjacent home of the O'Callaghan family, throwing open the doors and windows to let the 'holy smoke' waft through. Later the remains were buried in an unmarked grave in Mullawn Cemetery where they still lie.

Today the area around Tullow is signposted 'Father John Murphy's Last Journey' and is dotted with monuments and memorials: at the site of the O'Toole homestead, on the former O'Callaghan building (now offices), in Mullawn Cemetery, in Tullow square, at Ballon, Goresbridge and Kilcumney Hill. I had started out on my journey determined to find out as much as possible about Father John Murphy: the man, the legend and the song. As I drove out of Tullow I was satisfied that I had discovered a good deal about all three. Heading north I soothed my ragged emotions with the golden voice of Luke Kelly singing *Joe Hill*. This American song with its theme of martyred underdog struggling against overwhelmingly superior forces seemed appropriate also to the life of John Murphy:

'Takes more than guns to kill a man;
I never died', said he, 'I never died', said he.

The old coachhouse at Killan, meeting place of the United Irishmen.

Photo: John McLaughlin

7.
Kelly the Boy from Killanne

What's the news? What's the news? Oh my bold Shelmalier,
With your long barrelled guns of the sea.
Say what wind from the south brings your messenger here
With a hymn of the dawn for the free?
Goodly news, goodly news do I bring youth of Forth,
Goodly news shall you hear Bargy man,
For the boys march at dawn from the south to the north,
Led by Kelly, the boy from Killanne.

Tell me who is the giant with the gold curling hair,
He who rides at the head of your band?
Seven feet is his height with some inches to spare
And he looks like a king in command.
Ah, my boys, that's the pride of the bold Shelmaliers,
The greatest of heroes, a man.
Raise your beavers aloft and give three ringing cheers
For John Kelly, the boy from Killanne.

Enniscorthy's in flames and old Wexford is won
And tomorrow the Barrow we cross,
On a hill o'er the town we have planted a gun
That will batter the gateway for Ross.
All the Forth men and Bargy men will march o'er the heath
With Brave Harvey to lead in the van,
But the foremost of all in the grim gap of death
Will be Kelly, the boy from Killanne.

But the gold sun of freedom grew darkened at Ross
And it set by the Slaney's red waves,
And poor Wexford, stripped naked, hung high on a cross
With her heart pierced by traitors and slaves.
Glory O! Glory O! to our brave sons who died
In the cause of long downtrodden man.
Glory O! to Mount Leinster's own darling and pride,
Dauntless Kelly, the boy from Killanne.

Kelly the Boy from Killanne
Who is the Giant with the Gold Curling Hair?

This fine ballad by Patrick Joseph McCall commemorates John Kelly, a young man who played a short but dramatic part in the 1798 Wexford rebellion. Despite a tendency to go over the top at times, it is on the whole very rousing, is set to yet another classic marching tune and revived the memory of a man whom history had almost forgotten. A hundred years after the uprising McCall's ballad recreated the life of a man long dead, a mere historical footnote. Many other rebel leaders, Cornelius Grogan, Father Mogue Kearns, Matthew Keogh and Anthony Perry also lost their lives in the conflict but today they are largely unknown. Thanks to a song however, the name of John Kelly continues to resound down through the centuries.

McCall (1861-1919) was a founder member of the National Literary Society along with Yeats, Douglas Hyde and others, and published numerous volumes of poetry. He was the son of Dublin publican John McCall, originally from County Carlow, and a well-known collector of Carlow folksongs. Patrick McCall's mother was from Wexford and he himself kept a cottage there. Like his father he was also an avid collector of broadside ballads and drew much of his inspiration and basic atmosphere from them. His best songs were very individual in style and captured well the energy and spirit of nationalist sentiment around a hundred years ago. When the centenary of the rebellion came around in 1898 he was determined to make his own contribution to keeping the memory of the events alive. Another hundred years on it's apparent that he succeeded to an extent he could never have imagined.

By the 1790s Ireland had enjoyed a century of relative peace and a relaxation of the Penal Laws. However all this was thrown into turmoil by the outbreak of the French Revolution in 1789. Peasants and politicians throughout Europe were influenced by these cataclysmic events, but in Ireland the situation was exacerbated by religious differences and the still simmering resentment against the loss of land and the decline of Gaelic culture.

In 1793, regarded by some Wexfordians as the year of the 'first rebellion', around eighty Catholics had been killed in Wexford town during a demonstration against tithes, the tax on the whole community for the sole upkeep of the established Anglican church. Agitation and protest were commonplace and a French fleet threatened to invade at any time. In 1796 an *Insurrection Act* effectively negated the rule of law and the mood of political discontent was exacerbated by an economic one when the price of barley, a staple local crop, fell by 80 per cent in 1797.

Little detail is known about the life of John Kelly, for he came from humble origins and died young during chaotic times. However enough survives to make it clear that he was a decent young man who had striven heroically for the cause that he believed in. It's known that he was born and raised in the village of Killanne in the Barony of Bantry, Northwest County Wexford, not to be confused with the better known Bantry in County Cork of *Bantry Bay* fame. Killanne (*Cill Anna*) means 'church of Saint Anne'; the village and parish are situated in the shadow of *Stua Dhu*, Blackstairs Mountain, of which Mount Leinster, at 2610 feet, is the highest point. The name is derived from St Anne's holy well just outside of the village, a place of pilgrimage to this day. The village was also the home of noted rebel leader Father Philip Roche, executed in Wexford.

Kelly's father (1737-97), also called John, was born ten miles north of Killanne in the parish of Kilbrannish, three miles west of Bunclody. In the 1760s he moved to the townland of Wheelagower, three miles north of Killanne, where he met and married Mary Redmond around 1771, then settling in Killanne. (All of these very small places can be traced on the Discovery 1:50,000 Ordnance Survey Map, sheet 68). The couple had six children and John is thought to have been the eldest. John Kelly senior eventually became a prosperous merchant and ran a shop, pub and bacon-curing business as well as having fairly substantial farming interests. Just prior to the rebellion a government spy described him as 'a man of respectability in this neighbourhood' and John Kelly junior as 'of the better sort and a well conducted man'. We do not have Kelly's date of birth. It is given variously as 1773 and, on his memorial in Killanne graveyard, as 1776. Here the inscription, dating from 1898, reads:

> Erected in grateful memory of Captain John Kelly Killanne
> Born 1776 Executed 1798
> He was wounded whilst leading the insurgent troops
> at the Battle of New Ross.
> Was taken prisoner conveyed to Wexford
> and most cruelly executed
> At or near the old bridge.
> We revere his memory as a most ardent and exemplary patriot
> Who so honourably gave his young life, for his country's cause.

Bearing in mind that he was probably the first born of a couple married in 1771, the earlier year is probably closer to being correct. Neither do we have any reliable physical description of him but from the sketchy comments that have survived, he does seem to have been a man of well above average physical strength and mental resolve. When the rebellion broke out Kelly was planning marriage to a local girl called Doyle who is thought to have followed him to Wexford before fading from the pages of history after her sweetheart's death.

It is known that Kelly held the rank of Colonel, one of the most senior titles in the rebel ranks. The description of him in the memoirs of Miles Byrne (1780-1862) may be the basis of McCall's hyperbolic 'seven feet' giant. Byrne had just turned eighteen when the Rebellion broke out and he was present at many of the major battles. After Robert Emmet's rebellion in 1803 he escaped to France where he spent the rest of his life as an officer in the French army. He is usually regarded as a reliable witness and is one of the few participants in the rebellion who has actually written about Kelly.

> I must now speak of the ever-to-be-lamented John Kelly of Killanne, who was considered by all those who knew him, or who saw him in battle, to possess all the finest qualities of the truest patriot and the bravery and heroism of the greatest general of antiquity; this fine young man would have become the 'Hoche' of Ireland [General Lazare Hoche was the commander of the French expeditionary force to Ireland in 1796], had the war continued and succeeded. He was recovering fast from the wounds he received at Ross, when the relentless Orangemen of Wexford had him executed after the town was re-occupied by the king's troops.

It's difficult to know whether or not Byrne is exaggerating. However it's also difficult to imagine why he should have gone out of his way to heap praise on someone whom he could quite easily have ignored. He certainly wasn't looking for 'filler' material for his memoirs as they consist of three substantial volumes, which he hadn't completed before he died. It does seem certain that John Kelly was a young man of considerable presence, courage and character. In the many references to him that I have seen not one is negative and indeed most of them emphasise and praise his admirable qualities. Although a committed rebel, he fought on a purely military basis and respected Protestant civilians.

Kelly had been an active United Irishman since around 1796 and is believed to have travelled to Dublin to take the oath. The Killanne United men held many of their meetings in the coachhouse in the centre of the village and as the building still exists, this is now as close as it is possible to get to 'John Kelly the boy from Killanne'.

He joined the revolt on 28 May, just hours after news of the rebel victory at Enniscorthy, eight miles east of Killanne, had sent a surge of hope and confidence through the rebel ranks. He met up with the men of his district in Killoughram Forest, where he had been training the Bantry men for some months past, and crossed the Slaney to join the main rebel camp at Vinegar Hill. His first taste of battle came two days later at the Three Rocks on Forth Mountain, just west of Wexford town. Here the Bantry men led by himself, Thomas Cloney, Robert Carty and Michael Furlong defeated a detachment of General Fawcett's men in hand-to-hand fighting. It had not been a major battle but almost a hundred government troops had been killed, wounded or captured. The battle showed that the rebels had to be taken seriously as a military force, contributed to the surrender of Wexford without a fight and gave John Kelly an opportunity to prove himself as an able and courageous leader. Wexford town fell to the rebels later that day, the leader of the United Irishmen's political wing, Beauchamp Bagenal Harvey, was freed from prison and the insurgents had reached the zenith of their success. The Three Rocks engagement is commemorated by a modern sculpture, featuring five Wexford pikemen and inscribed:

> On May 30 1798 United Irish insurgent forces intercepted the reinforcements for the Wexford garrison near this place. The overwhelming of the troops resulted in the evacuation of Wexford by Crown forces. In this engagement Thomas Cloney, Colonel of the Bantry Battalion of the United Irishmen commanded the Insurgent forces. Nearby in the Church Meadow lie some eighty men of the Royal Artillery and Meath Militia who were killed in the battle.

> 'There is nothing surer than that Irishmen of every denomination must stand or fall together'.

> WILLIAM ORR, 1797
> [For information on William Orr, see *Henry Joy*]

By 4 June Kelly had been admitted to the rebel leadership inner circle of Harvey, Thomas Cloney and John Henry Colclough, who now headed an army of ten thousand men. They met in Talbot Hall, a mansion outside New Ross on the River Barrow, to plan their next move, the attack on the town.

'Tomorrow the Barrow we cross' was never to happen for the rebels though they did come very close. After a ferocious battle in which John Kelly was often literally 'the foremost of all in the grim gap of death' and in which he received a serious thigh wound that incapacitated him for the remainder of the campaign the rebels were driven back. It is interesting to note McCalls's use of the phrase 'grim gap of death', which crops up in various forms in a number of Irish songs. The best known is in the National Anthem, *A Soldier's Song* where it appears in its Gaelic form *bearna baoil*, literally 'gap of danger'. The phrase is also used in another old favourite, Thomas Davis' *Clare's Dragoons:*

> Our colonel came from Brian's race,
> His wounds are in his breast and face,
> The *bearna baoil* is still his place,
> The foremost of his bold dragoons.

For a time the tide of battle had swung in their favour when Kelly's Bantry men, the columns of John Boxwell, a Protestant rebel leader killed in the battle, and Thomas Cloney, fought their way street by street almost to the very heart of the town. Many of the inhabitants and defending troops had already retreated across the Barrow. However in the confusion, with fires raging and the inspirational Kelly out of action, the government troops gradually regained the initiative. The defeat at New Ross was a major setback for the rebels. Not only did they lose two thousand men and much of their weaponry but also the 'gateway to Ross' that could have opened up a whole new theatre of war in Kilkenny and beyond was closed.

The reference to 'Brave Harvey' refers, of course, to Beauchamp Bagenal Harvey (1762-98), the political and military leader of the early Wexford revolt. Harvey was a wealthy, Protestant landowner and barrister, a man of liberal and humane views. As a known prominent United Irishman he was arrested at his home of Bargy Castle on 26 May and imprisoned in Wexford jail. When the town fell to the rebels, he was released and assumed overall leadership of the revolt in Wexford, a position for which historians now agree he was ill-equipped. After the insurgents failed siege of New Ross he resigned and was replaced by Edward Roche. Three weeks later Harvey was hanged on Wexford Bridge and his decapitated body thrown into the River Slaney. This was a fairly common occurrence and the line 'Slaney's red waves' is little exaggeration. His body was later recovered and buried in St Patrick's churchyard in Wexford.

Certainly Harvey was an ineffective leader but he never claimed to be a military man. The position was thrust upon him against his better judgement. In addition the question has to be asked, 'Could *anyone* have led the rebels to success?' Harvey had an almost impossible task, as many of the rebels were largely untrained, undisciplined, unreliable and poorly equipped. In addition, the massacre of Protestant civilian prisoners at Scullabogue had left him disillusioned and disgusted. He had sacrificed great personal wealth, status and family life, having been married for only a year, to take up and lead a cause that he could easily have ignored. No one can grudge the unfortunate man McCall's description 'brave Harvey', despite the fact that his failure may not have been quite as 'glorious' as some. He is commemorated in *Bagenal Harvey's Lament*.

> Farewell to Cornelius Grogan and to Kelly ever true,
> Tom Cloney and good Father Roche, receive my last adieu
> And fare thee well bold Esmond Kyan, though cruel oppressor's laws
> Cause us to lay down our lives, still we bless our noble cause.

> Farewell to Bargy's lofty towers, my father's own estate
> And fare well to its lovely bowers, my own ancestral seat.
> Farewell each friend and neighbour that once I well knew there,
> My tenants now will miss the hand that fostered them with care.

Shelmalier (or Shelmaliere), *Siol Maoluidhir* ('place of the descendants of Maolughra'), East and West, are baronies to the north and west of Wexford town. Forth and Bargy are also barony names and lie to the south and west of Wexford. Both are well known for the survival there until about a hundred years ago of an ancient English dialect derived from Flemish, Welsh and English. A well-known example is this verse of an old song:

> Haraw ee bee, dhree yola mydes
> Fo naar had looke var to be brides
> Vo no own caars fadere betides,
> Dhree yola mydens.

> Here are we three old maids
> Who never had luck to be brides,
> Who no one cares whate'er betides,
> Three old maidens.

The term 'barony' was the old name for the territorial division of counties and fell into disuse about a hundred years ago. Within the thirty-two counties of Ireland there are two hundred and seventy-three baronies, then further subdivided into parishes and local areas called 'townlands', originally based on land owned by extended families. In 1798 regiments and other military groupings were often distinguished by the name of the barony that they came from, e.g. the Scarawalsh units, the Shelmalier Cavalry, the Gorey Yeomen, etc.

The townlands system is unique to Ireland and pre-dates the 12th century Anglo-Norman invasion. There are over 60,000 townlands, ranging in size from the single acre Mill Tenement in Lower Glenarm in Antrim to the 7012-acre Sheskin near Belmullet in Mayo. However these bland statistics do nothing to convey the tremendous power and influence of the townlands, and their Irish language names, on people for centuries bound to the land. They provide an almost indefinable sense of identity and belonging, creating an indelible bond between people and the place that they come from. For example, I am neither proud nor ashamed of the fact that I was born in Ireland but I am inordinately and irrationally proud of the fact that I was born in the townland of Crockglass ('green hill'). This at times mystical attachment to local landscape is a common theme in Irish literature, expressed in the concept of *dinnshenchas* ('topography'), with the legends, lore and love of familiar landscapes being handed-down, internalised and reinterpreted by each succeeding generation... *every stony acre has a name.* The concept has inspired much rich imagery and can be found in Irish writing from the 12th century *Book of Leinster* to the poetry of Seamus Heaney at the present time. However, in an ironic twist of historical fate, the most common townland name in Ireland is an English language word, 'glebe', land set aside for the upkeep of the clergyman of a parish.

After the Battle of New Ross, John Kelly was carried to his sister Anne's home in Wexford where he lay for about two weeks until he was arrested after the town was retaken by government forces. Not many of the rebel leaders escaped with their lives but if Kelly had been mobile, he would have stood a reasonable chance of reaching the Blackstairs Mountains as Father John Murphy and his men had done. Here on his own turf and with the support of the local people 'Mount Leinster's own darling and pride' may just have managed to survive until the worst of the reprisals were over.

There had been great courage as well as terrible cruelty on both sides. However social, economic and historical forces generally had conspired to ensure that there was little co-ordination, communication or military strategy in the rebel ranks. They had lost out to an overwhelmingly superior combination of more highly developed technology and resources. When it was all over, around thirty thousand people had lost their lives. No precise figures are available but it is estimated that about half those killed were non-combatants.

There were certainly ample atrocities on both sides, with one of the most infamous being the burning alive of a hundred, mostly Protestant, loyalist captives in farm buildings at Scullabogue, near Carrickbyrne, on 5 June. This had come in the wake of the rebel defeat at New Ross where around seventy insurgent wounded were burned alive as they lay in a makeshift hospital building hoping for medical treatment. The tone of the campaign had been set early on with the massacre of rebel prisoners at Dunlavin and Carnew on 24 and 25 May respectively.

The exact date of John Kelly's execution is uncertain but it is thought to have been around 28 June. After being hanged, his severed head was kicked around the streets of Wexford by government troops. This despicable treatment of his dead body can be taken as an indication that he had proved himself to be a formidable opponent.

Tributes to him were plentiful and generous but probably the most meaningful came from loyalist historians. The Reverend James Gordon, writing in 1805, described him as 'worthy of a far better cause and better associates. His courage and humanity being equal and conspicuous'. The Reverend William Hamilton Maxwell (1792-1850), no friend of any insurgent, wrote 'another rebel whose better qualities probably deserved an extension of mercy more than any other of the convicted was Kelly of Killanne. He had led the attack on [New] Ross, exhibited unbounded gallantry in action and great humanity when any opportunity to exercise it was presented. By a strange perversion his good properties were pleaded in aggravation of disloyalty and one who had every claim to commiseration was sacrificed to the turbulent spirit of the time'.

Henry Joy McCracken (1767 - 1798)

8.

Henry Joy

An Ulster man I am proud to be, from the Antrim Glens I come.
Although I labour by the sea I have followed fife and drum.
I have heard the martial tramp of men, I've seen them fight and die
And it's well that I remember when I followed Henry Joy.

I pulled my boat in from the sea and I hid my sails away.
I hung my nets upon a tree and I scanned the moonlit bay.
The boys were out, and the redcoats too, I kissed my wife goodbye
And there in the shade of a green leafy glade I followed Henry Joy.

Alas for Ireland's cause we fought and for home and her we bled,
Though our numbers were few our hearts beat true, but five to one lay dead
And many's the lassie mourned her lad and mother mourned her boy,
For youth was strong in the gallant throng that followed Henry Joy.

In Belfast town they built a tree and the redcoats mustered there.
I saw him come to the beat of a drum rolled out on the barracks square.
He kissed his sister and went aloft and bade his last goodbye
And as he died I turned and I cried, 'They have murdered Henry Joy'.

Henry Joy

The United Irishmen, Henry Joy McCracken
and the Battle of Antrim

This simple but very effective ballad deals in basic outline with the story of Henry Joy McCracken, one of the most charismatic, committed and radical leaders of the 1798 Rebellion. McCracken was a Presbyterian with links to both the Catholics and the ruling Episcopalians and was one of the few men who might have united north and south. The origins of the song are uncertain, with it being variously credited to Patrick Joseph McCall, William Drennan and T.P. Cuming. Some of the uncertainty is due to confusing it with an entirely different song called *Henry Joy McCracken*. In fact *this* song was written by McCall and first published in the *Shan Van Vocht* magazine. As with *Boolavogue*, McCall was again inspired by an older ballad, *The Belfast Mountains*. It may be that T.P. Cuming's association with the song is simply because he submitted it for publication to the *Irish Weekly* in the 1960s. It is very unlikely that he wrote it and authorship couldn't be attributed. My own introduction to it came from the recording by the inimitable Grehan Sisters about 1963.

The song uses the effective device of telling the story through the eyes of a humble foot soldier whose loyalty and devotion are so strongly felt that the listener immediately wants to know more about the mysterious and obviously heroic character called *Henry Joy*. It is very spirited, full of atmosphere and colour, is set to a marvellous melody and serves as a useful introduction to the fascinating but typically tragic story of Henry Joy McCracken (1767-98) and the United Irishmen in Belfast and County Antrim.

The Society of United Irishmen was founded in Belfast in October 1791 by John Campbell, Henry Hazlett (or Haslett), Thomas McCabe, William McCleery, Gilbert McIlveen, Samuel McTier, Samuel Neilson, Thomas Russell, Robert Simms, William Simms, William Sinclair, William Tennent and Theobald Wolfe Tone. Tone, a barrister from Dublin, was the invited speaker at the inaugural meeting and addressed the assembled company on the subjects of electoral reform and Catholic emancipation.

His recent pamphlet, *An Argument on Behalf of the Catholics of Ireland*, advocating Catholic civil rights, had caused a sensation and had sold by the thousand. All the founder members of the United Irishmen were Presbyterians, with the exception of Russell and Tone who were Episcopalians. Tone himself had little of the common Protestant dread of 'Popery' as his mother Margaret Lamport was a Catholic who didn't convert to Protestantism until he was eight years old. Now Tone set out, politically speaking, to become 'a red hot Catholic'.

At this time Belfast's population of around eighteen thousand was about over ninety per cent Protestant and there was none of the sectarian strife that was to plague the city so much in the future. However it was also a 'pocket borough' with both of the city's MPs being nominated by Lord Donegall – a situation strongly resented by the town's increasingly literate and demanding Presbyterian middle class who were strongly influenced by the democratic ideals of the French and American Revolutions. The Dublin branch of the Society was formed in November 1791 by Tone, Russell and James Napper Tandy (1740-1803), with about half the membership there being Catholic.

The United Irishmen had no single leader but coalesced from the ideas of a number of men over some years. Three who made major early contributions were Tone, Doctor William Drennan (1754-1820) of Belfast and Samuel Neilson (1761-1803), from Ballyroney near Rathfriland in County Down. Both Drennan and Neilson were the sons of Presbyterian ministers. Tone was a Dubliner who wrote, 'I am a Protestant of the Church of Ireland, as by law established'. He was heavily involved in the early days of the movement and on the second anniversary of the storming of the Bastille wrote down the three basic principles on which the Society was founded a few months later.

> July 14 1791. I sent down to Belfast resolutions... reduced to three heads. That English influence in Ireland was the greatest grievance of the country, that the most effective way to oppose it was by a reform in Parliament, that no reform could be just or efficacious which did not include the Catholics.

Drennan was one of the earliest radicals, concluding in the mid-1780s that the best solution for Ireland's problems was complete separation from Britain – radical indeed as the two nations had been united for around six hundred years under a common monarch. His thinking was influenced by the writing and preaching of a number of liberal 'New Light' Presbyterian clergymen of a generation earlier, notably John Abernethy (1680-1740) and Francis Hutcheson (1694-1746) who opposed the Penal

Laws in the belief that 'men of integrity and ability' were not limited to a single denomination. In 1784 Drennan proposed the establishment of a 'secretive organisation' to work towards independence and in 1791 suggested that the body might be called The Irish Brotherhood. However Tone's suggestion, The Society of United Irishmen, was adopted instead. A rather timid theorist, Drennan withdrew from active politics in 1795 after narrowly surviving a trial for sedition. He is also remembered as a minor poet, famed for having originated the phrase 'The Emerald Isle' in his poem *Erin* (1795).

> When Erin first rose from the dark-swelling flood
> God bless'd the Green Island, He saw it was good,
> The Emerald of Europe, it sparkled, it shone,
> In the ring of this world, the most precious stone!
>
> In her sun, in her soil, in her station, thrice blest
> With back turn'd to Britain, her face to the West,
> Erin stands proudly insular, on her steep shore
> And strikes her high harp to the ocean's deep roar.
>
> But when its soft tones seem to mourn and to weep,
> The dark chain of silence is cast o'er the deep
> At the thought of the past, tears gush from our eyes
> And the pulse of the heart makes her white bosom rise.
>
> O, sons of green Erin! Lament o'er the time
> When religion was – war, and our country – a crime,
> When men, in God's image, inverted his plan
> And moulded their God in the image of man.
>
> Arm of Erin prove strong, but be gentle as brave,
> And, uplifted to strike, be ready to save,
> Not one feeling of vengeance presume to defile
> The cause of the men of the Emerald Isle.

However Drennan's best-known poem is *The Wake of William Orr*, the Antrim United Irishman (born 1766) whose execution, on a dubious charge of administering illegal oaths in 1797, shocked and appalled the United Irishmen of the north. Orr went to his death with the words:

> My comfortable lot and industrious course of life best refute the charge of being an adventurer for plunder but... to have felt the injuries of the persecuted Catholics and to have united with them and all other religious persuasions in the most orderly and least sanguinary means of procuring address, if these be felonies, I am a felon, but not otherwise. I am no traitor. I die for a persecuted country. Great Jehovah, receive my soul. I die in the true faith of a Presbyterian.

To some extent the execution was a political miscalculation. It was intended to cow the radicals but instead it inspired many of them with the slogan 'Remember Orr'. On his arrest after the collapse of the rebellion Henry Joy McCracken was found to be wearing a green shamrock ring inscribed 'To the sacred memory of Mr. Wm. Orr who died for his country at the altar of British tyranny'. *The Wake of William Orr* consists of twelve verses. Here are a few of them.

There our murdered brother lies,
Wake him not with woman's cries,
Mourn the way that manhood ought,
Sit in silent trance of thought.

Why cut off in palmy youth?
Truth he spoke and acted truth.
'Countrymen UNITE!' he cried
And died for what our Saviour died.

Hapless Nation, rent and torn,
Thou wert early taught to mourn,
Warfare of six hundred years,
Epochs marked with blood and tears.

Monstrous and unhappy sight,
Brothers' blood will not unite;
Holy oil and holy water
Mix, and fill the world with slaughter.

Samuel Neilson was possibly the most radical of the trio and held such advanced views that even Tone called him the Jacobin, after the extremist French republicans. He founded the Society's newspaper, *The Northern Star*, and devoted his energies to the Movement throughout the 90s. He was wounded trying to free Lord Edward Fitzgerald and was twice imprisoned, including three years with Thomas Russell in Fort George. Freed in 1802, subject to staying out of Ireland, he went to America where he died of yellow fever in 1803. The fair-minded loyalist historian W. T. Latimer, writing in 1897, summarised his career:

Although Neilson was rash, he was exceedingly resolute in carrying out his plans. Animated by strong sympathy for the oppressed, he sacrificed his health, his property and the worldly prospects of his wife and family, whom he loved dearly, for what he was convinced were the interests of his country. He was one of the many Ulster patriots who may have adopted a wrong course but whose honour, honesty and unselfish fidelity to principle, should make their memory revered by Irishmen throughout all generations.

Although he had suffered terribly, including having to cope with the deaths of three of his children while on the run and in prison, he remained true to his principles until the end. Just before he died he wrote to Archibald Hamilton Rowan:

> Neither the eight years hardship I have endured, the total destruction of my property, the forlorn state of my wife and children... have abated my ardour in the cause of my country and of general liberty. You and I my friend will pass away but the truth will remain.

Initially the United Irishmen's goals were reformist only: universal male suffrage (a truly revolutionary concept as it didn't happen until 1918), civil rights for Catholics (though some members had certain reservations about this) and the removal of English control over Irish economic and commercial affairs. The radical Tone dismissed it as 'sad nonsense' the fears that some Protestants had of Catholics in government. The movement was founded as an open and legal debating forum and pressure group and remained so until it was outlawed in 1794 after contacts were discovered with revolutionary France, then at war with Britain, through Tone and William Jackson (1737-95). Two of the main factors which turned the movement from reform to revolution were the outbreak of war with France in February 1793 and the banning, the following month, of the Volunteer Movement. This had been formed in the late 1770s as an armed, loyal, patriotic and exclusively Protestant national defence force at a time when the greater part of the regular army was engaged in North America. Most members of the McCracken family were enthusiastic Volunteers. The movement provided an existing foundation for the United Irishmen whose members now had to decide which way to turn. The most determined and dedicated chose rebellion and revolution.

Henry Joy McCracken was the radical son of a prominent Belfast Presbyterian family, a grandson of Francis Joy who had founded the *Belfast News-Letter*, possibly the world's oldest newspaper, in 1737. He was descended from Huguenot stock on his mother's side, her family name having originally been Joyeuse. He had been in touch with Tone, Neilson and Russell since 1790 but it seems that he didn't formally join the Society until 1795. He was certainly politically active long before this. Although he came from a well-to-do business background, he abhorred the social divisions created by poverty and was always concerned about the condition of the poor. Along with Thomas Russell he worked hard to encourage the Catholic secret society, the Defenders, away from their entrenched sectarianism and into the ranks of the United Irishmen.

He was also instrumental in founding Belfast's first Sunday School in 1792, which taught girls as well as boys and 'did not presume to impart religious knowledge but taught their scholars how to obtain it for themselves, by which every sect might equally profit'. His prominent role within the United Irishmen led to imprisonment without trial in Dublin's Kilmainham Jail for fourteen months over 1796-97. Family influence and poor health played their part in his release. Once free, he immediately assumed overall leadership of the northern insurgents after the resignation of Robert Simms, just a few days before the Uprising in the first week of June 1798. After initial successes, such as the capture of Ballymena, Larne and Randalstown the inexperienced, poorly armed and organised insurgents were defeated at the Battle of Antrim on the 7th of June.

McCracken had displayed considerable personal bravery during the Battle and when it became apparent that it was lost, it is said that he had to be restrained by his men from the suicidal folly of throwing himself on the enemy lines. Instead he was persuaded to escape to the remnants of the rebel camp at nearby Donegore Hill, east of Antrim town. At first he hoped to try and join up with the County Down or even the Wexford rebels but when it became apparent that this was futile, he resolved to try to reach republican America.

After Antrim, it's thought that initially he headed north towards Ballymena and then hid on Slemish Mountain. Initially his group was over two hundred strong and they either slept rough or were put up in friendly houses, which for 'Henry Joy' were still plentiful. Next they headed southeast towards Glen Whirry, hiding out on the slopes of Wee Collin, east of Ballyclare. After being disturbed there by troops, he headed south in the direction of Lisburn in the vain hope of joining forces with the Down or southern rebels. It was in this area, on Bohill, a few miles west of Belfast that he met with his sister Mary who had been trekking the hills in search of him for two days. He had written to her on the 18th of June, an angry, bitter and understandably rather hysterical letter, but which contained two memorable phrases which have contributed to the McCracken legend: 'These are times that try men's souls' (a quotation from Thomas Paine) and 'The rich always betray the poor'.

By now it was obvious that the Uprising had failed and that his only hope was to flee the country. His family had obtained false papers and arranged passage for him on an American ship out of Greencastle (now part of north Belfast). He set off in that direction and is thought to have spent a final night at the cottage of his old friend David Bodle on Cave Hill, which he had a special, personal reason for doing.

As he attempted to rendezvous with the ship, he was arrested about a mile outside Carrickfergus on 7 July and transferred to Belfast for the formality of a trial. McCracken had been recognised by a local yeoman called Niblock who, confronting him, said, 'Mr McCracken, you have changed your name since I knew you'. Perhaps he had allowed himself to become careless about his security because he had managed to evade capture for so long and because he was so close to making his escape. When arrested, his group of comrades was reduced to two, John Queeny and Gavin Watt. Not being major figures, both avoided the hangman, with Watt getting seven years penal servitude and Queeny being transported for life.

After refusing an offer of his life for the names of his associates, in particular that of Robert Simms, who lived on until 1845, Henry Joy McCracken was hanged in Belfast on 17 July 1798. As he walked to the scaffold the severed heads of four previously executed rebels stared down at him. These included William Dickey, who had commanded at Ballymena, and John Storey, who had shared a cell with McCracken in Kilmainham Jail. Despite this horror, by all accounts he went resolutely to his death. After witnessing prison hangings, 'borne with the greatest fortitude', and hundreds of deaths at the Battle of Antrim, he now had 'a sort of carelessness about death'.

His sister Mary Ann, mentioned in the final verse of the ballad, outlived her brother by some sixty-eight years. She was a remarkable woman, a tireless pioneering worker for human rights and on behalf of the poor, who went on to establish a reputation as one of the most admired women that Ireland has ever produced. She lived to be ninety-six and continued to campaign against slavery in the United States well into her eighties. She had been 'romantically attracted' to Thomas Russell but he himself suffered unrequited love for Eliza Goddard. After he was executed along with Robert Emmet in 1803 she never married.

She did however have the consolation of being able to raise Henry's 'illegitimate' four-year old daughter by Mary Bodle, the daughter of David Bodle, in whose cottage on the Belfast side of Cave Hill he had often found refuge. Mary Ann hadn't known of the existence of the child until after Henry's execution. In the death cell he had struggled for the courage to tell her but such was the strength of the social mores of the times that, although he could face the hangman, he couldn't tell his sister that he had a daughter born 'out of wedlock'. The child went on to have a long and happy life and lived until 1878.

Today the bones of Henry Joy McCracken are thought to have been reburied with those of his sister in Belfast's Clifton Street cemetery appropriately, perhaps, at the Antrim Road end. When I visited there, I found the cemetery locked and fortified, for this is a troubled part of the city. Later I discovered that access for bona fide visitors can be arranged through Belfast City Council. The green military uniform that he wore at the Battle of Antrim is on display in the Ulster Museum on Belfast's Stranmillis Road in the grounds of the Botanic Gardens.

It is almost essential to make the short trip out to Cave Hill as McCracken, Tone, Russell, Neilson, the Simms brothers, William Putnam McCabe and others had done in June 1795. This was just prior to Tone's banishment to America and the group climbed to the ancient symbolic site of McArt's Fort on the Hill's summit. Here they made their famous 'solemn undertaking never to desist in our efforts until we had subverted the authority of England over our country and asserted our independence'. The panoramic views over Belfast, northwest to Lough Neagh, Antrim town, and south to the Mountains of Mourne are spectacular and include most of the locations that figure prominently in the story of Henry Joy McCracken: the 'Blue Hills' and 'Green Glens' of Antrim and towards Donegore and Slemish. Also visible are Carnmoney Hill and the Pool of Garmoyle in the area where he was finally captured between Cave Hill and Carrickfergus. The 1,200-foot summit is easily accessed from the grounds of Belfast Castle, about four miles north of the City centre.

After singing the ballad of *Henry Joy* for almost forty years but without ever knowing much about the person on whose life the song was based, it had eventually led me to many of the historically most interesting corners of Belfast and the North. It had also led me to discover the career of an Irishman for all seasons and for both traditions. Perhaps the most appropriate tribute came from his friend Jemmy Hope, who was with him during 'the times that try men's souls' and who had stayed with him until the final days: 'When all our leaders deserted us, Henry Joy McCracken stood alone faithful to the last'.

Courtesy Linenhall Library

General Henry Monro

9.

General Monro

Did you hear of the Battle of Ballynahinch,
When the country assembled in their own defence.
They assembled together and away they did go,
Led by their two heroes, Clokey and Monro.

My name is George Clokey, my age is nineteen,
In many a battle and skirmish I've been
And many great dangers I did undergo
With that brave Irish hero General Monro.

Monro took the mountains; his men took the field
And swore to the tyrants they never would yield
And the sound of the cannon never daunted us so
When commanded by Clokey and General Monro.

Monro being wearied and in want of a sleep
Gave a woman ten guineas, the secret to keep.
When she had the money the devil tempted her so
She sent for the army who surrounded Monro.

If you'd seen the cavalry when they came there,
Their horses did caper and prance in the rear,
The traitor being with them as you may all know.
'Twas out of a haystack they hauled poor Monro.

Monro he was taken and brought to the hall,
He sought to escape but he could not at all.
They marched him to Lisburn without more delay
And put his head on a spear the very same day.

In came his sister well clothed in green,
A sword by her side, both long, sharp and keen.
Three cheers she did give and away she did go
Saying, 'I'll have my revenge for my brother Monro'.

Monro he is taken and brought to a tree.
'Farewell to my wife and my children three
And let every brave man who hates Ireland's foe
Fight for her freedom like Henry Monro'.

Here's a health to each hero, who for freedom stand.
May their souls rest in peace for they died for their land.
Remember those martyrs, all slain by our foe –
Brave Emmet, Fitzgerald and General Monro.

General Monro
Henry Monro, the Down Rebellion
and the Battle of Ballynahinch

The subject of this fine historical ballad is Henry Monro, leader of the County Down United Irish insurgents of 1798, who was executed following the Battle of Ballynahinch. The song is plain and simple but probably more authentically 'folk' than many of the popular songs of '98 which, though invariably of good quality, were often written long afterwards through rose-tinted glasses. This 'minority' version is from a mid 19th century broadsheet in Oxford University's Bodleian Library. Recently I was pleasantly surprised to see the song featured in a loyalist collection for this is a song that can be appreciated by everyone irrespective of political straitjackets.

The song has entered the folk tradition and there are so many variants that it is virtually impossible to say what is 'correct' and what isn't. In the most popular version the narrator is 'George Campbell' whose age is given variously as sixteen, eighteen and nineteen. If he ever was a real person, he seems to have disappeared completely from the pages of history.

The only reference to authorship of the song that I have managed to trace comes from the 1968 reprint of W.G. Lyttle's *Betsy Gray or Hearts of Down*. This edition includes an Appendix largely based on research carried out by the County Down antiquarian Colin Johnston Robb. He attributes the song to 'an old poem written by a John McMullan, a native of Magheratimpany', a townland three miles south of Ballynahinch. (Robb's great grandfather, James Robb, was a yeoman officer at the Battle of Ballynahinch, in which his brother John fought for the rebels. Almost inevitably, tradition asserts that the two brothers met face to face during the Battle.)

Henry Monro (1758-98) is probably the least known of all the major rebel leaders and information about him is sometimes contradictory. His date of birth is sometimes given as 1768, though this seems unlikely. He is also often described as being Scottish but in fact he was born in Lisburn in Country Antrim. The surname Monro has numerous variant spellings (Monroe, Munro, and Munroe) and I have opted for the lesser-used variant of Monro as this seems to have been the form that he used himself.

Henry Monro was a direct descendant of Robert Munroe, the Scottish General defeated by Owen Roe O'Neill at the Battle of Benburb, County Tyrone, in 1646 during the Confederate War and co-incidentally immortalised in the popular nationalist song *Come to the Bower.*

You can visit Benburb by the storied Blackwater
Where Owen Roe met Munroe and his chieftains did slaughter.

In 1794 Henry Monro revived his local Masonic Lodge, probably as a front for United Irish activity, before he actually joined the Society the following year. At this time the majority of Freemasons in Ireland were Catholic, despite Papal Bulls in 1738 and 1751 condemning the practice. Though he later repudiated the organisation, Daniel O'Connell joined the Dublin Lodge in 1799. Eventually though, Catholics drifted away from the movement.

By all accounts Monro was a man of high moral principles in business, in politics and even in war. He is said to have refused to consider a night attack at Ballynahinch on the grounds that this would be ungentlemanly and unfair, though this story may be apocryphal. These principles he had imbibed from a strict Episcopalian upbringing that stayed with him until the day he died. In Lisburn he was well known and respected as a prominent merchant in the linen trade. He also had a reputation for being outspoken in favour of parliamentary reform and Catholic civil rights. The former in particular was a very dangerous public position to adopt in the political climate of 1790s Ireland (and Britain).

When the Uprising broke out in County Down the insurgents gathered at Creevy Rocks on the road between Saintfield and Ballynahinch. Monro fled there fearing arrest because of his reputation as an outspoken liberal with military experience gained in the Volunteers. One account attributes his flight to his witnessing 'a brother mason named Hood being scourged' to extract a confession. Such floggings, as well as house burning, pitch-capping and murder, were common occurrences. Large areas of the country were under martial law and troops, who were virtually a law unto themselves, were 'free quartered' in private homes. The line from *General Monro* 'when the country assembled in their own defence' is therefore more than propaganda. The rebels were predominantly Presbyterian, from such towns as Bangor, Donaghadee, Greyabbey, Lisburn, Killinchy, Newtownards and the Ards peninsula. They must have felt a real sense of grievance against the Episcopalian-dominated establishment to risk everything on what more cautious counsels regarded as a reckless, hopeless adventure.

Due to his political and military reputation Monro was hurriedly acclaimed 'General' of the Down rebels after the arrest of the Rev. William Steele Dickson (1744-1824), a Presbyterian minister, who was to be imprisoned for four years without trial. Immediately Monro led his force of around seven thousand men to their camp on Ednavaddy Hill to prepare for the assault on Ballynahinch. The Battle raged from 12 to 13 June; one version of the ballad contains the line 'they fought for twelve hours and never did yield'. During the night the government troops of the Monaghan Militia, mostly Catholic, ran amok, raiding pubs, getting drunk and burning and looting. As a general rule the Militia were mostly Catholic, with Protestant officers, and the Yeomen exclusively Protestant. Both were of course government forces though it was widely suspected that if the Uprising looked like being successful most of the Militia would defect to the rebels. Next day the Battle resumed with the government troops taking the initiative. As so often during the Uprising the inadequately armed and trained amateur insurgents lost out to their better-equipped and more professional adversaries. Ednavaddy was stormed, the Battle and the Uprising in the North was over.

Around five hundred of the rebels were killed, including about two hundred in the vicious mop-up operation. It was at this point that eighteen-year-old Betsy Gray, famed in song and story, was killed at Ballycreen along with her brother George and her sweetheart Willie Boal. It's thought that the two men could have escaped but went back to help Betsy and were themselves also killed. Betsy is commemorated in a long eponymous ballad and also in the very successful novel by W. G. Lyttle, *Betsy Grey or Hearts of Down* (1888). Today a mural in the centre of Ballynahinch also pays tribute, an earlier monument having been destroyed over a hundred years ago when it became a contentious local political issue.

After the Battle Monro remained at large for two days before being captured hiding in the countryside at Clontanagullion, between Ballynahinch and Dromara. It would appear that the ballad is at least half-accurate on this point. A local farmer, William Holmes, promised to hide him and fellow refugee William Kean in an outhouse but then betrayed them to the authorities. According to Latimer, Holmes had accepted 'five pounds and a parcel of linen shirts' to hide Monro in his pig-sty or 'crew' under some 'waps' of straw ('from out of a haystack they hauled poor Monro') until the hue and cry had died down. However, as the ballad puts it, 'the devil tempted' Holmes and he opted for the substantial reward, at least fifty guineas. No sooner were Monro and Kean secreted in the outbuilding, than Holmes' wife, the 'woman' of the ballad, hurried off to Hillsborough and betrayed them to the local corps of Yeomanry known as the Black Troop. Tradition asserts that 'a worse fate was reserved for Holmes. He was held in scorn and contempt by people of every class and creed in his neighbourhood, shunned in his private life and avoided in the marketplace... his descendants to the present day [1888] have the slur cast in their teeth'.

William Kean was Monro's *aide de camp* and had been employed by the *Northern Star*, the United newspaper whose offices in Belfast had been smashed by government troops in 1797. Not being regarded as a major leader, Kean wasn't summarily executed but was instead lodged in The Prevot, the Donegall Arms Inn in Belfast, which had been turned into a temporary military prison. In the early hours of 2 July he somehow managed to get a ladder into the yard and make his escape, never to be recaptured.

Monro however was not so fortunate. He was immediately taken to Lisburn, tried in the morning and hanged in the afternoon of 16 June outside his own home and shop. In 1798 'justice' was indeed dispensed with a terrible, swift sword. It's reported that as Monro mounted the scaffold the bottom rung of the ladder snapped but he quickly scrambled onto the platform saying, 'Gentlemen, I am not cowed '. It would be an injustice to the memory of Harry Monro if this account of his execution didn't note the composed and courageous demeanour that he displayed throughout the ordeal. Eyewitnesses from the execution party record that he went calmly to his death with a prayer and a short statement: 'Tell my country I demand better of her'. He then dropped a handkerchief, a signal to the hangman that he was ready for the rope to be sprung. However the first attempt failed and he had to go through the agony again. At the second attempt he leapt from the platform of his own accord with the cry 'I die for my country'. He was then decapitated and his head placed on a spike in the centre of town.

Surprisingly both his wife and his mother are often reported to have witnessed the execution from the adjacent family home. Latimer however disagrees with Madden on this point, stating that 'Mrs Henry Monro was removed to her father's the Friday before the Battle of Ballynahinch'. The widow, Margaret Johnston of Seymour Hill, Dunmurry, 'a renowned beauty', is thought to have lived on until 1840. Despite the ballad's reference to 'children three' the couple are not in fact thought to have had any children. Today the Monro family home, a simple terraced building, still stands on Bow Street in the centre of Lisburn. The execution site, just across the street, is now a small sunken garden. No monument marks the spot though a local official told me that a memorial might be erected in a more favourable political climate.

The ballad's reference to 'George Clokey' raises an interesting historical question. A number of men called Clokey are known to have taken part in the rebellion, though I have been unable to trace one called George. One possible candidate is Andrew Clokey from Spa, two miles south of Ballynahinch at Annaghmore, who is known to have been a rebel Brigadier General. Colin Johnston Robb, who came from nearby Magheratimpany and who spent much of his life researching the Down rebellion, was certain that the 'Clokey' of the ballad was Andrew Clokey,

> The Clokey brothers from Spa were dedicated United Irishmen and were among the officers who fought at Ballynahinch... the Clokey referred to [in 'General Monro'] was Andy Clokey... He was secretary of Spa Volunteers and for a time was First Lieutenant of Volunteers. He was a friend of Wolfe Tone whom he met in his brother's house in Ballynahinch when Tone was on a visit one time to Lord Moira at Montalto [at Ballynahinch]. Clokey escaped to America [but] returned home in 1825 and lived to a good old age [known as] 'Clokey the last of the rebels'. By that time the 'liberalism' of the area had almost disappeared and it had become a very loyalist district.

The friendship with Wolfe Tone is corroborated by Tone's *Journal* entry of 16 August 1792.

> Arrive at Ballynahinch late. Introduced to Clokey, a proper man. A new corps raised there on Peep-of-day boy principles, converted by Clokey, who in return is chosen their lieutenant. The Catholics and they are now on such good terms that the Catholics lend them their arms to learn their exercise and walk to see them parade, both parties now in high affection with each other, who were before ready to cut each other's throats. All this, done in about two months by the exertions of one obscure man. What might not have been done by the aristocracy of County Down if they were actuated by the same spirit? Damn them!

Two other historical characters, Emmet and Fitzgerald, are mentioned in the ballad. Robert Emmet (1778-1803), a major nationalist icon, led the ill-fated 'two hour' revolt of 1803 in Dublin for which he was later executed. He was an idealistic young man, inspired like so many of his generation by the revolutionary fervour in America and France. His brother Thomas Addis Emmet (1764-1827) was also a senior United Irishman. The Emmets were a prominent Dublin Episcopalian family and Robert was engaged to Sarah Curran, the daughter of Whig MP and liberal lawyer John Philpot Curran. His son Henry Grattan Curran (1800-76) wrote, or at least collected and adapted, the classic patriotic song *The Wearing of the Green*. It's one of the ironies of Irish history that a song now so strongly associated with Catholic nationalism was written by a Protestant.

Emmet's speech from the dock has gone down in history as one of the great pieces of nationalist rhetoric. Unfortunately the speech wasn't accurately recorded and it's likely to have been embellished over the years though the essence of it seems to be authentic enough. A comprehensive version, probably the basis of all others, is given by R.R.Madden, the great if partisan chronicler of the United Irishmen. On the authenticity of the speech Madden wrote:

> The report of Robert Emmet's speech in the Hibernian Magazine of 1803 is far more simple, and equally correct, as far as it goes; but there are likewise many omissions. It was only by submitting the various versions of the speech to the revision of persons who were present at the trial and had a strong recollection of the discourse pronounced by Emmet, and comparing different passages, that a copy could be obtained, wherein the omitted matter was supplied and the additions were struck out.

Excerpts, taken from Madden, include the following:

The Clerk of the Crown:
What have you therefore now to say why judgement of death and execution should not be awarded against you according to the law?

Robert Emmet:
My lords, as to why judgement of death and execution should not be passed upon me I have nothing to say... but as to why my character should not be relieved from the imputations and calumnies thrown out against it I have much to say... I am charged with being an emissary of France, it is false... never did I retain the remotest idea of establishing French power in Ireland. Were the French to come as invaders I would oppose them with all my strength, I should meet them upon the beach with a sword in one hand and a torch in the other, I would animate my countrymen to immolate them in their boats before they had contaminated the soil of my country... I would dispute every inch of ground, burn every blade of grass and the last entrenchment of liberty should be my grave.

When my spirit shall have joined those bands of martyred heroes who have shed their blood on the scaffold and in the field in defence of their country, this is my hope that my memory and name may serve to animate those who survive... your executioner may abridge the period of my existence, but while I exist, I shall not forbear to vindicate my character and motives from you aspersions. As men my Lords we must appear on the Great Day at one common tribunal and it will remain for the Searcher of all hearts to show a collective universe who was engaged in the most virtuous actions.

There are men concerned in this conspiracy who are not only

superior to me but even to your own conception of yourself my Lord. Men… who would not disgrace themselves by shaking your bloodstained hand.

My race is run, the grave opens to receive me and I sink into its bosom. I have but one request to ask at my departure from this world. It is the charity of its silence. Let no man write my epitaph, for as no man who knows my motives dare now vindicate them, let not prejudice or ignorance asperse them. Let them rest in obscurity and peace, my memory be left in oblivion and my tomb remain uninscribed, until other times and other men can do justice to my character. When my country takes her place among the nations of the earth, then and not til then, let my epitaph be written.

Lord Edward Fitzgerald (1763-98), another nationalist icon though not so celebrated in song and verse, was a militant senior United leader who was killed on 19 May during the struggle that ensued on his arrest just a few days before the Uprising proper had broken out. He too had become imbued with the democratic ideals of the French Revolution and had been drummed out of the Army for proposing a toast against hereditary titles, though he himself was the son of the Duke of Leinster. For the record, both Emmet and Fitzgerald were Protestants.

When I first heard *General Monro* I had assumed that the reference to 'Monro's sister' in verse eight was simply an irrelevant piece of defiance on the part of the writer. However a number of historical references to her indicate that she too was prominent within the local United movement. Martha McTier, wife of United founder member Samuel McTier and sister of William Drennan, wrote that one of the women 'taken up and lodged in the Prevôt and bail refused' was 'Miss Munroe, sister to the man who was hanged'.

Another fascinating reference is by a Belfast Yeoman called Poyntz Stewart, who was in love with her. Recorded in November 1804 it contains the following:

Margaret Monro, the beloved sister of the late Harry… well set up and handsome beyond a fair description… when the United Irish Society established a club of their craft here Margaret Monro became the mistress of the great dinners and suppers at their assembly rooms in Castle Street… she it was who founded the first quiltings, where the object of the social evenings was to discuss the political affairs of the day… and render signal service in the days of uprisings against the Government in this Kingdom… always dressed in the Dublin fashion… green and orange ribbons always

graced her head dress. I chanced to meet her at an assembly in the rooms in Lisburn about the latter end of May in the year of the rebellion. I was, for my part, in the full regimentals of my Corps of Yeomen. When I asked her to accompany me to the great repast of that evening she hotly declined and remarked 'Mr. Stewart Sir I would sorely disdain to accompany any gentleman who bears arms against his fellow-countrymen in their hour of fight for the freedom of Ireland'. ... I was perturbed and felt the rebuff, but I did admire the great spirit of woman-hood which rebuked me so...
I decline to reveal what I know of Miss Monro during the days of the Rising but after it was over she was living with Mr. Johnston [her brother-in-law] of Seymour Hill... for two years I carried a warrant for her arrest but I did not effect it nor did I wish to do so.

Stewart later records: 'She was thrown in Carrickfergus Gaol on no charge as yet known to me. I shall interest myself in bringing about her release at an early date if possible'.

A corroborative paragraph is given by Madden:

Mr. Munro's sister Margaret was obliged to leave the country for a length of time after her brother's death. On returning she was imprisoned for twenty-three weeks in Carrickfergus and was only liberated on procuring bail to a large amount.

Today the name of Henry Monro is not as well known as it deserves to be, though the recent bicentennial of the Uprising brought some welcome attention. A '98 re-enactment in Lisburn brought an appreciation of him to a modern audience. Many local people would have been pleased to learn that their town had produced such a brave and decent man, even if for the majority of present day Lisburn residents, he did fight on the 'wrong' side.

The wonderfully evocative place name of Ballynahinch is derived from the Irish *Baile na hinse* meaning something like 'settlement on the low ground beside the river'. Today the still small town has expanded just a little from its origins on the low ground by the Ballynahinch River. It is conscious of its place in history and the Battle site is signposted as you drive into town. Like most towns in the area it is a workaday sort of a place well off the tourist trail. Nevertheless I found it a pleasant overnight stop, allowing me to quietly commemorate 'that brave Irish hero', *General Monro*.

Photo: John McLaughlin

Memorial to Roddy McCorley, Toomebridge

9.
Roddy McCorley

See the fleet-foot host of men who speed with faces wan
From farmstead and from fisher's cot along the banks of Bann.
They come with vengeance in their eye, too late, too late are they,
For young Roddy McCorley goes to die on the bridge of Toome today.

Ireland, mother Ireland, you love them still the best,
Those fearless brave who fighting fell upon your hapless breast,
But never a one of all your dead more bravely fell in fray
Than he who marches to his fate on the bridge of Toome today.

When he last stepped up that street, his shining pike in hand,
Behind him marched in grim array a stalwart earnest band.
For Antrim town for Antrim town, he led them to the fray
And young Roddy McCorley goes to die on the bridge of Toome today.

His grey coat and his sash of green were brave and stainless then,
The banners flashed beneath the sun over those marching men,
His coat hath many a rent this noon, his sash is torn away,
For young Roddy McCorley goes to die on the bridge of Toome today.

Oh how his pike flashed to the sun then found a foeman's heart.
Through furious fight and heavy heart he bore a true man's part
And many a redcoat hit the dust before his keen pike play,
But young Roddy McCorley goes to die on the bridge of Toome today.

Up the narrow streets he stepped, smiling and proud and young.
About the hemp rope on his neck, the golden ringlets clung.
There was never a tear in his blue eyes, both glad and bright are they,
For young Roddy McCorley goes to die on the Bridge of Toome today.

Because he loved the motherland, because he loved the green
He goes to meet the martyr's fate with proud and joyous mien.
True to the last, true to the last he trod the upward way
For young Roddy McCorley goes to die on the bridge of Toome today.

Roddy McCorley

Hero or Villain on the Bridge of Toome?

T he 1798 rebellion produced many unlikely heroes, whose deeds have been commemorated in song. One of the most famous is Roddy McCorley, 'on the bridge of Toome today'. The ballad was written by Ethna Carbery (1864-1902), the pen name of Anna MacManus, daughter of prominent Belfast Fenian Robert Johnston. It was first published in her poetry collection *The Four Winds of Eirinn* (1902).

Despite living and dying relatively recently, a good deal of uncertainty surrounds 'Ethna Carbery'. Before examining the historical Roddy McCorley, it is worth taking a closer look at the life of the woman who wrote the stirring ballad about him, one of the finest of all the rebel songs. Most of the information contained in the next three paragraphs is based on recent research carried out by Helen Meehan, a local historian from Mountcharles, Donegal, just a mile from where the Roddy McCorley lyricist is buried.

'Ethna Carbery' was born in Bryans Street, Ballymena, about ten miles north of the hamlet of Milltown, a mile east of Toome, where Roddy McCorley had been born, or certainly lived, around a century earlier. (Some accounts give McCorley's birthplace as Bellaghy.) Ethna Carbery was born as Anna Isabella Johnson. Later the family opted to spell the name as 'Johnston', to conform to the perceived Belfast form. The origin of the name 'Ethna Carbery' is uncertain. However Helen Meehan, who is related to Carbery through marriage, and who has researched the subject carefully, has written 'if she took the pen name from a relative it must have been from the Donegal born wife of her great grand uncle, John, not from a grandmother'. Uncertainty also surrounds the date, and even the year of her birth. Virtually every book published gives it as 1866. However Helen Meehan has established that she was born on 3 December 1864. She has also traced Carbery's ancestors back to before 1750, when the poet's great, great, great grandfather John Johnson (no 't'), from Lisnahilt in Crebilly parish, near Slemish Mountain, Antrim, married a 'Barcley [Barclay?] girl from Broughshane'. Carbery's parents married in 1861 and were to have seven children. Her mother, Marjery Magee, had strong family connections in Donegal, near Pettigo. Her father, Robert Johnston, born on St Patrick's Day 1840 and known as 'Johnston of the North', was a senior Fenian, representing Ulster on the Supreme Council of the Irish Republican Brotherhood. He was a close colleague of James Stephens, Charles Joseph Kickham and, later, of Parnell and Maud Gonne. His ancestors had been active United Irishmen, so the author of *Roddy McCorley* was born into a family steeped in republicanism, past and present. It is not too surprising therefore that she was attracted to the heroic image and local legend that was Roddy McCorley. Shortly after the collapse of the Fenian Revolt of 1867 the Johnston family moved to Belfast.

Carbery married the Mountcharles, Donegal, novelist Seumas MacManus (1868-1960) in Belfast on 22 August 1901. Seven months later she was dead. MacManus later remarried, to Margaret McCollin, and raised a family. He died in New York, where he spent much of his life and where he enjoyed a successful literary career. In 1961 his remains were reburied in the same little churchyard at Frosses, Donegal, where his first wife had been buried fifty-nine years earlier.

There is also some confusion over the year of Ethna Carbery's death, with one standard reference book giving it as 1911, and some accounts even placing her in the General Post Office in Dublin during the 1916 Rising. The latter is possibly the result of confusing her with Winifred Carney, secretary to James Connolly. However her death notice in the Irish News Thursday 3 April 1902 confirms that she died in 1902.

> MacMANUS – On Wednesday at Revlin House, Donegal,
> Anna, wife of Seumas MacManus.
> Interment on Friday, Frosses, Inver, Donegal.
> Funeral leaves at one o'clock
> SEUMAS MacMANUS

I started out therefore with some relish to research the famous ballad, which just exudes rebel spirit and is one of the most effective and evocative in the entire rebel repertoire. However I was to be greatly disappointed, for the name of Roddy McCorley didn't appear in any of the dozens of general histories that I checked. Next I turned to Jonathan Bardon's nine hundred page *History of Ulster* which I was sure would deal in some detail with a name that is a household one in the North. Not so; again Roddy McCorley doesn't get a mention. Finally I turned, by this time more in hope than expectation, to specialist histories of the Uprising in the North. Gradually I began to come across fleeting references to someone who from here on I will simply refer to as 'Roddy'. In a sense these references only increased the mystery, as they couldn't even agree on such basic facts as his religion and the date of his execution, which is given variously as 1798, 1799 and 1800. The implication of this was that few documented facts about Roddy are known.

However I had long been aware of the existence of a much older ballad, entitled *Rody McCorley*. In the original edition of Ethna Carbery's poetry the name is also given as 'Rody'. The name is an anglicised form of *Ruiadhrí* or Rory and also occurs as Roger, Rodger and Roderick. I had never previously paid much attention to the older ballad probably because I had never heard it sung and anyway, surely it couldn't rival the Carbery classic. On closer inspection however it transpires that this song is crammed with detail, was probably composed within living memory of the events described and has a more authentic flavour to it than Carbery's romanticised composition. The key verses from the total of twelve are as follows:

> In sweet Duneane this youth was born and reared up tenderly,
> His parents educated him, all by their industry.
> Both day and night they sorely toiled all for their family
> Till desolation it came on all by cursed perjury.

> 'Twas first the father's life they took and secondly the son.
> The mother tore her old grey locks, she says, 'I am undone,
> They took from me my property, my houses and my land
> And in the parish where I was born I dare not tread upon'.

> 'Farewell unto you sweet Drumaul, if in you I had stayed,
> Among the Presbyterians I wouldn't have been betrayed.
> The gallows tree I'd never have seen had I remained there
> For Dufferin you betrayed me, McErlean you set the snare.

> In Ballyscullion I was betrayed, woe be unto the man
> Who swore me a Defender and a foe unto the Crown,
> Which causes Rody for to lie beneath the spreading thorn,
> He'll sigh and say, 'Alas the day that ever I was born'.

> They called on Father Devlin, his reverence came with speed.
> 'Here's one of Christ's own flock', he said, 'ye shepherds for to feed'.
> He gave to him the heavenly food that nourishes the soul
> That it may rest eternally while his body is in the mould.

This tells us much and though it can't be taken as fact, it must surely have some basis in reality. For example, it tells us that Roddy was born in the parish of Duneane, just east of Toome, that his father had a deadly brush with the law, that Roddy had some connection with the Presbyterians and that he was 'betrayed' by people called Dufferin and McErlean. Both of these characters are now lost to history but some speculation is possible. Both are thought to have belonged to local

Catholic families. 'Dufferin' is often also spelt as 'Duffin' and it is known that a Captain William Duffin of Ballygarvey, near Ballymena, was a local rebel commander. It is noted that he ordered 'some of the rebels on the street of Broughshane to wear green cockades'. On 17 October 1798 he was tried and acquitted, though he was given 200 lashes for 'prevarication'. I have found no evidence that this is the 'Dufferin' of the older ballad but the name, the area and the politics coincide.

McErlean, or MacErlain, is of particular interest as this was Roddy's mother's maiden name. Could a relative, who would have been likely to know the location of his hideout, have betrayed him? Strangely though we aren't told why Roddy was executed (apart from a passing reference to him having been a Defender, the exclusively Catholic agrarian secret society) or why he was considered to have been such a hero in the first place. There is no reference to any military or political activity, let alone to heroic exploits. Surely if this had been the case, the ballad maker would have featured such exploits prominently. Or maybe he is just taking it for granted that everyone would have already been aware of these. Another verse refers to Roddy's 'locks of yellow hair' which in Ethna Carbery's ballad become 'golden ringlets'.

During one of my many visits to 'Roddy country', I discovered a booklet entitled *Roddy McCorley: a Study of Evidence*, written by Anne Fay, undated but published in 1989. The study raises the fundamental question: was Roddy a political martyr or a common criminal? Some of the main points, with additional material, are summarised as follows:

1. Roddy's religion is usually given as being Presbyterian but the more I investigated the topic, the more I became convinced that he was probably a Catholic, though I have found no conclusive evidence either way. The surname McCorley is generally regarded as a 'Catholic' one by local people and in my conversations in the Toome area I was assured that it is *very* Catholic'. It is a variant of Torley or Curley, which is derived from the Irish *Mac Thoirdealbhaigh*, meaning 'son of Turlough'.

2. In 1907 Duneane Church of Ireland graveyard contained two headstones, now vanished, inscribed as follows:

   This stone belongs to John McCorly
   Here lieth the body of Felix McCorly
   Who died the 13th April 1768 aged eleven months
   And Ann McCorly who died June the 1st 1769 aged 4 years

   I.H.S.
   This to the memory
   Of Roger McCorly
   Who departed this life
   May 12th 1772 aged 61 years

No attempt is made to establish the identity, or religion, of any of those named or of any relationship to Roddy though it is assumed that he belonged to this family. In 1852 Roddy's remains were disinterred by his nephew, Hugh McCorley of Ballymena, and reburied in this family plot. 'Roger' named above could have been Roddy's grandfather or, less probably, his father.

In 1920 two young brothers, Roger (born 1901) and Felix McCorley, both Catholics, joined the IRA. Roger, who later became leader of the organisation in Belfast, claimed, according to IRA historian Uinseann MacEoin who interviewed him, 'descent from the legendary Roddy of Toome'. It's likely that he was indeed descended from Roddy, possibly a great grandson or great grand nephew. ('IHS', ancient Greek for 'Jesus' offers no clue to the McCorley family's religion, as it is a term used by both Catholics and Protestants.) The McCorley gravestones have not survived. According to one account they were 'blown up in January 1969', according to another, 'thrown down a well'.

3. At this time Catholics were often buried in the local Protestant church cemetery.

4. Roddy's mother was a McErlean from Bellaghy, north-west of Toome across the River Bann. McErlean is also regarded as an almost exclusively 'Catholic' name. It is derived from the Irish *MacFhirleighinn* ('learned man').

5. The McCorley family owned the local corn mill in the townland of Lismaclosky, about a mile east of Toome, adjacent to Duneane Church of Ireland Church. (This should not be confused with the more modern Duneane Presbyterian Church, a mile further east). Today the hamlet there is still called Milltown. On the six-inches-to-one mile Ordnance Survey map of 1834, marked at Duneane are 'Corn Mill', 'Mill Dam', 'School Ho[use]' and 'Church'.

6. According to various local traditions, Roddy's father had been transported, either for sheep stealing or for making pikes, or he had been hanged. The latter is supported by the older ballad, 'twas first the father's life they took'. It is also the view taken by Bobby Sands in his 17-verse poem *Rodai MacCorlai*.

> My greying mother, Tara the Pity, cut my silent father free,
> Where he danced like a ship on an angry wave from yonder hanging tree
> And he felt no touch nor heard no scream, his deathly gaze a loss
> As he slumped into her cradled arms, like Christ did from the cross.
> I am Rodai of Duneane – MacCorlai – Antrim born!
> This day in Toome I met my doom for an oath that I have sworn
> On yonder oak on Roughery Hill a jackdaw I have heard;
> It waits to steal my very soul, 'tis surely the devil's bird.

7. At some point Roddy's mother moved back to her own people (on the death or transportation of her husband?). She later returned to

Lismaclosky and remarried (possibly to a man named Orr, though definitely not William Orr, the executed local United Irishman whose life is well documented).

8. In 1907 the *Irish News* and *Belfast Morning Post* published an article by Francis Joseph Bigger entitled 'Roddy McCorley - Who Fears To Speak of '98?' This is an anecdotal and plainly biased piece, which, referring to Roddy's re-interment, includes the following: 'not one bone missing... it was a great funeral... the whole countryside was there to honour one who had laid down his life for his country'. Ironically Bigger's own grave was blown up by 'loyalists' in the 1970s. However the article does contain a number of interesting points. Bigger asserts that just prior to his execution 'Rody was attended to by Father Hugh Devlin', which, if true, would almost certainly mean that he was a Catholic. Bigger also gives an additional verse to the older ballad, not found elsewhere.

> Young Rody he stepped forward then, the scaffold he ascends,
> He looked east, he looked west, to view his loving friends,
> And turned round unto the north, he cried 'O, cruel Sam,
> It was you who proved my overthrow, you brought me as I am'.

'Cruel Sam' is thought to have been Samuel Finneston, captain of the band of Yeomen who finally captured Roddy. Interestingly, Bigger also refers to Ethna Carbery as 'that fine Ulster *singer*'.

9. Roddy became an outlaw at some point, whether before or after the Uprising isn't known.

10. In July 1798 a general amnesty pardoned all rebels except named leaders for whom a reward of fifty guineas was offered. (These men were known as the 'Fifty Pounders'). Roddy's name wasn't on the list. At this point he was therefore, at least theoretically, in the clear.

11. By the turn of the century Roddy and his outlaw band, led in fact by a shoemaker from Ballymena called Thomas Archer, had lost any initial public sympathy and was preying on the community. The gang committed serious crimes including murder during the course of robberies. Prior to the Uprising Archer had been a government militiaman but had deserted, joined the United Irishmen and had apparently fought with considerable courage at the Battle of Antrim. Even Archer, who was widely recognised as a thoroughly dangerous desperado, had a ballad composed in his honour.

> Archer the bold mileshyman [militia], turned out in '98,
> Not a sodger o' the King, but his yeos to bate.
> Hunted by the bloody Fencibles in places remote
> Betrayed was he to die a slave on Ballymena's Moat.
> ['Moat' is a variant of motte, an ancient earthen fortification.]

Archer was captured and hanged in Ballymena on the 10 March 1800. The blunderbuss with which he tried to fight off the Rasharkin Yeomen is now on display in the Ulster Folk and Transport Museum in Cultra.

12. Roddy was denounced from the pulpit by the local parish priest (this would also imply that he was a Catholic). The name of that priest was Hugh Devlin, the same as that of the priest in the older ballad who had administered the last rites.

13. This denunciation so infuriated Roddy that he marched into the church, grabbed the ciborium from the priest's hands and threw it on the floor.

14. This sacrilegious act finally turned the locals against Roddy and the location of his hideout at Ballyscullion East was disclosed to the authorities.

15. He was arrested, tried and hanged on the Bridge of Toome on 28 February 1800. Unfortunately we are not told specifically what the charges were, though it is clear that they were regarded as criminal in nature. He was buried beneath the road at the spot where he was hanged.

16. There seems to be no firm evidence either way as to whether or not he was ever a United Irishman or a Defender or whether or not he took any part in the rebellion.

17. A report in the *Belfast News Letter* of Tuesday 4 March 1800 includes the following account of Roddy's execution:

Extract of a letter from Ballymena, Sunday, 2nd March.

Upon Friday last, a most awful procession took place here, namely the execution of Roger McCorley who was lately convicted at a Court-martial, to the place of execution, Toome Bridge, the unfortunate man having been born in that neighbourhood. As a warning to others, it is proper to observe that the whole of his life was devoted to disorderly proceedings of every kind; for many years past, scarcely a Quarter-Sessions occurred but what the name of ROGER McCORLEY appeared in a variety of Criminal cases! His body was given up to dissection, and afterwards, buried under the gallows.

If the report is accurate, as seems likely even allowing for political bias, it would mean that Roddy was actually known as 'Roger' and that the date of his hanging was Friday 28 February 1800. (Although dividable by four the year 1800 was not a leap year, otherwise the date would have been 29 February). Despite the claim in the older ballad this was not Good Friday as Good Friday 1800 was 11 April. Perhaps this was an attempt to add dramatic symbolism by implying that Roddy was a Christ-like sacrificial figure. However as the trial was held before a 'court-martial', as also stated in the older ballad, this could imply that it had military as well as criminal implications.

The report continued: 'Thus, of late, we have got rid of six of those nefarious wretches, who have kept this neighbourhood in the greatest misery for some time past, namely, Stewart, Dunn, Ryan, McCorley, Caskey and the notorious Dr. Linn... the noted ARCHER will soon be in our Guard-room'.

This report seems to be a very damning piece of 'evidence', even allowing for the newspaper's pro-government line. Generally it has the tone of a genuine news report and gives the impression of having been written more in sorrow than in anger. Terms such as 'the most awful procession' and 'the unfortunate man' are very sympathetic in tone and not the sort of language that would normally be found in reports of political trials of the period.

18. Today Roddy's remains lie in an unmarked grave in Duneane Church of Ireland cemetery.

That then is an outline of the scenario but what is the reality? In the absence of firm evidence we can only make a relatively informed guess. My own feeling is that the story probably went something as follows. Roddy McCorley was born in the hamlet of Milltown, in the townland of Lismacloskey, in the Parish of Duneane, in the Barony of Upper Toome, sometime around 1770. The family owned the local corn mill and at some point Roddy's father committed some serious offence and was punished either by being transported or executed. One local tradition asserts that Roddy was aged twelve at the time. His family was evicted from their home and land. The punishment severely disrupted the life of Roddy's family, causing his mother particular grief and hardship. In reaction to this, Roddy embarked on a gradually escalating career of lawlessness. Possibly he joined, or at least established links with the Defenders. This is one area where it is definitely established that Defenders participated in the Rebellion.

When the Uprising came along Roddy joined the rebels, seeing it as an opportunity to hit back at the regime that had 'wronged' his family. Possibly his stepfather was a Protestant, which would have given him links to 'the Presbyterians of sweet Drumaul', the United Irishmen who in Antrim were almost exclusively Protestant. Almost certainly he would have fought at the Battle of Antrim on 7 June 1798. About ten thousand men took part and it must have produced many heroes. Of them all Roddy McCorley is the only one to have survived in the popular tradition. How did he gain this reputation? Surely the origins of the legend must have some basis in fact? However it has to be said that his modern reputation rests mainly on the Ethna Carbery ballad and she was primarily an imaginative and very political writer. She had co-founded the nationalist literary magazine *The Shan Van Vocht* (*Sean Bhean Bhoct*, 'the poor old woman', a symbol of Ireland under British rule). She also contributed regularly to *The Nation* and *United Ireland*. However even such a committed nationalist must surely have had some reason for regarding Roddy as a hero.

He had probably displayed bravery at the Battle of Antrim, though it is unlikely that 'For Antrim Town, he led them to the fray' as he is not mentioned in any historical accounts. Ironically Roddy was probably one of the Toome men who destroyed the famous bridge over the Bann to hamper government troop movements, little thinking that he would later be hanged there. He probably attained local legend status through an evolutionary process of exaggeration and distortion of the sort that feels sympathy for the outlaw and that tends to stress any positive points while ignoring the negative.

Why did he not take advantage of the July '98 amnesty? A pro-Roddy explanation would be that he refused to accept defeat and heroically continued the struggle as Michael Dwyer did in the south. However if this were the case surely the facts would have been well documented, as with Dwyer. The unfavourable explanation would be that he wasn't eligible for pardon as his major offences were criminal rather than political. The latter seems the more logical conclusion, though in fairness the question of surrender under the terms of the amnesty was not cut and dried. Although the rebels may have been amnestied by Lord Cornwallis in Dublin this didn't necessarily protect them from vengeful local yeomen. In addition General Gerard Lake, the national military chief, instructed his subordinates to ignore the amnesty.

Another wanted man, James (Jemmy) Hope (1764-1847), gave a clear account of why he refused to surrender.

> Having joined the Union in the spring-time of its strength, from a conscientious conviction of its principles being right, and having no reason to change my opinion when the Society was overtaken by adversity, I felt bound to that cause to which I had pledged my life. I considered surrender under that proclamation, was not only a recantation of one's principles, but a tacit acquiescence in the justice of the punishment which had been inflicted on thousands of my associates... looking to the Most High alone for protection I knew no danger but that of willfully and knowingly doing wrong... I resolved never to be taken alive.

Hope, a weaver who became a confidante of Henry Joy McCracken, Thomas Russell and Robert Emmet, is generally regarded as being incorruptible. He had fought heroically at the Battle of Antrim where he commanded the 'Spartan Band'. He remained on the run, even getting involved again with Emmet in 1803, meeting up with Michael Dwyer in Glen Imaal, always carrying 'a brace of pistols', never considering accepting terms, until 1806, by which time the political climate had changed. It's maybe a pity that Ethna Carbery didn't employ her poetic gifts to write a ballad about Jemmy Hope, a true working class Protestant hero. However given all that has happened in the past two hundred years, the legend, image and symbolic significance of Roddy McCorley, the heroic and handsome young rebel, far outweighs any possible negative reality and illustrates perfectly the power and influence of the political ballad in the popular consciousness.

The place name of Toome (or Toomebridge) derives from *Tuaim*, '[pagan burial] mound', the same as Tuam in County Galway. The original 'Bridge of Toome' was built in 1785, replacing the ford that had been used since ancient times. The River Bann rises in the Mountains of Mourne and flows through Lough Neagh eighty miles to the Atlantic beyond Coleraine. The 'fisher's cots' may be long gone but the River remains an important fishery, especially for eels, which are exported to Europe.

Present-day Toome, population seven hundred, has been badly scarred and depressed by the events of recent history. However, the legend of Roddy McCorley lives on and he is commemorated with a marble monument in the town centre, strategically located directly opposite the heavily fortified police station. The town's present day attitude to Roddy was probably fairly summed up by a local man, who over a few whiskies assured me, 'A great man, Roddy McCorley was a great man'.

Florence Mary Wilson (1874-1946)

11.

The Man from God Knows Where

Into our townland upon a night of snow rode a man from God knows where.
None of us bade him stay nor go, nor deemed him friend, nor damned him foe,
But we stabled his big gray mare; for in our townland we're decent folk
And if he didn't speak, why sure none of us spoke, and we sat till the fire burned low.

We're a civil sort in our wee place, so we made the circle wide
Round Andy Lemon's cheerful blaze, and wished this man his length of days
And a good end to his ride; he smiled in under his slouchy hat,
Says he, 'There's a bit of a joke in that, for we ride different ways'.

The whiles we smoked, we watched him stare, from his seat fornenst the glow.
I nudged Joe Moore; I said, 'You wouldn't dare to ask him who he's for meetin' there
Or how far he has got to go'; but Joe wouldn't dare nor Wully Boy Scott
And he took no drink neither cold nor hot, this man from God knows where.

It was closing time, and late forbye, when us ones braved the air.
I never saw worse, may I live or die, than the sleet that night, and I says, says I,
'You'll find he's for stoppin' there'; but at screek o' day through the gable pane
I watched him spur in the peltin' rain, an' I juked from his rovin' eye.

Two winters more then the Trouble Year, when the best a man could feel
Was the pike that he kept in hidin' near, till the blood o' hate an' the blood o' fear
Would be redder nor rust on the steel; an' us ones quiet from mindin' the farms,
Let them take what we gave wi' the weight of our arms, from Saintfield to Kilkeel.

In the time o' The Hurry we had no lead, we all of us fought wi' the rest
And if e'er one shook like a tremblin' reed, well none of us gave neither hint nor heed
Nor ever, even we'd guessed; we men o' the North had a word for to say
And we said it then in our own dour way, an' we spoke as we thought was best.

All Ulster over the weemen cried for the standin' crops on the land
And many's the sweetheart and many's the bride would liefer ha' gone to where he died
And have mourned her lone by her man; but us ones weathered the thick of it
And we used to dander along an' sit, in Andy's side by side.

What with discourse going to an fro, the night would be wearing thin,
Yet never so late when we rose to go, but some one would say, 'Do ye mind thon snow
And the man who came wanderin' in?' Then we be to fall to the talk again
If maybe by chance he was One O' Them, the man who rode like the wind.

'Twas gettin' on past the heat o' the year, when I rode to Newton Fair.
I sold as I could an' the dealers were near, only three pounds eight for the Innish steer
And nothin' at all for the mare; I met McKee in the throng o' the street.
Says he, 'The grass has grown under our feet since they hanged young Warwick here'.

And he told me that Boney had promised help to a man in Dublin town
Says he, 'If you've left your pike on the shelf, you better go hot fut home by yourself
And once more take it down'; so by Comber road I trotted the grey,
And I never cut corn till Killyleagh stood plain on the risin' ground.

For a wheen o' days, we sat waitin' for the word to rise an' go at it like men,
But no French ships sailed into Cloghy Bay, an' we heard the black news at the
    break o' day
That the cause was lost again; an' Joey and me an' Wully Boy Scott,
We agreed to ourselves that we'd lief as not ha' been found in the thick o' the slain.

By Downpatrick jail I was bound to fair, on a day I'll remember, faith,
For when I came to the prison square, the people were waitin' in hundreds there
And you wouldn't hear stir nor breath; for the sodgers were standin' grim an' tall
Round a scaffold built there, fornenst the wall, and a man stepped out for death.

I was brave an' near to the edge o' the throng, and I knowed the face again
And I knowed the set, an I knowed the walk, an' the sound of his strange up-
    country talk
For he spoke out right an plain; then he bowed his head to the swingin' rope
And I said 'Please God' to his dyin' hope, an' 'Amen' to his dyin' prayer
That the wrong would cease and the right prevail, for the man that they hanged in
    Downpatrick jail
Was the man from God knows where..

The Man from God Knows Where

Thomas Russell, Florence Wilson
and the 'decent folk' of County Down

This classic ballad revolves around the legendary United Irishman Thomas Russell. It's a dramatic, atmospheric, powerful and perceptive piece, written in 1918 by Florence Mary Wilson, a Quaker widow from Lisburn, the mother of nine children. However, although the lyrics form one of Ireland's most popular recitations, they are, as a song, virtually unknown.

The music wasn't provided for another sixty years, when it was composed by Tom Hickland, a prominent member of the Belfast folk scene in the 1960s. Later he joined the folk-group Five Hand Reel and *The Man from God Knows Where* was included on their album *A Bunch of Fives* which was released in 1979. The band included some of the best Irish and British folk musicians of the period and produced a number of distinctive and critically acclaimed albums. *A Bunch of Fives*, though, created barely a ripple and was to be the band's final release. Nevertheless it has stood the test of time well and is now something of a collector's item on the folk scene.

Five Hand Reel's personnel on the album was completed by Sam Bracken (Belfast), Bobby Eaglesham (Scotland), Barry Lyons (England) and Dave Tulloch (Scotland). A well-known former member, Dick Gaughan, had left the band the previous year. The background to *The Man from God Knows Where* was given to me by Bobby Eaglesham:

> My recollection of the Five Hand Reel version of *The Man from God Knows Where* is that it was the fiddle player Tom Hickland's project on the album. Tom probably came up with the main idea, with the rest of the band coming up with suggestions and changes. All FHR recordings were published jointly as all members had a hand in writing and arranging the material.

Tom Hickland remains modest and unassuming about his composition, though he did tell me that although *A Bunch of Fives* was the band's least commercially successful album, musically it remains his favourite. He will, in time, surely receive due recognition for his achievement of so effectively transforming one of Ireland's most loved recitations into one of her finest ballads. Sam Bracken too makes a significant contribution to the track, providing distinctive lead guitar as well as alternating lead vocals with Hickland. Both came from Belfast: Hickland, formely of the Winnowers, being a Catholic and Bracken, formely of Therapy, being a Protestant. It seems appropriate that Hickland was born in the same year, 1946, that Florence Wilson, the author of the lyrics, died.

The subject of the ballad, Thomas Paliser Russell (1767-1803) was born in the parish of Kilshanick, near Mallow in County Cork. He was a radical by nature and on his return to Ireland after four years with the army in India quickly became involved in subversive politics, firstly in Dublin with Tone and later in Belfast and the north. Russell was a charismatic personality and physically cut a striking figure. In 1803 his wanted poster described him as 'a tall handsome man... dark complexion, aquiline nose, large black eyes with heavy eye-brows, good teeth, full chested...[of] military appearance, speaking fluently with a clear distinctive voice and having a good address'. His image today, bolstered hugely by Florence Wilson's ballad, is that of the handsome, brave and idealistic hero, shrouded in mystique. In Ulster his name alone was said to be 'worth 50,000 men'. However the hardships he endured and the sacrifices he made took their toll and latterly he was virtually reduced to living on the charity of friends.

Russell was a complex character, who paradoxically combined devout religious belief with casual sexual affairs, heavy drinking and barrack room language, though he always strove to be true to his high moral principles. In 1792 he resigned from a potentially lucrative career as a magistrate in Dungannon because he 'could not reconcile it to his conscience to sit as a Magistrate on a bench where the practice prevailed of inquiring what a man's religion was before inquiring into the crime with which the person was accused'. On a more personal level he refused to use sugar because it was a product of slavery in the West Indies. Russell abhorred slavery and wrote poems such as *The Negro's Complaint*, *The Dying Negro* and *The Captive Negro*. Slavery was he wrote 'a system of cruelty, torment, wickedness and infamy... the work of wicked demons rather than men', the single issue 'of the greatest consequence on the face of the earth'. Russell was the great friend of Wolfe Tone and many's the philosophical and convivial evening the two young men spent together before their activities began to put their lives at risk. Tone, a religious sceptic and mischievous wit, gently mocked Russell for his devout religiosity, affectionately teasing him as 'PP', parish priest.

In the mid 1790s Russell went on reconnaissance and organisational journeys in Leinster and Ulster, trying to establish common cause between the Protestant United Irishmen and the Catholic Defenders. In 1796 he was arrested and imprisoned in Dublin. In 1799 he was transferred to remote Fort George near Inverness in the north of Scotland. He was held for six years, the longest of all the United Irishmen. Throughout his incarceration Russell was sustained by the Anglican faith instilled into him as a child, as well as by his certainty that his political cause was a just one. In a prison letter from 1800 he wrote, 'My long imprisonment does not prevent my being in perfect health. I trust that we shall meet again in Ireland, make some pleasant journeys, contemplating the works of nature and adoring its Divine Author'. The suicide and execution of his closest friends Tone and McCracken were severe blows but they did not deter him. He now wrote that he felt under a 'greater obligation to persevere in the great cause'. For Russell 'The Cause' overruled everything. His eventual release was conditional upon his going into exile. He did therefore spend some time in France but the fresh stirrings of revolt under Emmet were too much for him to resist and he returned to Ireland with three separate rewards on his head.

By now however Russell, ever the idealist, was out of touch with the new political reality and was pursuing a lost cause. The Presbyterians of County Down, driven to disloyalty and rebellion in 1798, had suffered badly as a result and were in the process of coming to terms with the *Act of Union* of the Irish and British parliaments in 1801. The vast majority were no longer prepared to take further risks.

Russell's 'revolt' unravelled around Loughinisland, between Ballynahinch and Downpatrick, as the local men who had turned out in such numbers five years previously now stayed home and the authorities began to make arrests. Russell managed to evade capture for a few weeks, staying in a number of friendly houses at various locations as far north as Belfast. Latterly he stayed at Ballysallagh near Bangor with Daniel and Ellen Rabb, employees of Mary Anne McCracken. On 25 August Rabb arranged for a fishing boat to take him as far as Drogheda. From there he made his way to Dublin on foot (Russell thought nothing of hiking thirty miles a day), having by this time discarded the green military greatcoat pressed on him by Emmet.

In the capital 'Mr Harris' was lodged in the home of Daniel Muley at 29 Parliament Street, at the very gates of Dublin Castle where Emmet, whom Russell planned to rescue, was being held. After a few days confined indoors he was betrayed by John Swift Emerson who curried favour with the Castle authorities. Emerson passed on his suspicions about one of Muley's rooms where the curtains remained drawn day and night, Russell was arrested by the ever-zealous town major Henry Sirr. Muley was a known United Irishman and in retrospect it seems incredible that his house, on the Castle doorstep, should have been chosen to hide the most wanted man in Ireland. Emmet and twenty-one others were executed on 20 September. Russell was taken north and imprisoned at Downpatrick where, said the Viceroy Lord Hardwicke, 'the example of his execution would have the greatest effect', proof that the government had decided prior to his trial that Russell wouldn't be allowed to survive. At his one day 'trial' he stated:

> I look back on the last thirteen years of my life in which I have interfered with the transactions in Ireland with entire satisfaction, though for my share in them I am now about to die... my death may serve as a memorial to others and, on trying occasions, it may inspire them with courage... I have travelled much [in India and on continental Europe] and seen the world and I think the Irish are the most virtuous nation on the face of the earth. They are a good and brave people and had I a thousand lives I would yield them in their service. I am perfectly resigned to submit to His Holy Will... as the soldier of the Lord Jesus Christ I will bow me down to whatever I may be ordained to undergo in this mortal world... I [am] about to pass into the presence of Almighty God... I feel no emnity to those who have given testimony against me and none to the jury who have pronounced the verdict of my death.

On 21 October 1803 Thomas Russell put the rope around his neck with his own hands and was hanged at noon. Afterwards his head was 'struck off and displayed'. Executed with him were local men James Drake and James Corry.

It is traditionally said that *The Man from God Knows Where* opens with Russell's arrival at the Buck's Head Inn in Killyleagh. Perhaps there is some good reason for this but I have been unable to trace any link with Killyleagh. Florence Wilson makes no reference to either the Buck's Head or to Killyleagh, simply introducing her poem thus:

> A County Down telling of the winter time of 1795 and the autumn of 1803... the man of the ballad was Thomas Russell, who organized County Down, but was in prison and was unable to lead in '98... at the opening of the poem, where he visits the inn in the depth of winter '95 we will suppose he does not make his name or mission known in mixed company or maybe does not suspect the possibilities underlying the dour reticence of the group of countrymen, though they afterwards gave a good account of themselves.

In fact the Buck's Head Inn was in Loughinisland. The name is derived from the 'Buck's Head', the local name for the Annadorn Dolmen, a nearby neolithic grave chamber. It was here that Russell, self-proclaimed General in Chief of the Northern District of the Provisional Government, desperately raised Emmet's standard of revolt on 24 July 1803, probably because he saw the Dolmen as a convenient symbol of Ireland's historic past. It is known that Russell definitely stayed at the Inn for a few nights as 'Captain Shiels', a horse dealer. The owner of the Buck's Head was James Fitzpatrick who on 26 July signed a deposition that implicated James Drake in the conspiracy but didn't name Russell, referring only to a 'stranger' who had spent 'about two hours' in The Buck's Head. 'Andy Lemon' is probably a fictitious creation by Florence Wilson although 'Lemon' is a fairly common name in the North. On a recent visit to the area an elderly resident pointed out the site of the Buck's Head and told me that 'it was demolished about fifty years ago for safety reasons'.

The Man from God Knows Where brilliantly and seemingly incidentally portrays the hopes and fears of local people as they become drawn into the conflict. It follows their hardships, disappointments and defeat to eventual peace and resumption of normal life ('us ones weathered the thick of it'). The historical events serve as a useful backdrop which provides sequence, rhythm and pace for what is in effect a vivid evocation of everyday life in that particular time and place. It's almost as atmospheric as watching a newsreel of the events as ordinary lives, attitudes and language are recreated from the pages of history. 'Wully Boy Scott', 'Joe Moore' and 'McKee' are probably generic, local worthy characters but 'Young Warwick' is a reference to twenty-nine year-old Archibald Warwick, a trainee Presbyterian minister who was executed on 15 October 1798. Warwick, from the townland of Drumawhey, near Six Road Ends, was on the government's 'Fifty Pounders' wanted list and is thought to have led the rebel attack on Portaferry on 10 June. Local tradition asserts that he was 'affiansed' to 'Mary Stewart', a close friend of Betsy Gray who came from nearby Gransha or Granshaw.

Two other ministers, also based in County Down, were executed. The best known is James Porter of Ballindrait in Donegal (born 1753) who was hanged at Grey Abbey on 2 July despite the pleadings of his wife and seven children. Porter hadn't participated in the revolt and was executed at the insistence of Lord Londonderry (Robert Stewart) in revenge for satirising him as 'Squire Firebrand' in *Billy Bluff and Squire Firebrand* (1796). The third minister executed was Robert Goudy, also of Grey Abbey who was an associate of Henry Monro. Today the remains of Archibald Warwick lie in his family grave in Newtownards, though the inscription, perhaps not surprisingly, makes no reference to any political activity. He lies buried just about six miles away from the woman who 120 years after his death immortalised his name.

Outwardly Florence Wilson may have been a conventional, middle class intellectual but a deep fire must have smouldered in her soul and she must have had great affection for the ordinary people of County Down. Her command of the idiom is unfailing and of course much of it is of Scottish origin. Note 'screek o' day' (the crack of dawn), 'juked' (ducked), 'liefer' and 'lief' (rather), 'wheen' (few) and the more obvious 'pelting' (pouring) and 'sodgers' (soldiers). Florence Wilson's own family origins were very probably Scottish as her maiden name of Addy originated in Angus. In nearby Dundee a branch of the Addie family was prominent in the jute trade and it is quite likely this was connection that brought Florence Wilson's ancestors to the linen town of Lisburn. The name is the Scottish diminutive form of Adams and occurs also as Adie and Eadie.

Florence Mary Wilson (1874-1946) was born in Lisburn, County Antrim where her father Robert was manager of the Island Spinning Mill. She was educated at the Friends' School, founded by the Quakers in Lisburn in 1774. In 1898 she married Frederick Wilson, a solicitor, and set up home in Bangor where she spent the rest of her life. Her husband, by whom she had four sons and five daughters, died in 1915. By all accounts she was a cultured, erudite woman whose main interests were literature, Irish history, archaeology, music and painting. She was a member of the prominent circle of intellectual Protestant nationalists of the period, including Francis Joseph Bigger, Alice Milligan and Sir Roger Casement, a large portrait of whom, I am told, hung above her fireplace. *The Man from God Knows Where* was included in her 1918 poetry collection *The Coming of the Earls* and has become a classic Irish recitation. She was probably attracted to writing about Thomas Russell because the two shared similar democratic principles, tolerant and idealistic minds and romantic personalities.

The reverse title page of The Coming of the Earls states: 'Of this book only 450 copies have been printed. The type has been distributed'. Florence Wilson dedicated the book to her seventeen-year-old son Niall who was then serving in the First World War. Later he also served in the Second World War. As the dedication is redolent with affection for her son, for nature, the Down landscape, Ulster, Ireland and for peace, it surely says much about the type of woman Florence Wilson must have been.

TO NIALL

Since all my love is yours, take this book too,
And when you have read its pages through,
Turn for a while from you dread battle-place
To these still Ulster woods – to one old wood,
Where blue-bells bloom in May: and where we stood
Together, listening to the cuckoo call,
By the dark lake, beyond the pine trees tall;
Before the lips of war had seared your face.

Again the cuckoo calls and blue-bells grow
Under the beeches out in Portavoe:

And through the happy fields the children play;
Hush! Dim, against the sun, you stand: you come
O lonely shadow, seeking Peace and Home -
Instead of Ireland and her singing trees,
Beloved, I can only give you these
Songs, heard by you, on some glad yesterday.

Portavoe and 'the lake', a reservoir, are on the Down coast, at almost the exactly the half-way-point of the famed 'six miles from Bangor to Donaghadee'.

Some further indications of Florence Wilson's character may be gleaned from her obituary in the *County Down Spectator* of 9 November 1946. Though not an historical document, it has the ring of reality about it, hinting at a woman with a prickly personality, who did not suffer fools or flippancy very gladly, but who was essentially an upstanding human being.

> A woman of great character... of great courage... and of rigidly moral standards. She experienced and endured with great gallantly many vicissitudes of fortune but her spirit never failed or flagged... she had a warm and generous heart, her words may at times have been critical or harsh, her deeds were always the opposite... may the friendly earth of County Down which she loved so truly lie lightly upon her.

On a visit to Bangor I managed to trace her final home in Groomsport Road. Sadly, the building has since been demolished to make way for redevelopment. The former owner, Mrs Mills, then in her eighties, bought the house from the Wilson family in 1947 and lived there for over fifty years. The ground floor, latterly a butcher's shop, once contained Florence Wilson's living room and kitchen. Mrs Mills, who knew the Wilson family before she and her husband bought the house, happily related many anecdotes providing a fascinating insight into the poet's everyday life. My favourite was of her once being so engrossed in composition, while the evening meal was cooking, that she nearly burned the house down. The blackened joint was rushed from the smoke filled kitchen and next day the children had to remind their mother that a couple of her pots and pans were still lying outside in the garden! Mrs Mills agreed in general terms with the obituary, saying that Florence Wilson was 'kindly but strict, she stood no nonsense!' She also described her as 'tall and thin'.

The Man from God Knows Where is also something of a geographical tour of County Down. Historically the area is strongly associated with Saint Patrick, hence the numerous references to churches and saints in the place names. Saintfield, a one street hamlet in 1798, was captured by the insurgents on 9 June but they quickly moved on to Ballynahinch and it was burned to the ground by government troops.

The origins of the place names referred to are:

> Cloghy Bay, (*clochaig*), 'stony place'.
>
> Comber, (*An Comar*), 'the confluence' [of the Enler River with Strangford Lough].
>
> Downpatrick, (*Dún Pádraig*), 'fort of Patrick', replacing an ancient ring fort, Dun Lethglaise.
>
> Kilkeel, (*Cill an Chaol*), 'church of the narrow place'.
>
> Killyleagh, (*Cill Ó Laoch*), 'church of the descendants of Laoch'.
>
> 'Newton' (probably Newtownards), (*Baile nua na hArd*), 'new town of the high point' – the Ards Peninsula'. There is also a County Down townland named Newton, a few miles north-west of Loughinisland.
>
> Saintfield, (*Tamhnach Naomh*), 'field of the saints'.

Today Downpatrick is the hub of the agricultural Lecale Peninsula, covering the county eastwards to Strangford Lough and the sea. Russell is buried in the parish church cemetery in English Street, with the gravestone, starkly inscribed 'The Grave of Russell', provided by Mary Anne McCracken. Further along English Street is the County Down Museum, once the prison where Russell was hanged from the door lintel. This is also the home of the Saint Patrick Heritage Centre. The supposed site of St Patrick's grave is at Down Church of Ireland Cathedral just a little further along the same street; he is thought to have died at nearby Saul.

This part of the county is 'scenic' in a low-key sort of way but can't compare with the nearby Mountains of Mourne. Allied with the persistent image of the 'troubles' among foreign tourists, the result is that it's very quiet at present making exploring all the more enjoyable. Cloghy Bay is located towards the southeast end of the Ards Peninsula, just south of the fishing village of Portavogie. It isn't certain that this is the spot where it was hoped to land a consignment of French rifles in 1798, though Florence Wilson believed it. A small island a few miles south is called Guns Island, conveniently reachable at low tide. However it's a mere academic point for indeed 'no French ships sailed into Cloghy Bay'.

The towns here have of course changed beyond recognition since the 'decent folk' of County Down were caught up in 'the time o' the hurry'. However here and there, in cemeteries, at monuments and historical sites it is still possible to find echoes of those days. Among the strongest are the spirit of a noble poet, Florence Mary Wilson, and the memory of a man who at the cost of his prospects, his freedom and his life championed civil rights and religious tolerance, Thomas Russell, *The Man from God Knows Where.*

12.

The West's Awake

When all beside a vigil keep,
The West's asleep, the West's asleep.
Alas and well may Erin weep,
When Connacht lies in slumber deep.
There, lake and plain smile fair and free
Mid rocks, their guardian, chivalry.
Sing oh! let man learn liberty
From crashing wind and lashing sea.

That chainless wave and lovely land
Freedom and nationhood demand.
Be sure the great God never planned
For sleeping slaves a home so grand
And long a brave and haughty race
Honoured and sentinelled their place.
Sing oh! not even their son's disgrace
Has yet destroyed their glory's trace.

For often in O'Connor's van
To triumph dashed each Connacht clan
And fleet as deer the Normans ran
Through Corrsliabh Pass and Ardrahan
And later times saw deeds as brave
And glory guards Clanrickarde's grave.
Sing oh! they died their land to save
At Aughrim's slope and Shannon's wave.

And if when all a vigil keep,
The west's asleep, the west's asleep.
Alas and well may Erin weep
That Connacht lies in slumber deep.
But hark! A voice like thunder spake,
The west's awake, the west's awake.
Sing ho! Let England quake,
We'll watch 'til death for Erin's sake.

Photo: John McLaughlin

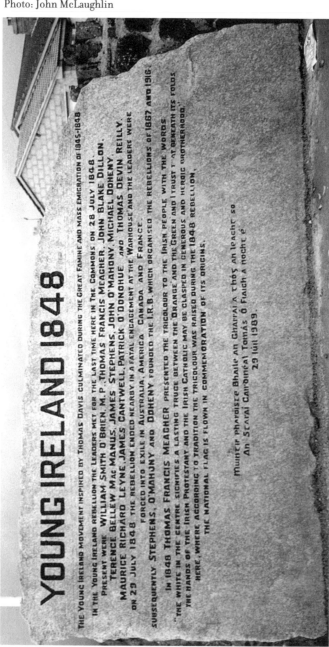

Young Ireland 1848 memorial, The Commons, near Ballingary, Co. Tipperary

The West's Awake

Thomas Davies, John Mitchel
and the 1848 Rebellion

This old nationalist favourite was written by a man who, although he died at thirty, is one of the most admired Irishmen of the 19th century, the gifted, versatile and prolific Thomas Osborne Davis (1814-45). For a hundred and fifty years it has stood the test of time, though the modern mind may now regard the lyrics as melodramatic and overly romantic. Nevertheless it is still difficult to imagine how the first and third verses in particular of a song written prior to the Great Famine and aimed at a popular audience could be much improved upon. It must surely be ranked among the greatest of Irish political songs

Thomas Davis, a Protestant of Welsh stock on his father's side, was born at 73 Main Street in Mallow, County Cork, but moved to Dublin at the age of four. Ironically, Davis, a major nationalist icon, may have been named after a major loyalist one, Sir Thomas Osborne, Marquess of Carmarthern (1631-1712), one of the 'Immortal Seven' who helped install William of Orange on the British throne. Educated in law at Trinity College, the charismatic Davis decided against a career at the bar and turned his talents to politics.

On my quest to see as many of the visible reminders of Irish history as I could, I made the pilgrimage to Mallow. A plaque on an outside wall confirmed that I had come to the right place.

'He served his country
and loved his kind'
Thomas Davis was born in this house
On October 14th 1814

The present owners of the property, now a small eatery, patiently answered my questions, let me take photographs, and even gave me some articles on Davis to take away and photocopy.

In 1842 Davis founded the *Nation* as a campaigning nationalist periodical and quickly achieved wide circulation. The magazine received about twenty new songs every week and Davis himself wrote over fifty during the three years prior to his death. He recognised the power and influence of song, saying 'music is the first faculty of the Irish', ballads are 'worth a thousand harangues' and 'we will endeavour to teach the people to sing the songs of their country that they may keep alive in their minds the love of fatherland'. Most of his lyrics were hurriedly composed to meet the *Nation's* weekly deadlines and were mainly a means to a political end.

Davis was the leading intellectual of the Young Ireland movement, which sprang up in the 1840s as Daniel O'Connell's Repeal [of the union with Britain] movement faltered. A handful of the more extreme Young Irelanders, disenchanted with O'Connell's increasing conservatism and outraged at British ineptitude over the Famine, attempted a revolt in July 1848. However the ill-conceived 'Uprising' led by landowner William Smith O'Brien (1803-64) was contained by forty-six policemen in what has come to be rather disparagingly dismissed as 'The Battle of Widow McCormick's Cabbage Patch', near Ballingarry in County Tipperary.

No matter how pathetic the action, I was determined to see the scene of it with my own eyes. However as I drove into the unprepossessing village of Ballingarry, my feeling was that I was going to be disappointed. Somehow it just didn't seem like anything of historical significance had ever happened there. Then on a wall of crumbling plaster I noticed the stark engraving '1848'. Hopes were renewed. I approached the nearest signs of life, four shell-suited teenage girls.

'Hello, girls. Are there any monuments about the revolt in 1848?' Blank looks. An older woman approached and I repeated my question. 'It's the Warhouse you want.' 'The Warhouse? I'm looking for anything to do with the 1848 rebellion. Widow McCormick's house, if it's still standing.' 'That's the Warhouse', she replied. Then, 'Have you seen the monument at the commons?' This sounded more like it and, now certain that I was finally on the trail of William Smith O'Brien, I drove the three miles north to the hamlet of The Commons (*Na Coímíní*) where I found a substantial monument.

YOUNG IRELAND 1848

The Young Ireland movement, inspired by Thomas Davis, culminated during the Great Famine and mass emigration of 1845-48. In the Young Ireland rebellion the leaders met for the last time here in The Commons on 28 July 1848.

Present were WILLIAM SMITH O'BRIEN, MP, THOMAS FRANCIS MEAGHER, JOHN BLAKE DILLON, TERENCE BELLEW McMANUS, JAMES STEPHENS, JOHN O'MAHONY, MICHAEL DOHENY, MAURICE RICHARD LEYNE, JAMES CANTWELL, PATRICK O'DONOHUE and THOMAS DEVIN REILLY, on 29 July 1848. The rebellion ended nearby in a fatal engagement at the Warhouse and the leaders were forced into exile in Australia, America, Canada and France. In 1848 THOMAS FRANCIS MEAGHER presented the tricolour to the Irish people with the words,

'The white in the centre signifies a lasting truce between the orange and the green and I trust that beneath its folds the hands of the Irish Protestant and the Irish Catholic may be clasped in generous and heroic brotherhood'.

Here, where according to tradition the tricolour was raised during the 1848 rebellion, the national flag is flown in commemoration of its origins.

I stood in contemplation for a few moments, took some photographs, then enquired of three men working on the roof of a house, 'Where's the Warhouse lads'? 'About a mile back down the road, first on your left.' These were the sort of directions that even I could follow so I set of confidently and took the first left. It was a narrow country lane with no passing places, covered in mud and other healthy residue of agricultural Tipperary. After about a mile of this I felt that I was going nowhere and stopped by a gate into a field. I was just about ready to give up and head for the comforts of Limerick when a young man came trundling up the hill on a tractor. 'The Warhouse?', I enquired. 'There, through those trees', he replied. By sheer luck I had stopped at exactly the right spot. 'Is it OK to go in?' 'Surely.' Off I went, at first trying to tiptoe through the mud, but quickly bowing to the inevitable and squelching on regardless. A couple of hundred yards later I came upon an old man, a young boy and a collie dog sitting on a crumbling wall by a dilapidated and obviously deserted old house. Summoning up what remained of my self-belief I asked, 'The Warhouse?' The old man replied, in English, though it might just as well have been in Irish, as I could barely penetrate the rural Tipperary accent, 'Aye'. He continued, 'That's it alright, the Warhouse. Mrs McCormick's house'. Then astoundingly, 'Bertie Ahern was here last year. They put up a plaque'. I dashed round to the gable end and there it was.

THE WARHOUSE
Scene of the 1848 Rising
Acquired by the State 1998
Taoiseach Bertie Ahern, T. D.

Now the boy took up the story. 'Sure they're spending two million pound doing the place up.' I had found Widow McCormick's 'cabbage patch' and the frustration of my journey through the mud-splattered highways and byways of Tipperary instantly vanished. I look forward to revisiting The Warhouse after restoration but I was glad to have seen it in its original state.

The 1848 'revolt' had petered out after two men had been killed during the assault on the police taking refuge inside the house. William Smith O'Brien himself referred to it as a mere 'escapade, not an insurrection'. O'Brien, a wealthy aristocratic Protestant and a former Tory MP was initially sentenced to death, later commuted to transportation to Australia. Whether Thomas Davis would have participated in the events had he lived is one of those things we will never know. His death had come suddenly after an attack of scarlet fever, the name being derived from the typical red rash produced. Today the condition is easily treated with penicillin. The whole country was stunned and Michael Doheny's description of the funeral typified the sense of shock and loss.

> How sincere and deep was the public grief no pen can ever tell ...in
> the procession that followed... every eye was wet and every tongue
> silent. If ever sorrow was too deep for utterance it was that which
> settled over the early grave of Thomas Davis.

Davis had tried to promote a sectarian free form of nationalism, based
on tolerance, reason and education with the slogan, 'Educate that you
might be free'. He also wrote *A Nation Once Again*, which with its famous
chorus once served as an unofficial national anthem.

> When boyhood's fire was in my blood
> I read of ancient freemen,
> For Greece and Rome who bravely stood,
> Three hundred men and three men,
> And then I prayed I yet might see
> Our fetters rent in twain
> And Ireland long a province be, a nation once again.

One of the most influential and radical of the Young Irelanders was John
Mitchel (1815-75), the son of a Unitarian minister from Dungiven in County
Derry. He had also qualified as a lawyer but nothing bored him more than
doing wills for Orangemen in Banbridge, County Down. He therefore
moved down to Dublin and became involved in journalism and politics.
Quickly Mitchel became the most incautiously outspoken and radical of all
the Young Irelanders, openly challenging and virtually taunting the
government with strong, forthright language and coldly logical analysis of
the Famine and the land question. He was reaching a large audience and
influencing public opinion through his hard-hitting articles in the *Nation*
and later in the *United Irishman*. The government decided that somehow he
had to be stopped. He was therefore shamelessly 'fitted up' by the Lord
Lieutenant, Lord Clarendon (George Villiers), 'Butcher' Clarendon in
Mitchel's acerbic language, on a specifically created new charge of 'treason-
felony'. He was hurriedly found guilty and immediately transported to Van
Diemen's Land (Tasmania) for fourteen years in 1848. Mitchel was torn
away from his wife Jenny Verner, the daughter of an Orangeman whom he
had married when she was sixteen in Drumcree Church after originally
eloping to England. It was a love match that despite severe trials and
tribulations lasted the rest of their lives. The faithful Jenny (1820-1900),
who had also contributed to the *Nation* under a pseudonym, is buried
beneath a Celtic cross in Woodlawn Cemetery in the Bronx in New York City.

After five years down under, Mitchel made a dramatic escape, which
involved long horse rides over the mountains, trips in small boats and
disguise as a priest, ironically amusing for the son of the manse. He was to

spend most of the next twenty years in America before eventually returning to Ireland where he was elected abstentionist MP for Tipperary in 1875, just before he died. His classic *Jail Journal* is still very readable today. Mitchel is commemorated in an almost forgotten ballad, *John Mitchel*, the final verse capturing something of the distress of transportation.

> Farewell my true-born Irishmen, farewell my country small,
> But leaving my own dear babes behind, it grieves me worst of all,
> There's one request I ask of you, when your liberty you gain,
> Remember Mitchel far away, a convict bound in chains.

The other most influential Young Irelanders, who with Davis co-founded the *Nation*, were John Blake Dillon (1814-66) and Charles Gavan Duffy (1816-1903). Dillon, from Ballaghadereen in County Mayo, was also a barrister. He participated in the 1848 revolt at Killenaule, near Ballingarry, fled to America via France, was amnestied in 1855 and died suddenly from cholera a year after being elected MP for Tipperary.

Duffy, from Monaghan, a Catholic educated at a Presbyterian school, was imprisoned for sedition in 1844. He supported the 1848 revolt and was again imprisoned for a short period. Gradually he became disillusioned with Irish politics and emigrated to Australia in 1855. There he became Prime Minister of Victoria in 1871 and accepted a knighthood in 1873. His grandson George later returned to Ireland and was a signatory of the Treaty in 1921.

Other leading members of the movement were Michael Doheny (1805-63), who wrote the classic nationalist song *The Shan Van Vocht*, James Fintan Lalor (1807-49), John Martin (1812-75), who was Mitchel's brother-in-law, and Thomas Francis Meagher (1823-67). At his trial 'Meagher of the Sword', the flamboyant young orator, remained defiant, telling the Judge, 'My Lord, this is our first offence, but not our last. If you will be easy with us this once, we promise on our word as gentlemen to try to do better next time'. Such language was not calculated to inspire leniency and Meagher was sentenced to death, commuted to transportation to Tasmania. Four years later he escaped to America where he became a General in the Union army and Governor of Montana.

Patrick O'Donohue commemorated on The Commons memorial, suffered badly for his part in the rebellion. Sentenced to death, later commuted to transportation for life, he managed to escape from Tasmania to America in 1853. However he was to die the following year, destroyed by separation from his wife and child, alcohol and neglect. Another prominent nationalist of the period was Kevin Izod O'Doherty (1823-1905) who was transported to Australia in 1849 where he qualified as a doctor and became a member of the Queensland government. He had married Mary Anne Kelly (1825-1910), the former girl poet of the Nation, known to her readers as Eva.

The West's Awake makes many references to places of historical importance. Connacht (*Connachtach*), 'land of Conn's descendants' is of course one of the four present-day provinces of Ireland. With an area of 6,610 square miles, it is the smallest province, consisting of counties Galway, Leitrim, Mayo, Roscommon and Sligo. The borders of present-day provinces were only drawn up in the 17th century and in ancient Ireland Meath (*Mide*), 'middle or central', was regarded as a separate province with Munster also sometimes divided into two. Irish successes in Connacht during the Nine Years War of the 1590s and in 1798 at Castlebar probably caused Davis to see it as a symbol of hope and of the whole country's untapped revolutionary potential. He had visited the area in 1843 and would undoubtedly have drawn inspiration from seeing the historic sites with his own eyes.

Aughrim (*Eachrim*), 'horse ridge', near Ballinasloe is the scene of one the most important battles fought in Ireland. On 12 July 1691 a twenty-five thousand strong Williamite army defeated about twenty thousand Jacobite troops. A total of about seven thousand men lost their lives, with the four thousand Jacobite dead being stripped and left to rot where they lay.

The decisive moment came when the Jacobite commander, the Marquis de Saint-Ruth, was decapitated by chainshot. The arrogant French aristocrat hadn't shared his battle plan with any of his subordinates who included Patrick Sarsfield. However it is difficult to get at the truth of the matter. One historian contends that if Saint-Ruth 'had lived one more hour he would have won' while another states 'it would be naïve to suppose that he (Saint-Ruth) had some masterly counterstroke up his sleeve' and that 'Ginkel possessed the initiative throughout'. (General Godard van Reede Ginkel (1630-1703) was the Williamite commander at both Aughrim and the second Siege of Limerick in 1691.) Effectively, the Jacobite defeat ended the Catholic cause in Ireland and any realistic hopes of independence until the 20th century. For nationalists, Aughrim is a symbol of despair, while for unionists its anniversary is celebrated almost on a par with that of the Boyne. Today at the Battle site there is an interpretative centre with many interesting and poignant exhibits, including weapons from the battlefield.

O'Connor (*Ó Conchobar*) was the ancient royal family of Connacht whose power waned after Felim O'Connor's Irish army was defeated by an Anglo-Irish force under William Liath de Burgh amid great slaughter at the Battle of Athenry, fifteen miles east of Aughrim, in 1316.

Corrsliabh Pass, 'pointed mountains', is located in the Curlew Hills on the Roscommon-Sligo border, a few miles north of Boyle. Historically it was of strategic importance as it commanded the road to Sligo town. Davis probably had in mind the Battle of the Curlews, which took place there in 1599. On this occasion the English were defeated. The Irish commander O'Rourke decapitated the English general Sir Conyers Clifford and sent the head to his lord Red Hugh O'Donnell.

Ardrahan (*Ard Rathain*), 'height of the ferns', is a village south of Galway City. It was here that the incident took place in 1225 that Davis may have had in mind when he wrote *The West's Awake*. A plundering Anglo-Norman force was attacked and routed by the Irish under Tuathal O'Connor. Today the ruins of a Norman castle built on the site of an ancient earthen fort still stand there. The reference to 'Shannon's wave' is probably an allusion to the final action of the Williamite Wars, the Siege and Treaty of Limerick in 1691. To a nationalist like Thomas Davis such events served only as sources of inspiration in the continuing struggle for independence. He wrote:

> I never heard of any famous nation that did not honour the names of its departed great, study the annals of the land and cherish the associations of its history... they are more enriching than mines of gold.

Clanrickard(e) is the title of the ancient, aristocratic, Old English Burke family of Connacht. Davis may simply have used the name as a symbol of 'noble resistance', or he may have had specific members of the Burke family in mind – for example, Ulick, 'the Great Earl' (1604-57) or John, the ninth Earl, the 'noble youth Lord Burke, Viscount of Galway, son to the present Earl of Clanrickarde', who survived the Battle of the Boyne but who lost his life in the Jacobite cause at Aughrim.

As I travelled round the country visiting all of these places, I wondered what Thomas Davis would have thought of Ireland in the modern world. In 1843 the *Nation* had written of 'the deadly bane of Ireland – DIVISION'. Undoubtedly therefore he would have mourned the partitioning of the country as well as, I suspect, the passing of some aspects of 'romantic' Ireland. However I concluded that overall he would probably be reasonably content with the liberal, confident and increasingly tolerant and mature society that has evolved in the 'twenty-six counties'. It is the type of independent and rational state that Thomas Davis could only dream about when he wrote *The West's Awake*.

Lord Roden (1788-1870)

13.

Dolly's Brae

Being on the 12th day of July, eighteen and forty-nine
the pagans of this country together did combine
to shoot and slay our Orangemen upon that glorious day,
they did encamp in thousands great at a place called Dolly's Brae,
they did encamp in thousands great at a place called Dolly's Brae.

Lord Roden was Grand Master of the Orangemen just then,
no better Chieftain could be found among the sons of men,
to humanists he would not yield, nor any Popish foe,
he firmly stood like Joshua on the plains of Jericho,
he firmly stood like Joshua on the plains of Jericho.

He sent an invitation to Rathfriland Orange corps
to come and spend the day with him at sylvan Tollymore.
The Orangemen they did obey their noble chief's command
so over Dolly's Brae they marched, a loyal stalwart band,
so over Dolly's Brae they marched, a loyal stalwart band.

We loudly cheered for Roden then and for the British crown,
Slieve Donard sent the echo back o'er Castlewellan town.
The pagans heard our loyal cheers as they lay on the hill,
awaiting there like hungry wolves our Orangemen to kill,
awaiting there like hungry wolves our Orangemen to kill.

Priest Mooney and Priest Murphy went through the rebel lines
distributing the wafer god among the Philistines.
Priest Mooney cursed the Orangemen with candle, book and bell,
the rebel crowd did cry aloud 'we'll drive them all to hell',
the rebel crowd did cry aloud 'we'll drive them all to hell'.

We formed in full procession and unfurled our flags once more,
we bade adieu to all the friends we left at Tollymore,
with fifes and drums and loaded guns we gaily marched away,
resolving to defend ourselves going home over Dolly's Brae,
resolving to defend ourselves going home over Dolly's Brae.

As o'er the Brae we did proceed, the road being very bare
the Ribbonmen advantage took and fired upon our rear.
Like lions stout we wheeled about, with powder and with ball,
the volley we sent into them caused scores of them to fall,
the volley we sent into them caused scores of them to fall.

The battle being over, the glorious victory won,
we reached our homes that evening by the setting of the sun.
Our wives and sweethearts met us returning home that day
with shouts of joy they greeted us safe back o'er Dolly's Brae,
with shouts of joy they greeted us safe back o'er Dolly's Brae.

So now my song I mean to end, my pen I will throw down.
I say success to every man who supports the British crown
and generations yet unborn shall sing this loyal day
and speak of those that beat their foes at famous Dolly's Brae,
and speak of those that beat their foes at famous Dolly's Brae.

Dolly's Brae

Orangemen, Ribbonmen
and Death on One Green Hill

Dolly's Brae, a narrow country road near Castlewellan, County Down, was the scene of one of the worst sectarian affrays of the 19th century. The 'battle', between the Protestant Orangemen and the Catholic Ribbonmen, took place on 12 July 1849. There were about equal numbers, twelve hundred, on each side but for some reason, never satisfactorily explained, other than in terms of superior Orange sharp-shooting, the Ribbonmen suffered substantial casualties while the Orangemen and attendant police and military suffered none. The actual battle took place on Magheramayo Hill, about a mile beyond the Brae, which had been the original focus of the confrontation because the narrowness of the pass made it a likely spot for an ambush. The place name is something of a mystery but may be derived from the nickname for a local man called O'Hara.

The Orangemen's annual march was returning in the evening to Rathfriland, ten miles west, from 'Lord Roden's Park' (Tollymore Forest Park), passing through the Catholic townland of Magheramayo. The two well-armed groups confronted each other and when a shot was fired the tension that had been building up all day exploded and both sides cut loose. The atmosphere was also probably influenced by an earlier confrontation on St Patrick's Day at nearby Crossgar when a policeman was killed. This too was worthy of a song, *The Defence of Crossgar*.

> You Protestant brethern of high and low station
> That dwell in this nation hear what I say,
> I pray pay attention, while briefly I mention
> The Thrashers' [Ribbonmen] intention on Patrick's Day.
> It's well understood that thousands were warned
> To clean up their pistols and guns for the war,
> By a secret council they basely determined
> Not to leave a Protestant soul in Crossgar.

At Dolly's Brae around thirty Catholics were killed but as they probably carried away some of the dead, the exact figure was never established. No one ever faced charges relating to any of the deaths.

Tragic as the incident was, it would now be no more than an historical footnote had it not been commemorated in song, further evidence of the power of the ballad in Irish political history and popular culture. This version is a mere selection of verses taken from the sixteen published by the Ulster Society, an organisation formed in 1985 'to promote an awareness and appreciation of our distinctive Ulster-British culture and heritage in all its richness and varied forms'; David Trimble was its Chairman until 1990. Trimble was concerned that Protestants were often perceived as 'having no culture', especially in England and America, thereby losing out in the propaganda battle to republicans whose 'culture' had a much better image.

The song appears to be a descendant of an earlier ballad, *Dolly's Brae No More*, whose first two verses are:

> Come all you loyal Orangemen, I pray listen unto me
> To I relate these verses of cruel Popery,
> For murder and confusion is all that they adore
> But they are down and ne'er to get up till time is no more.

> It being on the 12th day of July eighteen hundred and forty-nine
> Our Orange boys they met once more in honour of the Boyne,
> With heart and hand they did agree to march to Tollymore
> And the music did in glory play, 'Ye Croppies do give o'er'.

Inevitably both traditions have divergent views over the sequence of events. The Catholic version is that the Orangemen deliberately took a detour through a Catholic area to provoke the residents by parading their dominance and supremacy. They claim that the Orangemen fired the first shot. The Orangemen's version is that they had avoided the route the previous year in order to avoid trouble. They claim that this allowed the jubilant Ribbonmen to circulate scurrilous songs deriding them for their cowardice. The Orangemen claim that the Catholics fired the first shot.

The ballad is probably inaccurate regarding 'Priest Mooney and Priest Murphy'. According to Kevin Haddick-Flynn in his history of Orangeism, 'Father Patrick Morgan [not Murphy], the local parish priest and Father John Mooney spent several hours on the Hill arguing with them [the Ribbonmen] to return to their homes'. However 'their leader, Captain Lennon – a [Ribbonman] activist who a short time before had been discharged from police custody – was adamant that they should remain'.

The official government inquiry into the incident laid the blame, for what seems to have been more of a massacre than a battle, mainly on the Orangemen. Lord Roden (Robert Jocelyn, 1788-1870) and two other senior Orangemen were removed from their positions as magistrates. The 'battle' at Dolly's Brae has by no means been the only sectarian affray that has taken place during the 'loyalist marching season'. They have been a recurring social and political problem from the early 1800s. It's thought that the first deaths resulting from such marches were in Belfast on 12 July 1813.

At the 'Battle' of Garvagh in County Derry on 26 July, also in 1813, another death, that of William Doey, a Catholic 'mountainy man from Foreglen', occurred when about four hundred Ribbonmen, seeking revenge for a previous defeat, attacked the King's Arms, an Orange pub. More may have died, as an Ulster Society songbook states 'three [Catholics] perished on the field of battle and others, fatally wounded, died soon afterwards'. The Orangemen celebrated and commemorated the 'victory' with a sixteen-verse ballad *The Battle of Garvagh*, probably contemporary as it refers to the Catholics as 'tories'. It is still very popular today.

> The Day before the July [Lammas] Fair
> The Ribbonmen they did prepare
> For three miles round to wreck and tear
> And burn the town of Garvagh.

It was only around this time that celebration of William's victory at the Boyne in 1690 began to be celebrated. Previously the preferred date for homage had been his birthday, 4 November, and this was not considered to be predominantly sectarian. Many liberal and radical Protestants, who would have favoured Catholic civil rights, saw William's success as a triumph over arbitrary government rather than as a victory for Protestantism over Catholicism.

The 1820s were a particularly tense period. The *Unlawful Societies Act* of 1825 had banned both the Catholic Association, formed to campaign for Catholic Emancipation, and the Orange Order (which almost immediately reformed as Brunswick Clubs). In April 1829, Catholic Emancipation, which many Protestants had not seen as inevitable, became law; militant southern Catholics threatened 'the invasion of Ulster' and Protestant siege mentality reached fever pitch. It's no great surprise then that Orange parades during this period often resulted in pitched battles.

Accurate details of these are scanty but it is thought that at Stewartstown, Tyrone in July 1829 around twenty people died. A Ribbon ballad from the period contains the line 'To Stewartstown they did retreat at the loss of twenty three'. One Catholic, James O'Sullivan, was executed at Omagh Jail for his part in the affray. At 'the Battle of Macken' in County Fermanagh on 13 July 1829 'several' Orangemen were killed (another Catholic ballad puts the figure at six) when 'both parties they assembled each other to devour'. Nineteen Catholics were found guilty and transported to Australia. There was more trouble in 1830 and this time it was the turn of a number of Protestants to be transported to Botany Bay after Catholic homes had been burned in Maghera, County Derry.

After Dolly's Brae the government introduced the *Party Processions Act* (1850) which it vainly hoped would dampen all shades of controversial meetings and parades. For a while this was reluctantly accepted by the Orangemen but in the wake of the Fenian scare of 1867, William Johnston (1829-1902) led a protest campaign which resulted in the repeal of the *Act* in 1872. Johnston defied the government by leading illegal parades, was imprisoned, emerged a hero and was elected to parliament, defeating the official Conservative candidate in Belfast. From the townland of Ballykilbeg near Downpatrick, Johnston was a 'larger than life' character who spent his whole life campaigning against all things Catholic. He also coined the immortal phrase 'Home Rule is Rome Rule', though he defended his daughter when she converted to Catholicism, even driving her to Mass. The repeal of the *Party Processions Act* was hailed as an important victory and offset to some extent the disestablishment of the Church of Ireland three years previously. At the time this was regarded as the thin end of the wedge that would gradually lead to Home Rule and worse.

The Orange Order was formed in 1795 after another Protestant 'victory' in yet another sectarian clash, the Battle of the Diamond, near Loughgall in County Armagh, when about twenty Catholics were killed. The Ribbonmen, successors to the Defenders, were virtually a mirror image of the Orangemen, though they were an illegal organisation, taking their name from identifying white ribbons or handkerchiefs. Since its foundation, the Order has been an essentially grass roots movement pledged to maintain 'the Protestant Constitution and to defend the King and his heirs as long as they maintain the Protestant ascendancy'. This may have been a laudable enough aim in the political and religious climate of the 1790s but it finds little support in present-day British society.

Hence the Order has not enjoyed a favourable press or made many friends in recent years in the most powerful and populous part of the Union, liberal, post-Christian, secular, England. There, many of its actions have been seen as being of the 'own goal' variety, inflicting hardship on its own community and costing huge sums for security operations. However it would be too simplistic, looking at the Order as a whole, to see is as consisting of mere rabble-rousing bigots who make a lot of provocative noise every summer. Although it may be difficult for Catholics and for English Protestants, who have had an entirely different historical and cultural experience, to understand and accept, the Orange Order is an ancient, deep-rooted, cultural movement, providing expression and identity for many ordinary, decent Protestants. Historically this has been of great significance in a country where they have always been in a minority and have always lived in fear of rebellion and betrayal.

However elements within it are widely regarded as blatantly sectarian and it is difficult to see how it can survive in its present form in a world that has moved so far away from the kind of society in which the Order was founded. But changing deeply held beliefs in Northern Ireland is painfully slow. Too many roads still lead to Drumcree or Dublin, not Damascus. Change however is inevitable; it's just a question of how many years, or generations, it will take. It took republicans a long time, about two hundred years, to finally realise that their fundamentalist position was untenable. Hopefully it won't take the Orange Order until 2200.

Sinn Féin has now conceded the crucial principle that reunification can only happen through the democratically expressed will of the majority *in Northern Ireland only*, effectively recognising and accepting the previously unthinkable, partition. This is stated three times in the opening three paragraphs of the Belfast [Good Friday] Agreement of April 1998 and, in case anyone missed it, is repeated another three times towards the end of the document. This vital principle also received overwhelming support, 94.4 percent, in a referendum in the Republic. The Republic has also bitten the bullet of relinquishing its territorial claim on the North, an extremely difficult thing for many 'southern' Irish to accept. It has also revised the 'special position' of the Catholic Church in its Constitution. The Union therefore is now safe and unionists no longer have to fear a scheming, hostile neighbour to the south. Inevitably though the Union of the future will be very different from that of the past. The general social trend is towards secularism, pluralism, and the homogenisation of culture and society through travel, television and information technology. The global village is upon us. Sooner or later the two rival camps will have to 'adapt or die'.

Evolutionary change in political thinking, which will have repercussions for political life in Northern Ireland, is also taking place in Britain. The continued relevance of the *Act of Settlement* of 1701, banning Catholics from acceding to the throne, is coming under scrutiny. The idea is now widely regarded as outdated. The same applies to the monarch bearing the title 'Defender of the [Protestant] faith' in a multi-faith, atheistic and secular society, which bears no resemblance to that of 1701. Official British society now accepts Catholics as equals; indeed many senior British establishment figures such as the former Secretary of State for Northern Ireland (Dr. John Reid), the leader of the Conservative Party (Iain Duncan Smith), and the wife of the Prime Minister (Cherie Blair) are all Catholics. In January 2002 the Queen invited Britain's leading Catholic cleric, Cormac Murphy O'Brien, to preach at Sandringham, the first time since before the reign of William of Orange, signalling that the historical era of Catholicism as an enemy of the formerly Protestant British state is now over. Again, this did not happen overnight. Pope Clement XIII withdrew Church support for the Stuart dynasty in 1766!

It would indeed appear that the early stages of revising 'traditional' unionism, and ultimately fundamentalist Orangeism, have already begun. At the time of writing, a debate within unionism is taking place regarding the relationship between the Ulster Unionist Party (UUP) and the Orange Order. Pro-Belfast Agreement unionists are said to favour a loosening, if not a severance, of the ties between the two organisations, especially curbing the voting rights of the Order in UUP decision making. The process has been ongoing for some time but was given fresh impetus in 2000 during the Party leadership contest when the 120 Orange delegates, 15% of the total, voted unanimously for the Rev. Martin Smyth, a former Orange Order Grand Master.

With the constitutional position of the Union absolutely guaranteed in law and accepted by republicans, there is no need for unionism to be constantly looking over its shoulder. It can afford to be more accepting of the nationalist, Catholic tradition, which should itself reciprocate by being more tolerant of Protestant culture and tradition, and by renouncing political violence. Both traditions need to be less insular, paranoid, strident and shrill. They need to adopt a more inclusive form of 'civic unionism' and 'civic republicanism'. Encouragingly, despite the difficulties, not least the standoff at Drumcree, this type of language has recently been creeping into statements by some leading unionists and republicans. They realise that the time has finally come for both sides to recognise the negativity and futility of clinging to unrealistic, one-dimensional pasts. The real difficulty will be bringing their core constituencies with them.

Today at Dolly's Brae there is nothing to see but gently rolling countryside. However directions are given for those curious to see the historical site. From Castlewellan take the A50 road in the direction of Banbridge and continue for about a mile and a half by the edge of Castlewellan Country Park. Just beyond the end of the Park take the first right turn up a minor road signposted 'Leitrim', a small village in the area. Dolly's Brae, signposted with a normal street nameplate, is first left after about three-quarters of a mile. From here there is an excellent view west to Magheramayo Hill.

Leaving behind the historical horrors of Dolly's Brae, and still unresolved present-day divisions, the chief scenic attraction of the area is undoubtedly the Mountains of Mourne, famed in Percy French's great song of that name. At 2796 feet the highest point in the Mournes is Slieve Donard (*Sliabh*

Domhanghairt), 'the mountain of Domangand', a 5th century chieftain who became a disciple of St Patrick and is said to have built a stone prayer cell on the mountain's summit. On a clear day it's possible to see Scotland, England, Wales and the Isle of Man, which makes the long climb well worthwhile. Amid such serenity it is difficult to imagine that only a few miles away the members of two slightly differing sects of the same religion still act out thousands of action replays of events at Dolly's Brae.

Apart from Aughrim, the Boyne, Derry's Walls, Limerick and Dolly's Brae itself, most of my travels had taken me to nationalist shrines. Now I decided to put my head in the lion's den and pay a visit to the museum of the Orange Order at Loughgall in County Armagh. Admittedly I was nervous, but only a little. Having spent all of my adult life in Glasgow and having many Protestant friends, colleagues and neighbours, I was well aware of the baggage that we all carried. I also had first hand experience of Orange Walks, seeing and hearing them most weekends from May to September as they pass within a hundred yards of my front door in Glasgow. However I was also aware that Loughall had tremendous symbolic significance for both sides. Many of the Protestants drowned at Portadown in 1641 had come from the parish and it was here that the Orange Order had been founded. It was also here in 1987 that eight IRA men had been ambushed and killed by the SAS, 'butchered at Loughgall' in the words of a republican ballad. In the event my apprehensions quickly disappeared when I was introduced to Isaac Walker, the Museum's elderly caretaker.

Full of enthusiasm, Isaac took me in and showed me around. The subtleties of the various types of Orange regalia may have been lost on me but many of the items on show were of great historical interest. A couple of rifles from the Battle of the Diamond and the original table used at the first meeting in James Sloan's pub over two hundred years ago. From my point of view however the most interesting, and the most repellent exhibit, was the banner carried by the Rathfiland Orangemen at Dolly's Brae, a sad but very real physical link with one of the most tragic and symbolically significant incidents in Ireland's troubled past.

When I had knocked on Isaac Walker's door the first thing I said to him was, 'I'm a Catholic; can I see round the Museum?'. I was made welcome and ushered in. I wasn't asked for my name or for any form of identification and was allowed to take as many photographs as I wanted. Isaac had replied with a phrase, not used often enough in Northern Ireland, but one that will always stay with me: 'Sure you'll do me no harm'.

Photo: John McLaughlin

Famine graveyard, Carndonagh, County Donegal

14.
Skibbereen

Oh father dear, I oft times hear you speak of Erin's Isle,
Her lofty scenes, her valleys green, her mountains rude and wild.
You say it is a lovely land wherein a prince might dwell,
Then why did you abandon it, the reason to me tell.

My son, I love my native land with energy and pride,
Until the blight came o'er my crops, my sheep and cattle died.
My rent and taxes were too high, I could not them redeem
And that's the cruel reason why I left old Skibbereen.

It's well I do remember that bleak December day,
The landlord and the sheriff came to drive us all away;
They set my roof on fire with their demon yellow spleen
And that's another reason why I left old Skibbereen.

Your mother too, God rest her soul, fell on the snowy ground,
She fainted in her anguish at the desolation round,
She never rose but passed away, from life to mortal dream
And found a pauper's grave, my son, in dear old Skibbereen.

It's well I do remember the year of forty-eight
When I arose with Erin's boys to fight against our fate.
I was hunted through the mountains, as a traitor to the Queen,
And that's another reason why I left old Skibbereen.

And you were only two years old and feeble was your frame
I could not leave you with my friends; you bore your father's name.
I wrapped you in my cotamore at the dead of night unseen,
I heaved a sigh and I bade goodbye to dear old Skibbereen.

Oh father dear the day will come when vengeance loud will call
And we will rise with Erin's boys and rally one and all.
I'll be the man to lead the van, beneath the flag of green
And loud and high we'll raise the cry, 'Revenge for Skibbereen'.

Skibbereen

Famine, Eviction, Emigration, the Land War

This bitter 19th century ballad deals with many of the most basic themes in Irish history: famine, land ownership, eviction and emigration. It also hints at political action and influence from across the Atlantic, 'the biggest lake in Ireland'. The song's author is unknown but it almost certainly originated in East Coast America and was probably written by a radical ex-patriot such as O'Donovan Rossa (1831-1915). Rossa, poet as well as patriot, didn't write the song but he came from Rosscarbery, near Skibbereen, and may have been involved in its publication. Information on the song's origins have proved elusive but it seems to have been around for a good number of years before being introduced to a wider audience when included in a Herbert Hughes songbook in 1915. Surprisingly the fifth verse isn't always sung for it provides a direct political link with the Young Irelander's 'revolt' of 1848. 'Cotamore' means simply overcoat.

While the song may not be by or about O'Donovan Rossa, it does fit his situation almost perfectly: famine victim, political protest, American exile. His family suffered desperately in the Famine, being reduced to eating anything they could find, including the family donkey. His father sacrificed his own life to feed his children, leaving a large family helpless in a society with no concept of social security. The experience turned fourteen-year-old Rossa into a lifelong Fenian rebel. Later he wrote 'worse than the hunger... was the degradation into which want and hunger will reduce human nature'.

The Great Famine is probably the most difficult subject in Irish history to address. Apart from its sheer scale and the emotion generated, it is also hugely political. Whatever view one takes, inevitably it will upset someone else because in the final analysis, irrespective of the 'facts', 'objectivity' and 'balance' people will believe what they want to believe. The 'balanced view' is that the Famine resulted from an extremely unfortunate combination of ignorance, incompetence, providence, prejudice and neglect. The reality is probably that it is too complex to explain in any meaningful way, though that will never stop people having strong opinions on the subject.

The 'extreme', 'nationalist', view is the 'British plot to clear the land' theory and until recent times the Famine and the evictions and mass emigration that followed it have been the biggest sources of anti-British sentiment. The 'British plot' theory was classically summarised by John Mitchel: 'The Almighty sent the potato blight but the English created the famine'. Personally I find it very difficult to disagree with the essence of this statement and keep asking myself, 'Would such a disaster, on such a scale, have been allowed to run its course in the same way had it happened in England?'

It is undeniable that the government mostly looked on when it was economically and logistically possible to provide relief. It did make token efforts with the provision of cheap maize, workhouses, soup kitchens, etc., but this was nowhere near on the scale necessary. It is one of the major paradoxes of human history that this disaster took place in the United Kingdom of Britain and Ireland, then the richest country in the world, where ample food was available. The poor, however, had no cash to buy it on the open market and the government of the day was reluctant to intervene, influenced by the laissez faire theory of non-intervention in the economy. It wasn't therefore a true 'famine', as the main shortage was not food but political will.

The situation was also affected by a common British stereotyped view of the Irish people as uncivilised, undisciplined, ungrateful, feckless, superstitious, culturally and racially inferior. This Victorian outlook held that the Irish were born troublemakers, always drunk, forever complaining and constantly plotting rebellion – that through their indolence they had brought the horror down on their own heads, that they would have to live with the consequences and that they could only be redeemed by systematic moral regeneration. This view, to the modern mind racist and sectarian, was the legacy of the Penal Laws as a people deprived of education and the means of earning a decent living were then condemned for their ignorance and poverty. The Prime Minister Lord John Russell, with his dismissal of what he called 'Irish pauperism', exemplified this attitude.

Like other countries Ireland had for many centuries been subject to famine, the result of economic slumps, freak weather conditions and war. Thousands died in famines created by scorched earth policies in the 17th century. During the six hundred years from 1300 a famine in Ireland occurred, on average, every thirty years or so. However the first to result from a failure of the potato crop did not come until 1741, etched in the folk memory as *Bliain an áir*, 'the year of the slaughter', when about a quarter of a million people perished, ten per cent of the population.

It's not surprising that one of the best-known Famine songs is set in Skibbereen for in the mid-nineteenth century most people in this part of southwest Cork were dependent on the potato for survival. The awful accounts of the Famine that emanated from the area are well documented and even at the time it was known to be one of the regions worst affected. In Ireland as a whole about forty per cent of the population, three million people, were in the precarious position of almost total dependence on the potato. The Famine was to effectively reduce the food supply for these people by an average of one third for four consecutive years, or more. Modern scholars estimate that around a million people died of hunger and famine-induced disease. Connacht suffered the most, accounting for approximately 40 percent of all deaths. For Munster the figure was 30 percent, for Ulster 21 percent and for Leinster 9 percent. There was population decline in thirty-one of the thirty-two counties, Dublin being the only exception.

The Famine lasted from 1845 to 1849, in some areas to 1852, but even before that many peasants went hungry during *mí an ocrais*, 'the hungry month', between when the new crop was ready and the previous year's supply used. This already precarious situation was exacerbated by an increase in population from five to eight and a half million during the previous forty years. On the face of it this might look like 'ignorant Irish Catholics breeding like rabbits', while the rest of the UK exercised restrained responsibility. In fact statistics show that between 1801 and 1841 population growth in Ireland was almost identical to that of Scotland and fifteen per cent less than in England and Wales.

However for the Irish poor there was little accompanying economic growth. Even if peasants did somehow manage to increase production then their rents were usually raised, leaving them with no increase in disposable income. With so many more mouths to feed the available food supply had, effectively, been significantly reduced even before the Famine began. The situation was made worse as the increase in population also led to an increase in nuclear families and ever smaller and ever less efficient divided smallholdings. One thirty-seven acre farm in 1781 had by 1823 been divided into thirteen separate holdings. For these 'four acres and a cow' families Ireland was an accident waiting to happen.

By the autumn of 1845 it was obvious that there was a failure of the potato crop due to a 'blight' or 'typhus', later identified as the fungal disease phytophthora infestans. The result was that about one-third of the crop was lost and before the end of the year people were dying. In 1846 the disaster was much worse with seventy-five per cent failure. In 'black forty-seven' there was no blight but the crop yield was still low, as fewer seed potatoes had been available and were also more expensive. In 1848 a third of the crop failed with the shortage again exacerbated by low planting.

The cumulative effect of these statistics was calamitous with mass suffering and death through starvation, typhus, dysentery and relapsing fever as well as major social dislocation. In the workhouse at Skibbereen more than half the child inmates died and many more suffered blindness due to lack of vitamin A in their diet. People scavenged for any edible substance they could find – berries, roots, seaweed and nettles to make soup.

Although inevitably Catholics suffered most, the Famine was not confined to Catholic areas and in parts of Ulster death didn't discriminate. In areas with large Protestant populations, like the Barony of Tartaraghan (north of Armagh), 30.2 % of the population was dependent on relief, while in Portadown the figure was 18.8 %. In Lurgan more Protestants than Catholics died in the primitive, filthy and disease-ridden union workhouse. Lord Lurgan himself (of the well-known loyal Brownlow family) died in 1846, from typhus fever picked up at the workhouse. Alexander Irvine's *My Lady of the Chimney Corner* (1913) is a moving fictional account of the poverty and suffering of his Protestant forebears in Antrim town.

Many of the poor now faced a stark choice, starvation or emigration. Those who couldn't beg or borrow the fare stayed and many of them starved. There was also a hugely abnormal surge in emigration, some of it financed by the small amounts of compensation paid by landlords anxious to clear troublesome peasants off the land. Prior to the Famine the most popular destination had been Canada but now the US began to take about seventy-five per cent of the total and continued to do so until the First World War. Many emigrants went to Britain but nothing like the numbers that crossed the Atlantic. It's something of a cliché but America really was a land of opportunity with scope for employment in fast developing industries like mining, railway engineering and canal building. It also didn't have the same Old World restrictions of social class, religious discrimination and political exclusion. For many emigrants there would have been hardship and problems of separation and adjustment but eventually the Irish established themselves as the second most economically successful ethnic group in American after the Jews.

Official US Immigration statistics show that during the worst period of Famine, eviction and Land War agitation, from 1841-1900, a total of 3,611,385 Irish citizens emigrated to the US. Modern historians still debate whether or not the big increase between 1841 and 1860 can be directly linked to the Famine or whether it would have happened anyway due to changes in the Irish economy. This sort of question typifies the 'traditional/revisionist' Famine debate.

For the majority of emigrants the six-week sea passage was cramped and unhygienic with exploitation and profiteering rife. It's interesting to note the comments of Wolfe Tone on his transatlantic journey in 1795, when conditions may in fact have been better than fifty years later. Having just received a substantial 'redundancy' payment from the Catholic Association for services rendered, he and his family could afford to travel in comfort, on a 'stout vessel' with a 'civil captain' and hire a 'state room, eight feet by six'. He was however horrified at the conditions of some of his less fortunate fellow passengers.

> The slaves who are carried from the coast of Africa have much more room allowed them than the miserable emigrants who pass from Ireland to America. The avarice of the captains in that trade is such that they think they can never load their vessels sufficiently and they trouble their heads in general no more about the accommodation and stowage of their passengers than of any other lumber aboard.

It was little wonder then that many of these ships were breeding grounds for dysentery, cholera and typhus. Mortality rates averaged 'only' about two per cent but epidemics could multiply that figure by more than ten. For around thirty-six thousand people between 1845 and the early 1850s the term 'coffin ship' was a reality.

Those of the poor who had any money used it to buy food rather than to pay rent. The Famine therefore also led to a surge in the number of evictions for rent arrears. Not all landlords were ruthless exploiters but enough were to ensure that between 1846 and 1853 around a quarter of a million people were evicted. Increased peasant vulnerability resulting from the Famine provided a useful opportunity for many landlords to consolidate small, uneconomic parcels of land and to switch from tillage to more profitable pasture farming.

Evictions didn't stop after the Famine. Between 1854 and 1887 it's conservatively estimated that a further 350,000 were evicted, with the true figure likely to be about double this. Precise figures are unavailable as many evictions were unofficial and the police weren't present to oversee and record them. Even the lower figure gives an average eviction rate of over two hundred people per week for more than thirty years. Many had nowhere else to go and were turned out literally into the open without food or shelter.

One of the most notorious of all the evictions took place in 1861 on the Derryveagh Estate of John George Adair near Letterkenny in Donegal. Despite no rent arrears, forty-seven families, almost two hundred and fifty people, were evicted to make way for sheep. Adair however claimed that the Ribbonmen were active on his land. He blamed them, wrongly as it transpired, for the murder of his steward, James Murray, in November 1860. No one was ever charged with the crime but it later emerged that the resident magistrate believed that it had been organised by Murray's own wife who was having an affair with one of Adair's shepherds, the probable murderer. Three days after the funeral the couple moved in together.

The local priest and minister combined forces to oppose the evictions but to no avail and many of the victims emigrated to Australia with the aid of funds raised through a public appeal. In the 1930s the Estate was purchased by Henry P. McIlhenny, the grandson of a poor immigrant from nearby Carrigart, who made his fortune after inventing the gas meter in Georgia. After improving the Estate, he gifted it to the nation.

Evictions were by definition ruthless and heartless affairs, as the Derryveagh example shows, seen by landlords as the mere exercise of legal rights rather than human tragedies. Men, women and children often had to be physically removed from their homes, which were then usually damaged or destroyed by the 'crow bar men', as in *Skibbereen*, to make them uninhabitable. Verse four may seem melodramatic but this sort of tragedy probably did happen somewhere in Ireland, possibly at Skibbereen.

With the full weight of the law behind them evictions were almost impossible to resist, but occasionally an attempt would be made. For example, a bailiff and a policeman were killed at Ballycohey in Tipperary in 1868 as tenants united in opposition to eviction by their landlord William Scully. The event was 'celebrated' in *The Battle of Ballycohey*.

'Did you hear of Billy Scully?', said the Shan Van Vocht.
'And the boys of Ballycohey?', says the Shan Van Vocht.
'That day we showed them fun and we made the tyrants run,
With their double-barrelled gun', says the Shan Van Vocht .

Near Millford in Donegal one landlord, William Sydney Clements (1806-78), 3rd Earl of Leitrim, who owned over 94,000 acres of land, was bludgeoned to death by three local men, Fenians, Ribbonmen or both, who finally decided that they had taken enough. Lord Leitrim was a particularly obnoxious and obsessive megalomaniac who treated his tenants like objects, flouting the 'Ulster custom' (which gave tenants better rights than in the rest of the country), raising rents and ruthlessly evicting as he saw fit. He also forced himself sexually on local girls, one of whom afterwards drowned herself. None of those who assassinated him on 2 April 1878 was ever convicted. The only one charged, Michael Heraghty, died before coming to trial. The other two, Neil Shiels and Michael 'Mickey Rua' McIlwee were never charged. Despite everyone knowing who had done the deed, a reward of £10,000 went unclaimed. Leitrim had been so unpopular with his own class, the police and even with the Lord Lieutenant that the authorities were reluctant to proceed too vigorously. Neil Shiels lived on until 1924, maintaining his Ribbon oath of silence to the end.

Even as gruesome an event as this has found its way into a song, the little-known sixth verse of Michael McGinley's *The Hills of Glenswilly*, written in 1878.

Cursed be the vile tyrannic laws that grind our native isle,
Will Irishmen be always slaves or forced to live in exile,
Yet countrymen you struck a blow to punish tyranny
When Leitrim's Lord of Cratloe fell, not far from Glenswilly.

By 1880 tenants were resisting in a more co-ordinated and effective way in what was to become known as the Land War. The Irish National Land League, inspired by but more radical than the Irish Tenant League of the 1850s, was formed in 1879. It lobbied politicians, helped tenants resist evictions, provided legal advice and ostracised the more reactionary landlords and their agents. The most celebrated case, which added a new verb to the English language, was that of Captain Charles Boycott, an agent for John Crichton, Earl of Erne, on a 2,184-acre estate near Ballinrobe in County Mayo. (The Earl's main estate, consisting of 31,000 acres, was at Newtownbutler in Fermanagh.) When Boycott (1832-97), wholeheartedly supported by Lord Erne, threatened eviction for rent arrears in 1880 he was ostracised by local people. As the harvest faced ruin Boycott was forced to hire outside help and was assisted by volunteers organised by members of the Orange Order. However the security operation ran to over £10,000, which as Parnell said, was 'a shilling for every turnip dug'. The campaign to send Boycott to 'moral Coventry' had been so strong that he couldn't even book a hotel room in Dublin and had to leave the country for a time.

The principal architect of the Land League was Michael Davitt (1846-1905) whose own family had been evicted from their home in Mayo in the 1850s. As a young man Davitt had been an active Fenian. The *No Rent Manifesto* issued by the League after the arrest of its leaders, including Parnell, in 1881 contained the following:

Pay no rent under any circumstances... do not be wheedled into compromise of any sort by the threat of eviction... they can no more evict a whole nation than they can imprison them.

By the early 1880s the situation was improving as the government was pressured into introducing the *Land Law (Ireland) Act* (1881), finally granting the 'three F's': fair rents, fixity of tenure and free sale. Land ownership however remained unchanged. The establishment of the Land Commission (1881) to fix agreed rents and regulate agrarian problems and the *Arrears Act* (1882) marked further advances as well as a major change in government attitude. Various other *Land Acts* up to 1909 allowed tenants to purchase their land through loans provided at favourable rates by the British government. In 1885 the mortgage limit was upped from seventy-five per cent to one hundred per cent of the purchase price. By 1921, eighty-five per cent of farms were owner occupied.

The Land League has been well described by that least pretentious and most plain-speaking of men, the Protestant nationalist MP Alfred Webb (1834-1908):

> My belief is, there never was a movement other than the Land League... that against greater odds with less suffering all round, conferred greater benefits on a people... The much abused and much despised Land League movement raised the condition of the tenantry of Ireland from that of serfs to that of freemen. Well has Mr Davitt entitled his history of the movement 'The Fall of Feudalism'.

Feudalism in Ireland had indeed all but disappeared. My grandfather, born in 1881, was no longer a peasant but a proud owner of land, even if it was only seventeen acres. Three centuries after his arrival the ghost of Arthur Chichester had finally been banished from Inishowen. On hearing stories about the Land War as a very young child it angered me that my grandfather had to borrow money to buy back 'the land of his ancestors'. Later in life I came round to the view that it was all just an accident of history, with many similar examples in colonial situations around the world.

After Independence in 1922 repayment of 'land annuities' by the Irish government continued until De Valera finally reneged on them in the 1930s, resulting in an 'economic war' with Britain. Though Michael Davitt didn't quite live to see the final success of the movement he had founded, the cumulative legislation initiated by the Land League transformed the countryside and formed the basis for the establishment of Ireland as it is today.

Present-day Skibbereen (*An Sciobairín*), 'the place of small boats', has fully recovered from the tragedy of its past. Happily the time for any thoughts of 'revenge' has long past but it will be a longer time before Ireland *forgets* the tragedy of *gorta mhór*, 'the great hunger'. The memory will be kept alive by songs like *Skibbereen*.

John Goulding's Grave, Gerringong, Australia

15.
The Bold Fenian Men

See who comes over the red blossomed heather,
Their green banners kissing the pure mountain air,
Heads erect, eyes to front, stepping proudly together;
Freedom sits throned on each proud spirit there.
Down the hills twining, their field glasses shining,
Like rivers of beauty they flow through each glen,
From mountain and valley, it's Liberty's rally:
'Out and make way for the bold Fenian men'.

Our prayers and our views they have scoffed and derided,
They've shut out the sunlight from spirit and mind.
Our foes were united and we were divided.
We met and they scattered us all to the wind.
But once more returning within our hearts burning
The fires that illumined dark Aherlow Glen.
We raised the old cry anew, slogan of Conn and Hugh:
'Out and make way for the bold Fenian men'

We're men of the Nore, and the Suir and the Shannon.
Let tyrants come forth, we'll bring force against force.
Our pen is the sword and our voice is the cannon,
Rifle for rifle and horse against horse.
We made the false Saxon yield on many a red battlefield,
God on our side we will triumph again.
Pay them back woe for woe, strike them back blow for blow.
'Out and make way for the bold Fenian men'.

Side by side in the Cause have our forefathers battled,
Our hills never echoed the tread of a slave,
In many a field where the leaden hail rattled,
Through the red gap of danger they marched to their grave.
And we who inherit their names and their spirit
Will march neath the banner of Liberty then.
All who love foreign law, native or Sassenach.
'Out and make way for the bold Fenian men'.

The Bold Fenian Men

The Fenian Movement, the Fenians of Cahersiveen, the Manchester Martyrs

This great piece of romantic patriotism is one of the finest of all the rebel songs. I first heard it sung on record by Patrick Galvin in the 1960s and the images planted then have never been wholly dislodged. It's a stirring, proud and defiant rallying call, full of bold and effective imagery and rounded off by a terrific marching tune. Written by Limerick man Michael Scanlan (1836-1917), it was first published in Chicago in 1864. Scanlan, the 'poet laureate' of Fenianism, came from the parish of Mahoonagh (Castlemahon), south-east of Newcastlewest. When he was about fourteen his family emigrated to America where he became involved in the Fenian movement, the latest republican conspiratorial group, which believed that independence could only be achieved through military means.

Scanlan is the author of many songs, his best known including *The Jackets Green*, an imaginative historical romance that evokes the heroic image of Patrick Sarsfield, and *Limerick is Beautiful*, an impassioned allegory with Ireland depicted as Éire, a female lover, 'proud, passionate and free'. Both songs are laced with Scanlan's distinctive brand of emotional, effusive but very effective lyricism. His poetry collection, *Love and Land* was published in 1866.

The origins of the term *Fenian* go right back into the tribal folk psyche. It is derived from *fiann* ('warrior-band'), collectively *fianna*, elite hunter/warrior outlaws who followed mythical *Fionn Mac Cumhaill* (Finn MacCool) and *Cormac Mac Airt*, the semi-legendary High King from the 3rd or 4th century AD. The modern political use of the term is usually attributed to Ballingarry veteran John O'Mahoney (1816-77), though some scholars say that the English antiquarian Charles Vallancey (1721-1812) used it as early as 1804. The term also appears in the first issue of the first-ever Irish language magazine *Bolg an tSolair*, or, *Gaelic Magazine*, published by the *Northern Star* in 1795. The magazine contains *Laoi na Sealge* or, the famous Fenian poem, called *The Chase*. The term has proved to be one of the most resonant labels in Irish history, still in daily use through the name of one of Ireland's two main political parties, Fianna Fáil, 'soldiers of destiny'.

Fenianism had its origins in the Irish communities of North America in the 1850s. It marked a new beginning for the nationalist movement after the failure of the Repeal of the Act of Union campaign, the decline and death of Daniel O'Connell (1775-1847), the trauma of the Famine and the debacle of the Young Irelander's revolt. A bridge to Fenian activity was the raid on Cappoquin police barracks in Waterford in August 1849, led by James Fintan Lalor (1807-49), a pioneer advocate of land reform.

The best-known of all the Fenians was James Stephens (1824-1901), a Protestant railway engineer from Kilkenny. In Dublin on Saint Patrick's Day 1858 Stephens was instrumental in founding the Irish Republican Brotherhood, usually equated with the Fenian Movement. With his fellow conspirators he took a vow 'to renounce allegiance to the Queen of England... to take up arms and fight [for] an independent democratic republic'. However his reputation later suffered as a result of his cautious attitude to armed revolt, he was not an Emmet or a Patrick Pearse, and from 1865 onwards he ceased to be a leading player.

A Fenian revolt had been planned for February 1867 but this was called off when it was discovered that the government had found out about it through its network of spies and informers. However communications were poor; news of the postponement didn't reach some areas, so sporadic outbreaks occurred in various parts of the country. One of the most celebrated was at Cahersiveen in Kerry's Iveragh Peninsula, 'the Ring of Kerry'. With the benefit of hindsight it is apparent that this action was doomed from the start for as a later Kerry republican said, 'the Iveragh men rose but they rose alone'. The rebels, variously estimated at between a hundred and a thousand, did enjoy a minor success when they gained control of the coastguard station at Kells, one of the few 'military' successes of the entire Fenian revolt.

On 13 February 1867 the *Kerry Evening Post* reported that

'there were three persons arrested in Killarney late last night on suspicion of being mixed up in the reasonable designs of the Fenian conspirators. One is a stranger arrived here lately and gives the name of Moriarty, another is named Gaynor, the third, resident in Killarney, named Sheehan. They were brought into Tralee this afternoon by train, handcuffed and escorted by a strong force of police and at once marched off to jail'.

The 'Moriarty' referred to was certainly not David Moriarty (1814-77) the Catholic Bishop of Kerry, who declared 'hell is not hot enough nor eternity long enough for the godless Fenians!' At least one of the rebels, John O'Neil Goulding (or Golden, from the Irish *O'Gullin*) (1841-79) was transported to Australia and never saw Ireland again (see also *The Boys of Mullaghbawn*).

The Iveragh insurrection is commemorated in the rousing ballad *The Fenians of Cahersiveen*, a local folk song that came to national prominence when published by Herbert Hughes in 1936.

> The night of the rising it was a great sight
> To see all those brave boys all ready to fight
> With their swords and their bayonets, their pikes and their guns
> Oh 'twas glorious to see them all true Erin's sons.
>
> So hurrah for the Fenians of Cahersiveen,
> None bolder nor braver in Erin was seen,
> No braver battalion did fight for the green
> Than the true hearted Fenians of Cahersiveen.

Another revolt was attempted nationally in early March but this too was ineffective and quickly fizzled out, again defeated by poor organisation and infiltration by government agents. The Fenian revolt, like that of Robert Emmet in 1803 and Young Ireland in 1848, had, in military terms, been a disaster. Yet it provided another layer in the perceived tradition of an armed revolt per generation, with each new rising drawing on and feeding off previous ones. The Young Irelanders took inspiration from 1798, still within living memory, and used the struggle for publicity and propaganda. A good example of this was *The Memory of the Dead* by twenty-year-old student John Kells Ingram (1823-1907), first published anonymously in the *Nation* in 1843.

> Who fears to speak of Ninety-eight?
> Who blushes at the name?
> When cowards mock the patriot's fate,
> Who hangs his head for shame?
> He's all a knave or half a slave,
> Who slights his country thus,
> But a true man, like you man,
> Will fill your glass with us.
>
> We drink the memory of the brave,
> The faithful and the few,
> Some lie far off beyond the wave,
> Some sleep in Ireland too,
> All, all are gone, but still lives on
> The fame of those who died,
> All true men, like you, men,
> Remember them with pride.

Ironically, the author of these oft-quoted lines of nationalist sentiment became much more conservative in later life, eventually opposing even Home Rule, and not publicly acknowledging the rebellious song of his youth until he was seventy-seven years old. Similarly the Fenians used the memory of the United Irishmen, Emmet and the Young Irelanders as sources of inspiration, with one of the best-known Fenian songs, *The Rising of the Moon* by John Keegan Casey (1846-70) looking back to '98,

> They fought for dear old Ireland and bitter was their fate.
> Oh what grief and sorrow filled the year of ninety-eight.
> But thank God some hearts are beating still in manhood's burning noon
> Who will follow in their footsteps at the rising of the moon.

The song was an instant hit, being sung by the Fenian prisoners on the *Hougoumont* en route for Australia in 1867. Casey, from near Mullingar, also wrote the classic *Máire My Girl*. Sadly he died in his own 'manhood's burning noon' after contacting tuberculosis while in prison for his Fenian activities.

Some other leading Fenians included:

John Devoy (1842-1928), from the Kildare townland of Kill, who served six years in prison. He was born in the same 'cabin' as his mother's uncle who had been 'out' in 1798, as had both his grandfathers, so he had rebellion in his blood. A combative, irascible and uncompromising character, he lived to see his eighty-sixth birthday and was a rebel from the day he was born. He became an active one at the age of nine after a teacher smashed a slate over his head when he refused to sing 'God Save the Queen'. He was a tireless organiser, fundraiser and campaigner through *Clan na Gael* in America and conspired with most of the leading republicans and nationalists, including Davitt, Parnell, Casement and Pearse, who regarded him as the most single-minded of all the Fenians. Devoy was a highly intelligent man but never earned more than enough to keep body and soul together and lived most of his life in cheap hotel rooms in New York City. However he wasn't interested in wealth, never touching a penny of the hundreds of thousands of Fenian dollars that passed through his hands.

Charles Joseph Kickham, (1828-82), novelist and poet, a nephew of John O'Mahoney and a Fenian founding member. He was a strong advocate of armed revolt and was sentenced to fourteen years in 1865. At his trial he declared, 'I have endeavoured to serve Ireland and now I am prepared to suffer for Ireland'. Despite poor health and physical handicap Kickham returned to the movement, heading the Irish

Republican Brotherhood from 1873 until his death. Today he is best remembered as the composer of the anti-recruiting song *Patrick Sheehan* (sometimes called *Blind Sheehan*) and the love song *She Lived Beside the Anner*.

Thomas Clarke Luby (1822-1901), a Dublin Protestant and a founder member. He was involved with Young Ireland and also conspired with Lalor at Cappoquin in 1849. He accompanied James Stephens on his 3,000 mile fact-finding mission round Ireland in 1856. In 1865 he was sentenced to twenty years penal servitude, eventually serving six. On his release he was banished abroad, settling in New York where he worked as a journalist. He was never allowed to return to Ireland.

John O'Leary (1830-1907), from Tipperary, a leading writer and theorist. He abandoned his law studies when he discovered that barristers had to take an oath of allegiance to the British monarch. He served five years of the deliberately harsh prison regime inflicted on all the Fenian leaders. He is immortalised in Yeats' *September 1913*:

> Was it for this the Wild Geese spread the grey wing upon every tide,
> For this that all blood was shed, for this Edward Fitzgerald died,
> And Robert Emmet and Wolfe Tone, all that delirium of the brave?
> Romantic Ireland's dead and gone, it's with O'Leary in the grave.

Jeremiah O'Donovan Rossa (1831-1915), a lifelong patriot who served six years. At his trial he made an eight-hour speech in defence of the Fenian Movement. A somewhat erratic firebrand, he organised the indiscreetly named Skirmishing Fund in America, and bomb attacks in England in the 1880s. He often had to be reined in by more cautious exiles in America who nicknamed him O'Dynamite Rossa and, less flatteringly, O'Donovan Assa. Although he devoted his whole life to the struggle, today he is probably best remembered for the oration given at his funeral in Dublin by Patrick Pearse. 'Life springs from death and from the graves of patriot men and women spring living nations... they think they have pacified Ireland... the fools, the fools, the fools, they have left us our Fenian dead and while Ireland holds these graves, Ireland unfree shall never be at peace'.

No account of Fenianism would be complete without reference to the 'Manchester Martyrs', all recalled by name in the song *The Smashing of the Van*, learned from the recording by Enoch Kent almost forty years ago. Kent, one of Scotland finest folk voices of the '60s, says that he got the song in a Glasgow pub 'from an Irishman named Paddy', possibly Patrick Galvin, who both published and recorded the song. Surprisingly it is seldom sung nowadays for it is a decent historical ballad. 'Sorrow and excitement ran throughout all Lancashire' when an attempt was made to free Fenian leaders Thomas Kelly and Timothy Deasy 'in Manchester one morning in the year of '67'. After the demise of James Stephens, the Fenians had appointed Kelly as 'chief executive of the Irish republic'. He was a fanatical but very resourceful man who, with Devoy, organised Stephens' Richmond Jail breakout in 1865, with the help of one of the warders, Dan Byrne, and the Superintendent of the Hospital, John Breslin, who were paid-up Fenians.

John Joseph Breslin was to go on to have a long and successful Fenian career. His greatest exploit came when he travelled to Australia via New York and California and led the successful rescue of Fenian prisoners on the 'Fenian Whaler' *Catalpa* in 1876. Breslin is one of those immortalised, though not by name, in the *Galway Races* who 'brought home the Fenian prisoners from dying in foreign nations'. Devoy, the arch plotter, had masterminded the scheme but Breslin executed it, with aplomb. He is commemorated in the now virtually unsung ballad, *The Fenian's Escape.*

> On the seventeenth of April last the Stars and Stripes did fly
> On board the bark *Catalpa*, waving proudly to the sky.
> She showed the green above the red, as calmly she did lie,
> Prepared to lift the Fenian boys to safety o'er the sea.
>
> When Breslin and brave Desmond brought the prisoners to the shore
> They gave a shout for freedom, God bless them evermore
> And manned by gallant Irish hearts, pulled out the Yankee flag
> For well they knew from its proud folds, no tyrant could them drag.

The final line is literally true as the British gunboat *Georgette*, in close pursuit, could both outrun and outgun the *Catalpa*. However the latter's American Captain, James Anthony, played the 'how dare you fire on the American flag' diplomatic card and the British backed down. 'Desmond' was Tom Desmond, a deputy sheriff from Los Angeles, Breslin's lieutenant on the mission. The exploit left egg on the face of the Empire, gave the Irish a great psychological boost and provided the Fenians with a major propaganda coup.

Back in Manchester Kelly and Deasy were released by their comrades, 'but in blowing open off the lock they chanced to kill a man, and three men must die on the scaffold high for the smashing of the van'. Those hanged for the death of the policeman, Sergeant Charles Brett, were William Phillip Allen, Michael Larkin and Michael O'Brien. The man who had fired the fatal shot, Peter Rice, escaped and there were strong suspicions that the three men executed were mere scapegoats.

Like many before and since they died unrepentant. Allen, aged just 19, declared, 'I want no mercy... I die proudly in defence of republican principles'. O'Brien, from Cork, had participated in a number of Fenian actions including the capture of the police station at Ballyknockane and the derailing of the Dublin express. Another of those found guilty but reprieved because he was an American citizen, Edward O'Meagher Condon (1835-1915), shouted as he was being led from the dock, 'I have nothing to regret... God save Ireland'. Condon's defiant parting shot was later used by T.D. Sullivan (1827-1914) as the basis of his famous patriotic song *God Save Ireland (cried the heroes)*. This was to vie with Davis' *A Nation Once Again* for the honour of unofficial national anthem until *A Soldier's Song*, written in 1907 by Peadar Kearney (1883-1942), an uncle of Brendan and Dominic Behan, was officially adopted. Michael Larkin had the last word: 'God be with you Irishmen and Irish women'. The only other references to others of the 'rescue party' that I have found are MacEoin's note that James Stritch, 'one of the last of the active Fenians, [who] had taken part in the Manchester rescue of Colonel Kelly and Captain Deasy', died in 1933. The National Graves Association records that another member, J.W. O'Beirne, served on its Committee until his death in 1942.

Another Fenian rescue attempt went wrong the following December at Clerkenwell Prison in London when fifteen people died in a massive explosion as the Fenians attempted to free their second-in-command and armaments officer, Richard O'Sullivan Burke (1838-1922). One of the alleged bombers, Michael Barrett, was the last person to be publicly executed in England. Substantial doubts remain about his guilt. His defenders claim that he was in Glasgow at the time of the attack and couldn't possibly have participated. Tragic as these events were, they were intended solely as rescue attempts and not as deliberate acts to terrorise the English public. Although there had been some Fenian activity in England, the first orchestrated bombings didn't occur until 1883. Tom Clark, a signatory of the Proclamation of the Irish Republic in 1916, spent fifteen years in prison for his part in the campaign, organised as we have seen by old Fenians in America such as O'Donovan Rossa.

In Dublin an extremist Fenian offshoot, the [Irish National] Invincibles, carried out the Phoenix Park murders of Irish Chief Secretary Lord Frederick Cavendish, a nephew of Prime Minister Gladstone, and his Deputy, Thomas Burke in May 1882. Six men were hanged for the murders, Joseph Brady, Daniel Curley, Michael Fagan, Thomas Caffrey, Timothy Kelly and Joseph Poole. The latter is generally regarded as innocent as he had not been involved in the attack and was not an Invincible, though he was a well-known Fenian. The group had been informed on by their own leader James Carey, who cut a deal with the authorities. However he was murdered shortly afterwards on board ship for South Africa by a Donegal Fenian named Patrick O'Donnell, who himself was hanged in December 1883, thus concluding one of the darker episodes in Irish history. The Phoenix Park murders had been carried out with surgical knives, smuggled from London in the skirts of the wife of Frank Byrne who was Secretary of the Land League in Britain. The sense of shock and outrage created delayed the repeal of the Coercion Acts and set back the whole political process, which seemed to be moving towards Home Rule.

As a specific political movement Fenianism faded after the failure of the 1867 revolt as the Land War and Home Rule took centre stage. However Irish nationalism, of which Fenianism was merely the strongest expression of the times, never faded away. Many old Fenians lived to see the formation of the Irish Free State in 1922 and it is almost a statistical certainty that some even saw the Republic established on 21 December 1948.

The geography of *The Bold Fenian Men* is set very much in the south of the country, Michael Scanlan's territory. The River Nore (*An Fheoir*) rises in County Laois and flows through Kilkenny City before joining the Barrow some seventy miles later just north of New Ross. The River Suir (*Siúr*), 'sister river' (to the Nore and Barrow) is about ten miles longer. It rises in Tipperary and flows via Thurles, where Smith O'Brien was arrested in 1848, Carrick-on-Suir, the hometown of the Clancy Brothers, Mooncoin, famed in song, before meeting the Barrow and joining the sea beyond Waterford city. (For information on the River Shannon see *The Scarriff Martyrs*.)

The celebrated Glen of Aherlow is situated some five miles south of Tipperary town on the edge of 'the gay Galty Mountains', themselves often celebrated in song, and which peak at just over 3,000 feet. The Aherlow River joins the Suir near Cahir. Here Michael Scanlan imagined the 'men of the Nore, the Suir and the Shannon' as they set out determined to redress past wrongs, humiliations and defeats. Perhaps he also imagined them singing his own recently composed anthem 'out and make way for *The Bold Fenian Men*'.

Courtesy Green Collection and the Ulster Folk and Transport Museum

Hackler at work, Toome, 1915

16.

The Hackler from Grouse Hall

I am a roving hackler lad that loves the Shamrock Shore,
My name is Pat McDonnell and my age is eighty-four,
Beloved and well respected by my neighbours one and all,
On St Patrick's Day I might like to stray round Lavey and Grouse Hall.

When I was young I danced and sung and drank good whiskey too,
Each shebeen shop that sold a drop of real ould mountain dew,
With the poitín still on every hill the peelers had no call,
Round sweet Stradone I am well known, round Lavey and Grouse Hall.

I rambled round from town to town for hackling was my trade,
None can deny, I think that I, an honest living made,
Where e'er I'd stray, by night or day, the youth would always call
To have the crack with Paddy Jack, the hackler from Grouse Hall.

I think it strange how times have changed so very much of late,
Coercion now is all the row with Peelers on their bate (beat).
To take a glass is now alas the greatest crime of all
Since Balfour placed that hungry baste (beast), the sergeant at Grouse Hall.

This busy tool of Castle rule he wanders night and day,
He'll seize a goat all by the throat for want of better prey,
The nasty skunk, he'll swear you're drunk, though you had none at all,
There is no peace about the place since he came to Grouse Hall.

'Twas on pretence of this offence he dragged me off to jail,
Alone to dwell in a cold cell my fortune to bewail.
My hoary head on a plank bed, such wrongs for vengeance call,
He'll rue the day he dragged away the hackler from Grouse Hall.

Down into hell he'd run pell mell to hunt for poitín there
And won't be loath to swear an oath 'twas found in Killinkere.
He'll search your bed from foot to head, sheets, blankets, tick and all,
Your wife undressed must flee the nest for Jemmy from Grouse Hall.

Thank God the day's not far away when Home Rule will be seen
And brave Parnell at home will dwell and shine in College Green,
Our policemen, will all be then, our Nation's choice and call,
Oul Balfour's pack will get the sack and banished from Grouse Hall.

Let old and young clear out their lungs and sing this little song,
Come join with me and let him see, you all resent the wrong
And while I live I'll always give a prayer for his downfall
And when I die I won't deny, I'll haunt him from Grouse Hall.

The Hackler from Grouse Hall

Linen, Flax and a Drop of the Hard Stuff

This very skilfully constructed song is set against the background of the flax, linen and illicit whiskey or *poitín* ('poteen') trades in County Cavan towards the end of the 19th century. It's a real gem, full of sardonic humour and incidental social and political background detail. It's also not a bad advertisement for the *poitín* if Pat could still write as lucidly as this at the age of eighty-four!

The references to Balfour and Parnell date the song to between 1887 and 1891, when Arthur Balfour was the Chief Secretary of Ireland. As Parnell died in 1891, the song must have been written during this period. Charles Stewart Parnell, one of the major names in Irish history, a constitutionalist who bordered on the militant, was Member of Parliament for Meath 1875-80 and for Cork City 1880-91. His inspired and effective leadership of the nationalist movement through the Home Rule and Land War period was brought to a pathetic and premature end by a divorce scandal in 1889.

Balfour was dubbed 'Bloody' Balfour in 1887 when the police killed three demonstrators at a public meeting at Mitchelstown, County Cork during the Land War campaign. In the same year he also introduced the Criminal Law and Procedure Act, one of the many 'Coercion Acts'. These allowed for curfews, detention without trial and increased powers for magistrates. The line 'coercion now is all the row with peelers on their beat' probably indicates that the song was written in reaction to this Act.

Although he published an anti-Home Rule book in 1912, Balfour is usually regarded as a relatively 'constructive unionist'. In his final year of office he introduced the Congested Districts Board to fund the creation of larger holdings of land. By 1923 the Board had spent ten million pounds and redistributed more than two million acres. He became Tory prime minister in 1902 and supported the Anglo-Irish Treaty of 1921.

The Irish had of course been 'filling the air with the odour rare' of poitín, ('little pot') since time immemorial. In the old days local people distilled whiskey for their own use and it had no commercial value. There was no trade in it and everyone was happy. Then in 1661 the government introduced taxation but as this was largely unenforceable, it made little practical difference and poitín production carried on regardless. However the principle of a whiskey tax had been established and the old days were numbered. Things changed radically in 1779 when a *Revenue Act* came in, outlawing small stills and imposing a tax on others. Legal or 'parliament' whiskey became more expensive and people turned in increasing numbers to the illegal brew, which was also of superior quality. This drove many of the larger, legal distillers out of business and encouraged the small illicit ones to step production up even further.

Almost anyone could set up a still. All that was needed was a supply of running water and the 'instruments': still, head, 'worm' and the basic ingredient, barleycorn. In the rural areas such operations were virtually impossible to eliminate and by the 19th century the practice was widespread, especially in the North. Donegal became the top poitín - producing county, ahead of Tyrone, Derry and Mayo.

By 1817 the situation required that the newly-formed Peace Preservation Force be sent up to Donegal to clamp down. Around the same time the Irish Revenue Police were also established and by 1832 numbered five hundred men. The revenue men had reasonable success, their main weapon being the imposition of blanket fines, on both guilty and innocent, in any townland where poitín was found. Much of the Donegal liquor, as elsewhere, was for local consumption but substantial amounts were also 'exported', much of it 'spirited' across Lough Foyle in unlit fishing boats, earning valuable cash income, often the only time small farmers ever saw actual money.

Although in reality it was a serious business the poitín trade has been the source of much humour for if there's one thing the Irish like more than a wee drink it's putting one over on the authorities, probably a 'hangover' from outlaw rapparee times! Smuggling butter, bacon and other mundane household goods was fine but it was a double bonus to be able to turn a penny from the illicit brew. My father raised us on stories of how he smuggled the stuff across the border, in bicycle tyres! This was during the Second World War and later the government gave him a medal for keeping an eye open for German planes. However the Luftwaffe wasn't the only thing that he was watching out for! The ever-suspicious Guards, latter-day Grouse Hall men, often stopped him but always left empty-handed. If the old bike tyres trick was thought to be ingenious it was nothing to some of the schemes dreamt up by the 'cadgers', poitín distributors, over the centuries. A government report from 1823 stated 'some women have pockets made of tin and a breast and a half moon that goes before them and with a cloak around them will walk with six gallons and it shall not be perceived'. From Connacht came further tales of peasant cunning with one distiller manufacturing 'a tin vessel with the head and body the shape of a woman, dressed to resemble his wife' going quite respectably about his business.

The files of the *Derry Journal* reveal that others of my Inishowen clan also seem to have involved. In 1923, Patrick McLaughlin, a Carndonagh publican, was charged with having the stuff on his premises. He failed to appear in court but was fined £50 anyway. In the same year William McLaughlin, another publican, this time from Clonmany, was more inventive, obtaining a sick note showing that his wife, a necessary witness, couldn't attend the court. He got an adjournment and maybe came up with a plausible excuse by the time his case came round again, if it ever did. Generally though, if Donegal men were the greatest poitín producers, they weren't always the most imaginative in avoiding the clutches of the law. When caught red handed Neal Doherty of Ballyliffin desperately tried to drink the contents of the bottle. Stephen Butler of Carndonagh sought to disguise some bottles of the clear liquid in Old Bushmills bottles and a Mrs Harkin of Clonmany tried concealing it in her underwear. However, as with the Sergeant from Grouse Hall, the Guards did their duty; no matter how distasteful, the law took its course and the miscreants were all heavily fined. The Inishowen trade has also produced a number of decent folksongs including the following.

The Jolly Smuggler
I am a jolly smuggler and I keep the best of stuff,
I don't care much for Civic Guards from Carrowkeel to Muff,
Carndonagh or Culdaff, Buncrana or Moville,
I am at their defiance as I sit here by my still.

The Illies Still
If ever the North and South be united
It will be over the head of a glass of *poitín*
And it's not until then that wrongs will be righted,
In place of two Irelands, just one will be seen

The Shandrum Still
It is not my intention for to advertise the stuff
And when I make a few remarks, I think it is enough
For to convey my sentiments while attending on a spree,
The ould stuff was unsurpassed for strength and quality.

The hackler took his name from the tool of his trade, the hackle, a steel comb for splitting and combing flax fibres in the manufacturing of linen thread. Flax is defined as 'an herbaceous annual plant of the genus linum'(often called 'lint') whose stem fibres are used to make quality writing paper as well as linen. Its cultivation in Ireland long predates the Christian era but it did not reach its commercial peak until the 19th century. Linen production grew from its cottage origins to exporting thirty-five million yards in 1800, by which time mechanisation had largely taken over from domestic production. The North of Ireland became the world's greatest linen-producing centre and Irish linen enjoyed a fine reputation for excellence and quality.

Preparation of the flax was a lengthy, intricate and unhealthy process. Firstly the flax plant, which produces a beautiful blue flower, was sown in the spring and harvested in August. After being hand-pulled to maximise length, it was then 'retted' (rotted) by being soaked for two weeks in dams of water. Next the flax was dried out in huge ovens or kilns or naturally in the open air, weather permitting. The next stage was 'scutching', the separation of the flax proper from the woody plant stem. Finally came the 'hackling' process, as the flax was further refined prior to spinning.

In reality the hackler's trade was a dangerous one, with the men often suffering from 'hacklers' disease', an ailment of the throat and lungs, the result of swallowing 'pouce', the dust created by the hackling process. A report in 1894 was headed 'All the Hacklers Die Young' and in fact few lived beyond their mid-forties. The 'satanic mills' too were typical of 19th century capitalism: up to a fifteen-hour day, low pay, child labour, hazardous conditions and authoritarian and oppressive management regimes. However the culture of the mills also produced many excellent folk songs, including *The Doffin' Mistress, Fan-A –Winnow, The Next Market Day, The Rovers Meet the Winders, You Might Easy Know a Doffer*, and one of the classics of the entire Industrial Revolution, *Factory Girl*.

> As I went out walking one fine summer's morning,
> The birds in the bushes did whistle and sing,
> The lads and the lassies in couples were sporting,
> Going back to the factory their work to begin.
>
> I spied one among them, she was fairer than any,
> Her cheeks like the red roses that bloom in the spring,
> Her hair like the lily that grows in yon valley
> And she but a hard-working factory girl.
>
> I stepped up beside her more closely to view her
> But on me she did cast such a look of disdain,
> Saying 'young man have manners and do not come near me,
> Although I'm a poor girl, I would not know shame'.
>
> I have land, I have houses adorned all with ivy,
> I have gold in my pockets and silver as well
> And if you'll come with me, a lady I'll make you,
> No more need you answer that factory bell.

But she turned away from me and then she did leave me
And all for her sake I will wander yon dell
And in some deep valley where no one can hear me
I'll mourn for the loss of my factory girl.

Most towns had their own linen hall or market where the drapers sold their produce. This has given us the place name of Draperstown in County Derry, one of the few Irish place names derived from English rather than Irish. The name was changed in 1818 to mark the link with the London Drapers Company, the original name being *Baile na Croise* ('town of the cross'). It is even thought that the Orange Order at least partly owed its foundation in 1795 to the importance of retaining control of the 'linen triangle' of Belfast, Dungannon and Newry in Protestant hands.

Louis Crommelin (1652-1727), a French Huguenot who brought his linen expertise to Lisburn in 1698 even tried to concentrate control in Huguenot hands by insisting on lengthy apprenticeships for all non-Huguenots. He argued they were so far ahead of the Irish in technique that they needed less training. Had the ploy been successful, which it wasn't, it would have disadvantaged all the locals, Protestant as well as Catholic. The linen trade continued at high levels of production throughout the 19th century but declined after the First World War with the introduction of synthetic fibres and changing tastes in fashion.

Another great folk ballad from this part of the country is also set against the background of the linen trade. Ostensibly *Jackson and Jane* is about a horserace but in fact it also provides us with numerous passing references to social and economic life around 1800. The two heroes of the ballad are Hugh Jackson, a Monaghan landowner and linen producer, and his wondrous champion steeplechaser Jane, rumoured to have been a former fishcart horse! The first three verses of the ballad give a good flavour of its quality and style.

You Monaghan sportsmen, attention an ear,
A few simple verses I want you to hear.
It's all about a hero I've heard people say,
They call him Hugh Jackson from Creeve near Ballybay.

His mills, kilns and barns they make a fine show
And his cloths to the North and the city do go,
For bleaching and lapping he exceeds them all
And his cloths were first approved of at the Linen Hall.

No more of his praises I'm going to explain.
If you listen awhile I will sing about Jane.
You can search the world over from Cork to Kildare,
You'll ne'er find a match for Hugh Jackson's grey mare.

The rest of the ballad relates with great good humour how Jane and her jockey inflicted a humiliating defeat on the 'Bellamont sportsmen', allowing Hugh Jackson to claim his winnings at 'ten guineas to four'. Bellamont, a fine Palladian villa built in 1729, was the family home of Lord Bellamont (Sir Charles Coote). He seems to have been a man of some principle as he resigned from the Cavan Militia in 1797 in protest at their policy of repression.

Back on the racecourse, Jane's noble run ensured that 'the cup came with honours to Creeve back again'. The ballad also contains the line 'I notice that Corry by 'Spanker' is threw', possibly a reference to James Corry who was the Secretary of the Irish Linen Board from 1796 to 1828. 'Bleaching' and 'lapping' were later stages in the linen manufacturing process, with bleached linen being described as 'white' and unbleached as 'brown'. After going through the various stages outlined earlier, it was bleached naturally in the sun in open-air bleach greens or bleach fields. 'Lapping' was the spinning of the material on a spinning wheel prior to weaving into cloth.

The hackler would visit most of the farms in his area providing his specialist service and substance. I suppose that it is just possible, from time to time, maybe on special occasions such as St Patrick's Day, so as not to cause offence, that he may have had little option but to share a glass or two with grateful clients, especially after a hard day's work with the thirst-inducing 'pouce' in the air!

However to the Sergeant from Grouse Hall, who seems to have enjoyed great job satisfaction, carrying out his responsibilities with a diligence and enthusiasm above and beyond the call of duty, this would have been no excuse. But imagine searching a man's bed, and with Mrs McDonnell still in it! In fact this was a favourite hiding place for the *poitín* and the Sergeant would have been well aware of it. 'Tick' is the old word for mattress.

Just in case you're depressed at the thought of the Sergeant getting the better of the poor old Hackler you will be pleased to learn that in an almost equally hilarious sequel the Hackler gets his revenge, with the Sergeant 'despised and stigmatised for tyranny and wrong'. Entitled, *The Sergeant's Lamentation*, here are three verses, with the second striking a more serious tone.

> I am belied because I tried to enforce the law
> And keep the peace around the place with drunken roughs and all.
> Though my protest may be expressed in language rather strong,
> I think I'm bound for to confound the author of that song.
>
> The League 'tis true I did pursue, the priest why should I spare
> Who broke the laws and was the cause of bloodshed everywhere.
> But Martin's fall in Donegal will be avenged ere long;
> When Balfour's shears get round his ears he'll sing another song.

I'm well content for to be sent away this very day
To Cork or Clare, or anywhere, a hundred miles away,
This cursed Grouse Hall caused my downfall, I have been here too long.
Before I go, I wish to know the man who made that song.

The second verse is historically interesting and confirms that the Sergeant, 'Jemmy', was an actual historical person. The verse relates to him having been sent to Gweedore in County Donegal to deal with a 'troublesome' priest, Father James McFadden (1842-1917) who had been making 'seditious' speeches in favour of the Land League and who had been imprisoned in 1888 for encouraging tenants not to pay rent. In February 1889 Jemmy and his boss, Royal Irish Constabulary District Inspector William Martin, moved in to arrest the priest one Sunday morning after Mass at Derrybeg Chapel. Passions were running high, local men moved in to protect their priest, a scuffle developed and sadly the forty-five-year-old Inspector was killed, bludgeoned to death with paling posts. Father McFadden was arrested but later released though seven of his parishioners were jailed for up to ten years for manslaughter. By 1892 they too had all had been released. Ironically, in the *Hackler* context, Father McFadden, 'The fighting priest of Gweedore', was a prominent local campaigner against *poitín*. 'Balfour's shears' is a reference to a convict haircut.

The place names mentioned in the song are all Cavan villages or townlands and are clustered within a few miles of each other. The village of Stradone (*Srath an Domhain*), the only one of any size at all is situated a few miles west of Cavan town. The meaning is given as both 'river valley of the world' and as 'deep river valley'. Killinkere (*Cillín Céir*), 'little church of the candles', even smaller, is a few miles further southeast, just north of Virgina. Lavey (or Lavay—*Leamhach*), 'abounding in elms' is a parish/townland about four miles southeast of Cavan town on the N3 main road. (The 'a' is pronounced as in 'cat'.) It is too small to be marked on ordinary road maps. So too is Grouse Hall itself but I was given directions to it in the Lavey Bar. The townland, nowadays spelt as one word, Grousehall, is situated on the small Lough Acurry about five miles south east of Stradone on the road to Bailieborough. The name, being in English, is obviously a relatively recent one, the original Irish name being *Maigh Leacht* ('plain of the gravestone'). All of the place names referred to in *Hackler* can be traced on the Discovery 1:50,000 Ordnance Survey maps, sheets 34 and 35.

If ever you chance to pass this way you might like to raise a glass, legal or otherwise, to the man who has given us so much pleasure with his good-natured cavorting around these parts over a hundred years ago. *Sláinte!* Here's to both 'the man who made that song' and to Pat McDonnell, *The Hackler From Grouse Hall.*

17.

My Lagan Love

Where Lagan stream sings lullaby,
There blooms a lily fair.
The twilight gleam is in her eye
And the night is on her hair
And like a lovesick *leanan-sídhe*.
She hath my heart in thrall,
Nor life I owe, nor liberty
For love is lord of all.

Her father sails a running barge
Twixt Leamh-beag and the Druim;
And on the lonely river-marge
She clears his hearth for him.
When she was only fairy high
Her gentle mother died,
But dew-love keeps her memory
Green on the Lagan side.

And oft-times when the beetle's horn
Has lulled the eve to sleep
I steal unto her sheiling lorn
And through the dooring peep.
There on the crickets' singing stone
She spares the bog wood fire
And hums in sad sweet undertone
The song of heart's desire.

Her welcome, like her love for me,
Is from her heart within.
Her warm kiss is felicity
That knows no taint of sin.
And when I stir my foot to go
'Tis leaving love and light
To feel the wind of longing blow
From out the dark of night.
[Repeat verse one]

Courtesy John McLaughlin

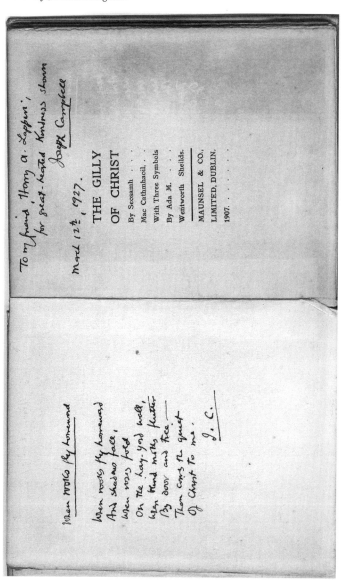

Title page of Joseph Campbell's *The Gilly of Christ*, signed by author. Harry Lapin, a wealthy Irish-American, was a benefactor of Campbell. 'When rooks fly homeward' is one of the poems in *The Gilly of Christ*.

My Lagan Love

The Mountainy Man, the Little People,
Hard Times in New York Town

This is one of Ireland's best-known and best-loved songs, described by poet the Robert Farren as 'the greatest song written by an Irish poet this century'. It has its origins between the hills of Donegal, where the melody was found, and the streets of Belfast where the lyrics were written. Musician Herbert Hughes (1882-1937) and antiquarian Francis Joseph Bigger (1863-1926) collected the traditional air in Donegal in 1903. Hughes wrote, 'I got this tune from *Proinseas mac Suibhne* [Francis McSweeny] who played it to me on the *fidil*. It was then sung to a ballad called *The Belfast Maid*, now forgotten in Cill-mac-nEnain [Kilmachrenan]'. Hughes was probably referring to the Barony of Kilnachrenan, the second most northerly in Ireland, after East Inishowen, rather than the town of the same name.

Hughes, a Methodist, and Bigger, a Presbyterian, both had a keen interest in Ireland's historic Gaelic culture and the Belfast home of Bigger, a wealthy solicitor and patron of the arts, was open house to like-minded people, irrespective of religious affinity. It was here that Hughes met Joseph Campbell (1879-1944), a Catholic, who was to pen the lyrics of *My Lagan Love*. Bigger was then editing the *Ulster Journal of Archaeology* and Campbell later remembered him as 'a diviner of thoughts, patron and friend, an urger of native effort, the loveliest soul, the lordliest type of mortal Irishman it has been, or will be, my lot to know'.

Herbert Hughes was a classically educated musician who provided the music for lyrics by Padraic Colum (1881-1972), both original and collected, like *Star of the County Down* and *She Moved Through the Fair*. He had gone on his first song-hunting trip to Donegal at the age of seventeen, co-founded the Irish Folksong Society in 1902 and spent his whole life collecting and publishing Irish songs. On his return from Donegal, Hughes collaborated with Campbell and their collection *The Songs of Uladh* [Ulster], including *My Lagan Love*, was published in 1904. The book was subsidized by Bigger and beautifully illustrated by Campbell's artist brother John (1883-1962) who had accompanied Hughes and Bigger to Donegal. It was prefaced:

> These songs were gathered from the Folk
> Who caught them from the Sidhe

Who sing them in the mountainy airs
To world-old minstrelsie
SEOSAMH MAC CATHMHAOIL

Joseph Campbell was born and educated in Belfast and was to establish a considerable reputation as a man of letters though he never seemed to quite fulfil his early promise. However he still has his adherents as the original Irish free verse poet. For a while it was fashionable to refer to him as 'The Mountainy Man' after his poem, *I Am the Mountainy Singer*, a title that reflected his mystical nature and his self-image as the voice of an idealised Ireland of days gone by. Also for a time he used the Gaelic form of his name, *Seosamh MacCathmaoil*, but dropped it he said, tongue in cheek, after hearing a girl refer to him as Sam McCatwail! He had rejected a conventional career in the family road-making business for the insecurity of the poet's calling and was often to be distracted by financial concerns. However he felt that he had no choice, believing that he had been gifted with bardic insight, a conviction evident in *The Herb-Leech* (1906):

All things on earth to me are known,
For I have the gift of the Murrain stone.

The murrain stone was a hollow, magical stone into which potions were poured for cattle to drink in the hope of preventing them catching the infectious and deadly disease known as murrain, which could bankrupt a farmer by wiping out his whole herd of cattle overnight.

Campbell was of partly Scots Protestant stock and although he was a lifelong republican he always retained a great affection for the Ulster Scots dialect and culture, learned first hand at his maternal grandfather's knee. However he was not an admirer of the more militant expression of that culture, exemplified by aspects of Orangeism. He also had a healthily sceptical attitude towards formal Catholicism, though he always practised privately, kneeling nightly to pray. Two verses succinctly illustrate this independent thinking.

The Orangeman
A monster? Not quite
As you may guess from my song,
But clay marred in the mixing,
God's image gone wrong.

Priests
You put a mask on beauty,
You bind the dancer's feet;
You bless the sad and bitter
And curse the gay and sweet.

Campbell's affection for Ulster Scots is evident in *'Tis Pretty Tae Be in Baile-Liosan* (1909), an adaptation of the great Antrim folksong *Ballinderry*.

'Tis pretty tae be in *Bailie-liosan*
'Tis pretty tae be in green *Magh-luan*
'Tis prettier tae be in Newtownbreda
Beeking under the eaves of June
The cummers are out wi' their knitting and spinning,
The thrush sings frae his crib on the wa'
And o'er the white road the clachan caddies
Play at their marlies and goaling-ba'.

The Scots dialect words are, *beeking*, basking; *cummers*, village women; *clachan caddies*, village boys; *marlies*, marbles and *goaling ba*, football. The poem is a nostalgic celebration of life in the village of Newtownbreda, County Down, in the 1880s, now swallowed up by the southern suburbs of Belfast, as have *Magh-luan* (Malone) and *Baile-liosan* (Ballylesson).

Campbell was equally influenced by the Gaelic culture of his paternal grandparents and as a boy was a frequent visitor to Flurrybridge, an Irish-speaking area of South Armagh, where his grandfather owned a farm.

After publishing volumes of songs, poetry and plays and living in Dublin and London, where he was Secretary of the Irish Society, he was back in Dublin at the time of the 1916 Easter Rising, which he supported but took no military part in. During the Civil War he was identified as a prominent republican, arrested and interned for seventeen months in Mountjoy Jail and in the Curragh, with devastating effect. Internment created unbearable strains, financial, psychological and sexual, on his 12-year old marriage to Nancy Maude, an upper middle class, English liberal Protestant who had married Campbell against the strongly expressed wishes of her parents and who had borne him three children. In 1922 he wrote to her: 'I am a broken a man… I had gifts to give my country and to humanity and they were spurned and rejected'. After the execution of Erskine Childers he cried despairingly, 'Where is Ireland's reputation for humanity and decency?' He emerged from internment alienated and disillusioned with politics, Ireland and organised religion.

In 1925 he emigrated to America where he earned a modest living as a lecturer in Irish literature at New York's Fordham University. However as his subject wasn't part of a regular faculty and having no formal academic qualifications, he had little job security and was paid considerably less than permanent staff. Everywhere he went though Campbell actively promoted Irish literature and culture and in New York founded the School of Irish Studies as well as editing the *Irish Review*.

My Lagan Love is now his main legacy though it is seldom attributed to him. It's sadly ironic that although the income generated by this song must be considerable, Joseph Campbell saw hardly any of it and spent most of his life struggling for the financial independence that would have allowed him to concentrate on his art.

The lyrics printed here are from *The Songs of Uladh*. It is an unusually powerful and atmospheric song, full of mystery and passion, seeming inspired almost as much by the landscape in which it is set as by an obsession for a beautiful woman. There is a strong supernatural element to it, conjuring up visions of mystical twilight, communing with nature as well as with the lady in question. The use of the term *leanan-sídhe* contributes powerfully to this atmosphere. Campbell describes this as,

> A fairy mistress [who] seeks the love of mortals. If they refuse she must be their slave. If they consent they are hers and can only escape by finding another to take their place. The fairy lives on their life and they waste away. She is the Gaelic muse, for she gives inspiration to those she persecutes. The Gaelic poets die young, for she is restless and will not let them remain long on earth, this malignant phantom.

It is generally assumed that geographically *My Lagan Love* is set in the valley of the River Lagan on the Down/Antrim border. No other possibility had ever entered my mind despite knowing and singing the song since hearing the recording by Lonnie Donegan around 1960. Recently however I have seen the suggestion that it may in fact be set in an area of Donegal also known as the Lagan (or Laggan). I have been unable to find any evidence to support this theory but there's no harm in exploring the idea.

The song is strikingly similar in style, atmosphere and language to *The Gartan Mother's Lullaby*, also by Campbell and included in *The Songs of Uladh*. This song is definitely set in Donegal as the Gartan Estate and Lough Gartan are located there. The first verse is:

> Sleep oh babe, for the red bee hums the silent twilight's fall,
> *Aoibheal* from the grey rock comes to wrap the world in thrall.
> A *leanbán* oh, my child, my joy, my love, my heart's desire
> The crickets sing you lullaby, beside the dying fire.

These lines have echoes of Brian Merriman's poem *The Midnight Court* (c.1780), set in County Clare at *Craig Liath* ('grey rock') and featuring *Aiobheall*, a queen of the *sídh* ('fairies'). *The Gartan Mother's Lullaby* also contains at least six similar, if not identical, words or phrases also found in *My Lagan Love*, 'twilight', 'thrall', 'heart's desire', 'crickets sing' 'lullaby' and 'dying fire'. Additionally there is the use of another fairy

creature name *Aiobheal* or *Aibell*, the Old Irish goddess or fairy queen said
to have been with Brian Boru at the Battle of Clontarf in 1014. *Leanbán*
looks similar to *leanan-sídhe* but is not related, meaning simply 'baby'.
The two are therefore virtually sister songs; both are set to melodies
freshly collected in Donegal, one of which is definitely set there. It is
difficult then to imagine why the author should separate them
geographically by setting one song a hundred miles away from the other in
a completely different part of the country.

However the place names of *Leamh-beag* and *Druim* from the second
verse of *My Lagan Love* almost certainly refer to the village of Lambeg and
The Drum, a bridge on the River Lagan, near south Belfast. The Irish form
of Lambeg is usually given as *Lann Bheagh*, meaning 'small church' – the site
of an old Franciscan friary, but the slight variation in spelling is unlikely to
be significant. Campbell had been born in Castlereagh Road in east Belfast
near this stretch of the river and often went for long rambles in the area. His
favourite spots were around Shaw's Bridge, at Milltown Road, and the
Giant's Ring, a prehistoric enclosure with a dolmen, or as some would have
it, a druid's altar, in the centre where the fairies were believed to live. The
landscape, legend and lore of the area would have been firmly fixed in
Campbell's receptive imagination. A further possible clue to the influence
of this landscape on Campbell's thinking may lie in the title of his 1907
poetry collection *The Gilly of Christ*. This translates from the Gaelic as
'servant, follower or devotee' and is the origin of the surname 'Gilchrist'
(*MacGiolla Chroist*). Another of the bridges on this part of the Lagan is called
Gilchrist Bridge. Legend has it that Christ once visited Ireland and was
shown round the country by an Irish boy named Gillachrist or Gilly. Later
Campbell gave the most unusual name of *Gilly* to his first born son.

The Lagan district of Donegal covers the area between Letterkenny,
Derry, Lifford and Stranorlar. The name is thought to mean 'low and level
country' and is the most fertile part of the county. In *The Laggan and its
Presbyterianism* (1905), the Rev. Alexander G. Lecky wrote that the Catholic
natives 'were at the time of the Plantation driven out of the Laggan to make
room for the English and Scotch settlers'. Almost until the Second World
War the area provided seasonal work for many young people, mostly from
the poorer parts of West Donegal, who used it as a training ground for
future trips to Scotland and further afield. The Rev. Lecky wrote of them
'going up to the Laggan to lift the Scotch', to learn English.

A number of written accounts of this experience have survived, the best
generally known being Patrick McGill's novel *Children of the Dead End*
(1914). McGill (1891-1963), from the Glenties, had been hired out at
Strabane Fair around the turn of the century. *Children of the Dead End*,

however, deals mainly with emigrant casual labourers in Scotland. Another, more local publication by Eoghan Ó Domhnaill in 1940, tells the story of Hiudai Sheainin who was hired as a fourteen-year-old at Letterkenny in 1857. Irish speaking, barefooted Hiudai earned one pound for his six months term, 'lifted the Scotch' and bought his first pair of shoes.

The hiring fairs were most common in west Ulster in towns like Derry, Letterkenny, Omagh and Strabane, peaking in the second half of the 19th century and continuing until the mid-twentieth. They were held twice a year, around 12 May and 12 November, with the earlier one being the bigger event as many more workers were needed over the summer. The experience was something of a lottery, though for all those involved it meant a difficult separation from home – just one step up from bonded servitude. The inherent social and economic difficulties were exacerbated by differences in language and religion – the workers being mostly Irish-speaking Catholics, the employing farmers English-speaking Protestants. The labourers, mostly children and teenagers, were allowed time off to attend Mass and were free to go home at any time. However, if they didn't complete the six-month contract, they received nothing.

The institution of the hiring fair has therefore engendered strong emotions, both in those who took part and in those who have written about it. Some saw it simply as good work experience, a rite of passage, a normal part of growing up, as well as a welcome opportunity to earn some hard cash. Others regarded it as little more than serfdom or slavery, with people having little choice but to work away from home, for long hours – six and a half or seven days a week, under strict and oppressive conditions, all for very low pay.

The Hiring Fairs of Ulster, a song from around 1880, is a glossy but nevertheless atmospheric evocation of the hiring fair experience.

> The plough boy with a steady hand, he will engage to plough the land.
> The dairy maid is well prepared to mind her milk and dairy.
> The cow boy with a staff or stave will mind his cows by brook or brae.
> The shoe boy too is wanted there, to polish boots for ladies.

> The kitchen maid can work or play, at certain times when not engaged,
> Sometimes she puts the hens to lay, and more times rocks the cradle,
> Sometimes she puts the geese to hatch, and other times she's cleaning flax,
> She'd dress the beds both soft and flat, and sleep till day is breaking.

> The farmer like a noble squire will come those servants for to hire
> And ask them what they require, with board and entertainment;
> They'll feed you well with bread and tea, if you comply to work sincere,
> Your dinner will have no delay, of butter, spuds and bacon.

The servants' wages now should rise as beef and butter got so high.
There's ten eggs sold at pence a piece, turkey eggs three ha'pence.
The paper states the London price of wheat and oats and bacon dry
And Gladstone seeking tenant right, it's now in contemplation.

The main duty of the 'cow boy' was herding cattle on the high ground,
which leads us back to *My Lagan Love*. The 'sheiling' of the third verse was a
primitive hut of sod and stone, built as a summer shelter for those tending
cattle on the higher ground. In addition to the purpose that it was intended
for, it also came to acquire something of a reputation for providing amorous
opportunities for young people, as shown in the survival in a Scottish
highlands place name *A'raidh na Suiridh*, 'the bothy (hut) of lovemaking'.
Whether Campbell's use of the term is a coded reference to this or whether
he would even have been aware of such a connotation I don't suppose we will
ever now know. Although not a philanderer he did have a number of lovers
after the break-up of his marriage shortly after emerging from prison a
changed man. Certainly the atmosphere of *My Lagan Love* is dripping with
sensuality. It is about passion, about 'love, the lord of all' and use of terms
like *leanan-sídhe* and 'sheiling' take it back into folk tradition and
mythology. The phrase 'crickets' singing stone' is not just atmospheric
scene setting. Campbell wrote,

> The cricket (Irish uirchuil, 'hearth-fly') is believed by our
> peasantry to be a very lucky little beast. In fact the phrase 'lucky as
> a cricket' has long since passed into proverb with them. Its
> presence in the kitchen-ends of farm-houses is supposed, too, to
> keep away all scathe [old dialect word meaning 'malevolence'] that
> otherwise might enter there. Many a time when as a child,
> holidaying among the mountains of South Ard-Macha [Armagh], I
> mind ferreting around the turf ashes (ar fud na gríosach) after
> dark-fall, looking, in my child's innocence, for the lively little lads
> with the cheery musical little 'cheep'. My grandmother, good
> woman, would never let me put a meddling finger on them,
> though, warning me off with the fearful words, 'If you touch the
> blessed creatures boy, they'll come out this very night, a whole
> school of them, and eat the heels out of your stockings!' That was
> enough to deter me from bothering with them further. To tell the
> truth, I have had a great and genuine respect for the crickets ever
> since... the crickets' luck is easily turned, they being whimsical
> and notionate in their ways. In South Ard-Macha, when a young
> married couple are about to take up house for themselves, it is a
> custom with them to carry a brace of crickets each in a match-box
> from the old parents hearths, these to bring luck to their own, and
> when secured to hold it there.

Although much of the language of *My Lagan Love* is strongly influenced by typical early Gaelic League enthusiasm, some might say affectation, the song nevertheless has certain timeless qualities that have given it a lasting hold on the imagination, both nationally and internationally. This attraction has proved irresistible to many of the greatest singers of the last hundred years. During that time, the song has been recorded by just about everybody who is anybody in Irish song including John McCormack in 1910. Usually though despite its peasant setting and folk atmosphere, it is somehow thought of as having more in common with the drawing room of the Big House than with the wee room in the back of the pub. However versions by Van Morrison with the Chieftains (1988) and Margaret Barry (1994, though recorded in the 50s) will have contributed to reclaiming it from the Big House. Margaret Barry (1917-89) was a great, natural soul singer, a Traveller from Cork who over the years was recorded by Peter Kennedy, Alan Lomax and Ewan MacColl.

The River Lagan itself rises on *Slieve Croob* near Ballynahinch and meanders forty-five miles to the sea by way of Dromore, Lisburn and Belfast. The meaning of the name is similar to that of the Laggan in Donegal. The original Irish name was *lao*, 'calf', a reference to the bovine goddess believed to inhabit its waters. Even as close to Belfast as Shaw's Bridge, Joseph Campbell's mystical silver stream is still 'scenic' and relatively unpolluted. I spoke with two boys fishing there and they assured me that they hoped to catch trout, maybe even salmon. The stretch of riverbank from here to Lisburn is now part of the Ulster Way long distance footpath.

After fourteen busy years in America Campbell returned home and spent the final five years of his life quietly in County Wicklow. He found a new outlet, broadcasting on Radio Éireann, boosting his self-esteem as well as his precarious bank balance. However by now he was overweight and suffering from a heart condition, his health problems exacerbated by being 'a terrible worrier'. His editor Austin Clarke wrote: 'In the spring of 1944 his nearest neighbours in the glen... noticed that no turf smoke was coming from the chimney and became alarmed. The poet was found dead where he had fallen across the hearth stone'.

Appropriately the last sounds Joseph Campbell heard were those that he loved and which had helped inspire his two best-known songs: 'The crickets sing you lullaby, beside the dying fire.'

18.

James Connolly

A great crowd had gathered outside of Kilmainham,
With heads all uncovered they knelt to the ground,
For inside that grim prison lay a true Irish soldier,
His life for his country about to lay down.

He went to his death like a true son of Ireland,
To the firing party he showed he was brave.
When the order rang out 'present arms, fire',
James Connolly fell into a ready-made grave

The Four Courts of Dublin, the English bombarded,
The spirit of freedom they tried for to quell,
But above all the firing, came the cry 'no surrender',
'Twas the voice of James Connolly, the Irish rebel.

The black flag they hoisted, the cruel deed was over
And gone was the great man that Ireland loved well
There was many a sad heart in Dublin that morning
When they murdered James Connolly the Irish rebel

Many years have gone by now since the Easter Rebellion
When the guns of Britannia they loudly did speak
And the bold IRA stood shoulder to shoulder
As the blood from their bodies flowed down Sackville
       [O'Connell] Street.

God's curse on you England, a cruel-hearted master,
Your deeds they would shame all the devils in hell.
Though no flowers are blowing, the shamrock's still growing
On the grave of James Connolly, the Irish rebel.

James Connolly (1868-1916)

James Connolly

The Republican Socialist and the Rising of 1916

James Connolly, the executed military leader of the 1916 Easter Rebellion, is one of the most revered patriots in Irish history and like all of them is widely celebrated in song. Without ranking among the greatest of political songs, *James Connolly* is reasonably effective, the least artificial of the many songs about Connolly. However he still awaits the truly great commemorative ballad, one with the essential blend of passion and poetry so apparent in the classics of the rebel genre, captivating the imagination like the best songs of Thomas Moore, Thomas Davis, Michael Scanlan, P. J. McCall and Peadar Kearney.

The Rebellion more generally though did produce a number of songs worthy of addition to the rebel canon. My personal favourites are Kearney's *Erin Go Bragh (A Row in the Town)* and *The Foggy Dew* by Father (Canon) Charles O'Neill. As well as being a more than competent lyricist, Kearney was also a practical revolutionary, having fought in the Jacob's Factory garrison in 1916.

> One of our leaders was down in Ringsend,
> For the honour of Ireland to uphold and defend,
> He had no veteran soldiers, just volunteers raw,
> Playing sweet Mauser music for *Erin go Bragh.*

Some misunderstanding surrounds authorship of *The Foggy Dew* because the author, Father Charles O'Neill (1887-1963), is sometimes confused with his brother Patrick who was also a priest. Born in Portglenone, Antrim, Father Charles spent all of his clerical life in the North at parishes in Belfast, Kilcoo and Newcastle, where he is buried. A photograph showing him in relaxed mood with De Valera and Frank Aiken confirms that he was at home in the highest of political circles.

Another song about Connolly, also entitled simply *James Connolly*, places the emphasis very much on the socialist aspect of his career. It is usually described as 'traditional' but was written by the Cork poet Patrick Galvin (born 1930) who is reputedly content to see the song pass anonymously into the folk tradition.

Where oh where is our James Connolly?
Where oh where is that gallant man?
He is gone to organise the union,
That working men may yet be free

Then who, then who, will lead the van?
Then who, then who, will lead the van?
Who but our James Connolly,
The hero of the working man.

Dominic Behan's *Connolly Was There*, set to the tune of *Brennan on the Moor*, also dwells mainly on Connolly's socialism.

There is a page in history when the worker first fought back,
When the might of exploitation first began to crack.
In farm and field and factory, in workshop, mine and mill
A flame was lit, a beacon bright, that flame is burning still.

Chorus
For Connolly was there, Connolly was there,
Bold, brave and undaunted, James Connolly was there.

William Martin Murphy and his Dublin millionaires
Tried bribery and corruption, hypocrisy and prayers,
To smash the Transport Union, their scabs they did enlist,
But all their graft was shattered by a scarlet iron first.

William Martin Murphy (1844-1919), from Bantry, Ireland's richest employer and bête noir of Irish socialists, was a press magnate and nationalist MP who described the Easter Rebellion as 'criminal and insane'. He is castigated in *Connolly Was There* because he founded the Dublin Employers Federation in 1912 to combat the Irish Transport and General Workers Union and because he led the employers during the Dublin strike and lockout of 1913.

The most recent song about Connolly, by Larry Kirwan of New York Irish band Black 47, contains a number of direct quotes from Connolly's speeches and writings. A storming piece of indignant and defiant rebelliousness, it is once again confusingly entitled *James Connolly*.

Marching down O'Connell Street with the Starry Plough on high,
There goes the Citizen Army with their fists raised in the sky.
Leading them is a mighty man with a mad rage in his eye;
'My name is James Connolly, I didn't come here to die,
But to fight for the rights of the working man, the small farmer too,
To protect the proletariat from the bosses and their screws.
So hold on to your rifles boys, don't give up your dream,
Of a republic for the working class, economic liberty'.

Connolly himself enjoyed a good chorus, mostly of the sentimental Irish variety and also tried his hand at versification with at least two of his lyrics being set to music.

A Rebel Song
Come workers sing a rebel song, a song of love and hate,
Of love unto the lowly, and hatred to the great,
The great who trod our fathers down, who steal our children's bread,
Whose hands of greed are stretched to rob the living and the dead.

Chorus
Then we sing a rebel song, as we proudly march along
To end the age-old tyranny that makes for human tears,
And our march is nearer done with each setting of the sun
For the tyrant's might is passing with the passing of the years.

The Watchword of Labour
Oh hear ye the watchword of labour, the slogan of those who'd be free,
That no more to any enslaver must we bend suppliant knee,
That we on whose shoulders are borne the pomp and the pride of the great,
Whose toil they repay with their scorn must challenge and master our fate.

Chorus
Then send it aloft on the breeze boys,
That watchword, the grandest we've known,
That labour must rise from its knees boys
And claim the broad earth for its own.

Although he didn't set foot in Ireland until he was fourteen years old and although he spent less than half of his life in it, there is no doubt about James Connolly's 'Irishness'. A principled moralist, a tolerant, honest and disciplined man, with little ego and no hypocrisy, who died as he had lived, poor but proud, he is enthusiastically welcomed into the pantheon of Irish heroes. Today his reputation rests mainly on his military role in 1916 but he is also admired for his life-long struggle to advance the social and economic conditions of ordinary people in an era when this was a daunting and thankless task.

He was born in Edinburgh in 1868, the third son of a poor Irish emigrant family. Little is known about the origins of his parents John and Mary (nee McGinn), thought to be from Monaghan. For a time John Connolly was employed as a carter removing the 'night soil' from the city streets, work that he must have found more congenial than trying to scrape a living in post-Famine Ireland.

The tenement where Connolly was born was demolished over a hundred years ago and the Sheriff Court now occupies the site. He is commemorated with a bronze plaque in the Cowgate, a continuation of the Grassmarket, at the southeast abutment of George IV Bridge.

To the memory of James Connolly
Born 6th June 1868 at 107 Cowgate
Renowned international and trade union
And working class leader
Founder of Irish Socialist Republican Party
Member of Provisional Government
of Irish Republic
Executed 12th May 1916 at Kilmainham Jail Dublin

Connolly had started work at the age of eleven and at fourteen joined the British Army where he gained the military experience that was to prove useful thirty years later. The boy was well informed, for he had joined a regiment that he knew was to be posted to Ireland. While still a teenager he was by his own admission a 'nationalist of the extreme type' who 'devoured the publications of the Land League'. In 1890 he married Lillie Reynolds, a Dublin Protestant. The couple were to have a large family and to remain devoted to each other for the remainder of their lives. Over the next few years they lived in Dundee and Edinburgh with Connolly scraping a living from labouring jobs, including 'carting' like his father, while immersing himself in self-education and socialist activism. In 1896 he returned to Ireland to work for the Dublin Socialist Club and founded Ireland's first socialist newspaper, the *Worker's Republic.* In 1903 he went to America where he spent the next seven years, working as a labourer, journalist, union organiser and political propagandist. However, although he could earn a living wage there, he never settled and was always on the lookout to return to Ireland.

The poverty in the Irish countryside prior to the land reform of the 1880s is well known. However the abysmal circumstances of many in the towns has received less attention. Even Connolly, who had personal experience of slum conditions in both Edinburgh and Belfast, was shocked at what he found in Dublin. Many families lived in one-roomed, damp and disease-ridden slums with hopelessly inadequate sanitation and sewage services. Tuberculosis was rife and the infant mortality rate was the highest in Western Europe. In truth it was said that the slums exhibited 'filth and stench inconceivable' and the disparaging British First World War recruiting slogan, 'The trenches are safer than the Dublin slums', had at least the virtue of being accurate. Perhaps the most telling statistic was that the average Dublin income was only 54 per cent of that in London although food prices were 7 per cent higher.

The long process of reform began with the arrival of Jim Larkin (1876-1947) in Belfast in 1907. That year the Dockers' Strike found the workers depressed and divided by sectarianism. Larkin struggled, without much success, to overcome this, though it was said 'half a dozen words from Jim Larkin and you were all together'. Despite support from the Independent Orange Order, the strike ended in failure after six months that had seen hardship, riots and the deaths of two innocent people shot by troops in the Falls Road. In the wake of the strike the Irish Transport and General Workers Union (ITGWU) was founded in 1909.

Relations between Larkin and Connolly were often strained, Connolly stating 'the man is utterly unreliable... he does not seem to want a democratic Labour Movement [but] a Larkinite Movement only'. 'I don't think I can stand Larkin as a boss much longer... he is consumed with jealousy and hatred of anyone who will not cringe to him.' Although Connolly 'cringed' to no one, his prime objective was to resist exploitative employers and he avoided an open confrontation with Larkin.

When Larkin was imprisoned in 1913 Connolly assumed the poisoned chalice of leadership of the labour movement. By this time the general political situation was in ferment and Connolly became involved in the republican as well as the socialist dimension of the struggle. The third Home Rule Bill of 1912 cleared the House of Commons and looked set to be approved by the reformed House of Lords. In the North the loyalist Ulster Volunteer Force was formed in January 1913 to defend the Union at all costs, or at least to keep Ulster, or as much of it as possible, British. For republicans however, the limited autonomy of Home Rule, with continued loyalty to monarch and empire, was of no interest. From Connolly's socialist perspective there was no point in swapping British capitalist 'masters' for Irish ones. As Larry Kirwan paraphrased Connolly:

> Oh citizens, this system is a curse,
> An English boss is a monster, an Irish one even worse.

The great Dublin 'Lockout', which began as a strike by the tramway workers employed by William Martin Murphy, started in August 1913. After six months the almost literally starving workers drifted back, beaten and humiliated. As Connolly put it, 'We Irish workers must again go down into hell'. At the outset of the strike Connolly had been jailed for three months but was released after a week on hunger strike. On 31 August the police killed two demonstrators in O'Connell Street and in response Connolly formed the Irish Citizen Army, whose flag was the Plough and Stars. A few weeks later the Irish Volunteers were formed as 'the open arm of the Irish Republican Brotherhood', according to Tom Clarke's widow

Kathleen, largely in response to government tolerance of the UVF in the north. In addition the underground Irish Republican Brotherhood (IRB), the remnants of the Fenian movement, was now plotting open revolt.

With the outbreak of the First World War in August 1914 Home Rule was suspended and Connolly, incensed at what he saw as working class Irishmen going off to fight Britain's 'capitalist' war, joined the IRB. The organisation was headed by Denis McCullough (1883-1968) but was dominated by its secret Military Council: Patrick Pearse, Eamonn Ceannt (Kent), Joseph Plunkett, Tom Clarke and Sean MacDiarmada (MacDermott). The driving force of the Military Council was Clarke, the most senior member and, after fifteen sanity-taxing years in a British prison, also the most uncompromising. By now Connolly was one of the leading advocates of armed revolt and mindful of Tone's dictum 'England's difficulty is Ireland's opportunity' stated, 'the time for Ireland's battle is NOW, the place for Ireland's battle is HERE'. On joining the IRB he discovered that the date of the Rising had been decided upon some six months previously, Easter 1916, chosen by Pearse as a quasi-religious symbol of resurrection and renewal.

Just before they set out from Liberty Hall, the Headquarters of the ITGWU, Connolly told the rebels that there would be no more Citizen Army and no more Volunteers, just a new unified organisation called the Irish Republican Army. Initially the rebels had entertained realistic hopes of military success as they calculated that there were only 6,000 troops and 10,000 police in the country whereas the Volunteers numbered 18,000. However various factors, not least the failure to secure arms from Germany, caused such hopes to be virtually abandoned. By now the rebel leaders, if not the rank and file, accepted that they had little hope of military victory, Connolly supposedly admitting, 'we are going to be slaughtered' and Michael 'The' O'Rahilly yelling, 'It is madness, but it is glorious madness'. By this time their aim was limited to making a dramatic, valiant and idealistic gesture, hoping to stir the latent nationalist sentiments of the vast majority of ordinary people.

On Easter Monday 24 April, on the stroke of the 'Angelus Bell o'er the Liffey's swell' at noon, Connolly issued the instruction, 'Left turn - the GPO – Charge!' and the rebellion had begun. An hour earlier Pearse, a thirty-six year old ascetic bachelor poet, a barrister and head of his own private school, had left his mother's middle class home in south Dublin, an overcoat covering his military uniform, and quietly cycled off to lead the rebellion. It took the government largely by surprise and the rebels seized control of a number of strategic buildings in the centre of Dublin, both north and south of the River Liffey. The main garrisons and commanders were:

The General Post Office, O'Connell Street: Pearse, Connolly, Plunkett, Clarke and MacDiarmada.

The South Dublin Union Workhouse, James's Street: Ceannt and Cathal Brugha.

Jacob's Biscuit Factory, Bishop Street: Thomas MacDonagh and John MacBride.

The Four Courts, Inns Quay: [John] Edward (Ned) Daly.

Mendicity Institution, Usher's Island Quay/Bridgefoot Street: Sean Heuston.

The Royal College of Surgeons, St Stephen's Green West: Michael Mallin and Constance Markievicz.

Boland's Bakery, Grand Canal Street: Eamonn De Valera.

Outside the front door of the General Post Office (GPO) orator supreme Patrick Pearse read out the Proclamation of the Irish Republic. It was signed, in the following order, by Clarke, MacDiarmada, MacDonagh, Pearse, Ceannt, Connolly and Plunkett, all members of the IRBs Military Council, Clarke's name appearing first in deference to his senior status. He may also have been offered the Presidency of the Provisional Republic and turned it down. Most modern historians attribute the provisional Presidency to Pearse. However Clark's widow Kathleen, admittedly not the most objective of commentators, disputes this, saying that in the death cell Clarke informed her that he had accepted the Presidency. What is not in dispute is that Clarke's name did appear first on the Proclamation and is the only one given a line to itself. The signing had taken place the previous Wednesday, 19 April, in an upstairs room of the home of the Wyse-Power family at 21 Henry Street. Mrs Jennie Wyse-Power was a founder member and vice-president of Cumann na mBan, 'the league of women', the female auxiliary corps of the Irish volunteers. Two and a half thousand copies of the Proclamation were then run off at Liberty Hall.

The Commander-in-Chief of the Irish Volunteers, Eoin MacNeill (1867-1945) had also been given the opportunity to sign but refused. A realist not a mystic, MacNeill, who had been kept ignorant of the Rebellion plans, ordered that the Rising be cancelled with a coded message in the *Sunday Independent*: 'All orders given to the Irish Volunteers for Easter Sunday are hereby rescinded'. The Military Council overruled this but the confusion resulted in delaying the Rebellion to Monday rather than the more symbolic Easter Sunday.

The rebels were quickly hemmed in by government troops and surrendered unconditionally on Saturday 29 April after the GPO and Liberty Hall were seriously damaged by relentless bombardment. Conditions in the GPO gradually became unbearable as heat, dust, stench and sleeplessness took their toll. It is no exaggeration, or nationalist propaganda, to say that the rebels fought with great courage and also acquitted themselves well militarily. Incredibly, Pearse, despite taking a 'sleeping draught', remained awake throughout the entire six days. No military strategist, he didn't personally fire a single shot, but he did demonstrate his incredible will and that his mystical rhetoric could inspire men to fight.

A few uncoordinated supportive actions, confused by MacNeill's cancellation order, had taken place in other parts of the country but these were of little military significance. Ten policemen lost their lives during the capture of their barracks at Ashbourne, Meath on 26 April. Near Fermoy, Cork, Royal Irish Constabulary Officer William Nelson Rowe died as Thomas Kent resisted arrest. The first fatal victim of the Rising had been forty-five year old Constable James O'Brien of the Dublin Metropolitan Police, on guard duty at the gates of Dublin Castle, the symbol of British occupation. He was killed by a shot from Sean Connolly, no relation to James, a captain in the Citizen Army. Sean Connolly was himself killed later in the week.

Although the Rebellion had lasted only six days, the willingness of the rebels to sacrifice their lives left the government in what was effectively a no-win situation. With a final death toll of 132 troops and police, 64 rebels and about 250 civilians, it could hardly ignore what it defined as treason, especially while engaged in a world war. Yet it was well aware that to execute the rebels would turn men widely regarded as cranks into martyrs and national heroes. Nevertheless it opted for execution and from the British perspective of the time it is difficult to see how they could have done otherwise. At least a further 2,000 were injured and much of O'Connell Street was a smoking ruin. Initially one hundred and twelve rebels were sentenced to death but only fifteen executions went ahead. The execution timetable read:

May 3: Patrick Pearse, Thomas MacDonagh, Thomas James Clarke
May 4: Edward Daly, Micheal Oh-Annrachan (Michael O'Hanrahan), William Pearse, Joseph Plunkett
May 5: John MacBride
May 8: Eamonn Ceannt, Cornelius Colbert, Sean Heuston, Michael Mallin
May 9: Thomas Kent (in Cork City)
May 12: Sean MacDiarmada, James Connolly

The less well-known names from the above deserve some consideration.

Oh-Annrachan: (born 1877) from New Ross, a writer and a life-long nationalist. Like many of the rebels he was of rebellious stock, with family members 'out' in both 1798 and 1867. An admirer described him as 'one of those modest, silent, earnest workers who do not seek applause'. To the British, 'he was an officer in the rebel army. There had been heavy firing and casualties in the neighbourhood where this man surrendered, [Jacob's Biscuit Factory]'.

Daly: (born 1891) from Limerick, an ardent republican whose father Edward had been jailed for Fenian activities as a seventeen-year-old in 1865 and whose uncle, John Daly, had served twelve years in prison with Tom Clarke. His sister Kathleen married Clarke in 1901. He was his parents' first-born son after eight daughters and, particularly as his father had died just before he was born, he occupied a special place in his mother's affections. She never fully recovered from his execution. Daly was described by the British as 'one of the most prominent extremists'.

Colbert: (born 1888) from Athea in County Limerick. *His* father too had been an active Fenian. He was a devout Catholic, fluent in Irish, a non-drinker and non-smoker, totally dedicated to his cause and consciously prepared to die for it. He commanded the garrisons at Watkins Brewery (Ardee Street) and Jameson's Distillery (Marrowbone Lane). The British described him as 'one of the most active members... took a prominent part in the organisation of the rebel army'.

Heuston: (born 1891) from Dublin. Like most of the rebels he joined and rose through the ranks of the Irish Volunteers. He worked as a clerk in Kingsbridge Railway Station, now Heuston Station. On Easter Monday morning he left his mother's house saying only that he was going on a 'route march'. The next his family heard of him was that he was being held in Kilmainham Gaol as one of the leaders of the Rebellion. He was described by the British as being 'in constant communication with the [rebel] leaders'.

Mallin: (born 1874) was a Dubliner, again of Fenian stock. Like Connolly, he joined the British Army as a boy soldier and served in South Africa during the Boer War, an experience that influenced his gradual evolution from loyal Crown servant to active Irish rebel. In civilian life he worked as a weaver and became Secretary of the Silk Weavers' Union in 1909. By 1914 he had risen to Chief of Staff of the Citizen Army. The British said of him, 'he commanded the rebels who occupied Stephens Green and the College of Surgeons [where there were] many casualties both among the military and civilians'.

The executions were by firing squad and took place in the yard at Kilmainham Gaol. The bodies were buried in quicklime without coffins in an attempt to destroy the remains, to prevent the graves within the grounds of Arbour Hill prison becoming political shrines. Before he died Connolly, who had long lapsed from the Catholicism of his youth, saying that he possessed 'not the slightest tincture of religious faith', for reasons known only to himself, went to confession and received communion from Father Aloysius, a Capuchin friar. The only rebel leader not held in Kilmainham, he was executed at the opposite end of the yard from the others, presumably because it was nearest to the gate that he was brought through from Dublin Castle. A simple black cross marks the execution spot.

The executions proved to be a serious political miscalculation and as the news spread, the public mood changed. Their drip-drip effect and the particularly emotive circumstances of some of them contributed to this. Connolly had been badly wounded by a dumdum bullet in the ankle. Despite the drugs, he suffered severe pain and had to be stretchered in and strapped to a chair to be shot. Plunkett was already dying from tuberculosis and added to the pathos by getting married just hours before his death. (His widow Grace Gifford, whose sister Muriel was married to Thomas MacDonagh, would later be held in Kilmainham during the Civil War.) Willie Pearse was just one of about sixteen hundred ordinary volunteers, victimised because he was Patrick's brother. Daly and O'Hanrahan were not considered major leaders and Sir Roger Casement, executed in London on 3 August, had never hurt anyone. Non-participant journalists Patrick McIntyre and Thomas Dickson were shot dead on 26 April. Francis Sheehy-Skeffington, a well-known pacifist writer was also shot after witnessing another murder by a British officer, who was found guilty but of 'unsound mind' and released after eighteen months. By the end of the year public opinion had changed irrevocably and celebratory bonfires and torchlight processions greeted the return from internment in Wales of six hundred previously suspect and often-despised rebels. The new political reality was confirmed at the ballot box on 3 February 1917 when a revamped Sinn Féin, which had not participated in the Rising and previously without enough support to even put up candidates, enjoyed its first ever electoral success at Roscommon. The victorious candidate was Joseph Plunkett's father. Westminster was now ignored in favour of the provisional Dáil in Dublin. The once great Nationalist Party of Parnell was finished. Home Rule was no longer enough.

On the first anniversary of the Rising the orange, white and green flag, symbolic of Catholic and Protestant equality and reconciliation, flew at half-mast from the GPO and people stopped in the street to salute. On 10 July 1917 De Valera, just out of prison, won East Clare for Sinn Féin. On 25 September Thomas Ashe, leader of the Ashbourne raid, died on hunger strike. In December 1918 in the first General Election under a new franchise, which had almost tripled the electorate, Sinn Féin won 73 of the

105 seats throughout Ireland. In Ulster though Unionists won 23 seats. The country was ominously divided.

On 21 January 1919 the IRA ambush at Soloheadbeg launched the War of Independence, leading to the eventual establishment of the Republic and the creation of Northern Ireland. The struggle for Irish independence, which might be said to have begun with Hugh O'Neill's victory at Clontibret in 1595, was finally though not completely successful. Today the names of the men who had brought it about are liberally commemorated in the streets, stations, public parks, bridges, buildings and songs of Ireland. Foremost among them is a man described by the British surgeon who attended him in his final hours as 'the bravest man I have ever known', *James Connolly*.

Photo: John McLaughlin

The Shannon Bridge (looking towards Ballina) where the Scariff Martyrs died

19.

The Scarriff Martyrs

The dreadful news through Ireland has spread from shore to shore
For such a deed no living man has ever heard before,
The deeds of Cromwell in his time I'm sure no worse could do
Than those Black and Tans who murdered those four youths in Killaloe.

Three of the four were on the run and searched for all around
Until with this brave Egan in Williamstown was found.
They asked him were the boys inside, to the rebels he proved true
And because he would not sell the pass he was shot in Killaloe.

On the 16th of November, that day of sad renown
They were sold and traced through Galway to that house in Williamstown.
They never got a fighting chance but were captured while asleep
And the way that they ill-treated them would cause your blood to creep.

They shackled them tight both hands and feet with twines they couldn't break
And they brought them down to Killaloe by steamer on the lake.
Without clergy, judge or jury on the bridge they shot them down
And their blood flowed with the Shannon convenient to the town.

With three days perseverance their bodies they let go.
At ten pm their funeral passed through Ogonnoloe.
They were kept in Scarriff chapel for two nights and a day,
Now in that house of rest they lie, kind people for them pray.

If you were at their funeral, it was a dreadful sight
To see the local clergy and they all dressed in white.
Such a sight of these four martyrs in one grave was never seen.
They died to save the flag they loved, the orange, white and green.

And now that they are dead and gone I hope in peace they'll rest,
Like all brave Irish heroes forever with the blessed.
The day will come when all will know who sold the lives away
Of young McMahon, Rodgers, brave Egan and Kildea.

The Scarriff Martyrs

The War of Independence, the Black and Tans, Death on the Shannon

This bleak ballad, set during the War of Independence, tells the story of four IRA men shot dead on 17 November 1920 *while in police custody*. Appropriately the melody is slow and sad and, coupled with the resigned tone of the lyrics, results in a bitter lament that tugs hard at the emotions. The men were shot on the Shannon bridge that connects Killaloe in Clare with Ballina in Tipperary. The four who died were Michael Egan, Lieutenant Martin Kildea (or Gildea), Adjutant Michael 'Brud' McMahon and Captain Alphonsus 'Alfie' Rodgers (or Rogers).

Mike Egan was, if not an IRA member, certainly a sympathiser, providing shelter for the 'three of the four [who] were on the run'. The song's reference to Galway is misleading for although Williamstown is a North Galway village the men were not in that area, or even in that county. Martin Kildea however was a Galway man and perhaps this is the source of the confusion. It's known that they were in hiding at Williamstown House, in County Clare, where Mike Egan was employed as a handyman.

The murders marked the culmination of a chain of events that began with De Valera's East Clare election victory in 1917, confirming the sea change in Irish politics brought about by the Easter Rebellion. His first campaign speech had been in Scarriff and locals believed that the town was thereafter singled out by the 'security forces' for special attention. The IRA, sometimes in groups two hundred strong, became very active in the area. By spring 1920 the police had withdrawn from barracks in Tuamgraney, Mountshannon and Whitegate, all in the Scarriff area. The Scarriff courthouse was also attacked and set alight, court records destroyed, 'British justice' in flames. On 18 September 1920 the barracks in Scarriff itself were besieged, the attack lasting five hours, to three o'clock the following morning. A local unionist, Robert Hibbert, complained 'as there are no police and no petty sessions there is no redress'. British control was slipping away.

The security forces would have had a good idea of the identity of some of the men behind the attacks and determined to get even, one way or another. Williamstown House was a local 'Big House' where Mike Egan, age 27, lived in one of the outbuildings. The house was located near Whitegate, a few miles north east of Scarriff, on the shores of Lough Derg, the 'lake' of the ballad. At midday on 16 November about thirty-five Auxiliaries under a Colonel Andrews, almost certainly acting on a tip-off, raided the house as the IRA men slept, presumably having been 'out' the night before. There was no chance of a warning as the 'Auxies' had approached unseen and unsuspected from the Lough, short-circuiting the IRA's effective, but land-only, lookout system. They had commandeered *The Shannon*, the 'steamer on the lake', a familiar vessel belonging to the Shannon Navigation Authority, whose apparently routine approach to Williamstown Harbour aroused no suspicion. Mike Egan was busy trimming a hedge when he was seized.

The four men, along with two passers-by, brothers John and Michael Conway, were arrested and transported south to Ballina, arriving at dusk. The prisoners were taken into the Lakeside Hotel where they were interrogated and tortured. The Conway brothers were threatened and roughly handled but not tortured. John Conway later revealed, 'Alfie Rodgers was pumping blood... I'd say he had lost all his blood before he was shot at all.' At midnight a party of Auxiliaries and Black and Tans, by now drunk, manhandled the semi-conscious men halfway across the bridge and shot them dead. Aware that they were about to die the men pleaded, in vain, for a priest. However on hearing the shots, priests on both sides of the bridge gave 'conditional absolution'. Afterwards Father Russell, in Ballina, stated, 'God heard their last request'.

Next day autopsies revealed that the men had all been shot from the front at point blank range, unlikely if not impossible of men trying to escape. Each body had at least seventeen bullet wounds. In the House of Commons the Chief Secretary, in reply to a question from Galway MP T.P. O'Connor, stated, 'The police and military were entitled to fire on persons attempting to escape who refused to halt when called upon'. For Britain it was just another incident in a dirty war and for them the matter was closed. On 18 June 1921 Williamstown House was burned down, a probable indication that it was seen as the source of the information that 'sold the lives away'.

Such events were all too common, now of necessity grouped together by historians as 'several atrocities', all but forgotten, except by the ballad singers. For example, a very similar 'incident' took place in Roscommon in April 1921 when John Bergin and Stephen McDermott were also summarily executed after being taken prisoner, commemorated in *The Woodlands of Loughglinn*.

A noble Irishman was he, John Bergin was his name.
He belonged to Tipperary and from Nenagh town he came,
But now thank God that he has gone away from harm and sin.
He fought till death and then he left the Woodlands of Loughglinn.

McDermott too was brave and true from the plains near Bellanagare,
He's missed at many's the fireside in homes both near and far,
He's missed at home in Blackloon by his own dear kith and kin,
His comrades true will miss him too in the Woodlands of Loughglinn.

The killings took place during the War of Independence (or Anglo-Irish War), a guerrilla struggle, vicious, bloody and unpredictable, fought out between the IRA and the Royal Irish Constabulary, later augmented by the 'Black and Tans' and the Auxiliary Division: 'Peelers, Tans and Auxies'. Officially the War ended in 1921 but the long and tortuous process that began in 1916, or maybe 1169, has continued intermittently until the present day.

The conflict is usually dated from 21 January 1919 after the Soloheadbeg Ambush at a quarry about two miles directly north of Tipperary town, ostensibly in search of explosives. Two policemen were killed, James McDonnell, from Belmullet (born 1862) and Patrick O'Connell, from Coachford (born 1882). The attack was carried out by a group of nine men, including Dan Breen of Grange, near Donohill (1894-1969), Sean Hogan of Donohill (1900-68), Sean Treacy of Soloheadbeg (1895-1920) and Seamas Robinson (1890-1961). This quartet has gone down in history as 'The Big Four'. The group was completed by Tadgh (Tim) Crowe of Soloheadbeg, Patrick [O'] Dwyer of Hollyford, Michael Ryan of Grange, Patrick McCormack of Dundrum and Jack O'Meara of Ballyhone, Emly, who was killed in action in 1921. With the exception of Robinson, who was from Belfast, the men all came from within a few miles radius of Soloheadbeg. Robinson, having fought in the Easter Rising and being imprisoned in its aftermath, was elected Commandant. The fatal shots are usually said to have been fired by Sean Treacy. Patrick McCormack, the last surviving member of the ambush party, died in 1982.

The attack was a calculated attempt to raise the political stakes by provoking a British reaction. A few months beforehand Treacy, a local farmer frustrated at the lack of activity had said, 'we'll have to kill someone and make the bloody enemy organise us'. Breen concurred: 'The gelignite was only incidental'. In his memoirs, published in 1924, he showed little remorse at the police deaths, dismissing the dead men as 'peelers, deserters, spies and hirelings', guilty of collaborating with a foreign government. Later in life, however, he stated that he had a 'horror of taking life', but believed the British treatment of Ireland left him with no choice. 'The thing that always hurt me', he said, 'was... the taking from us of our culture and the genocide of the starvation in '47'. He could also remember 'the last eviction which took place one mile from Grange.

Michael Dywer Ban, a relative of ours, was ejected from his home and died on the roadside. This event left an indelible impression on my mind'.

In his brief military career Sean Treacy became an IRA legend after being killed in a gun battle in Dublin. He was due to be married eleven days later. Treacy, an ascetic young man in the mould of Pearse and the yet unborn Sean South, was driven, as historian Calton Younger has written, 'by the silent power of a high voltage electric current'. Like most patriots before and since he is commemorated in numerous ballads, most famously in *Tipperary So Far Away*. The first and last verses are:

> The sun had set with its golden rays and the bitter fight was o'er.
> Our brave boys sleep beneath the clay, on this earth they are no more.
> The moonbeams shone on the battlefield where a dying rebel lay,
> His arms were crossed on his body outstretched and his life's blood
>   flowed away.

> The soldiers of Ireland bore him on high, on their shoulders with
>   solemn tread
> And many a heart with a tearful sigh wept for our patriot dead.
> In silence they lowered him into the grave to await for the reckoning day,
> Sean Treacy who died his home to save, Tipperary so far away.

Another bitter ballad, *Sean Treacy*, commences:

> Give me a Parabellum and a bandoleer of shells,
> I'll wait in ambush for some men and I'll blow them all to hell.
> For just today I heard them say that Treacy met defeat.
> Our lovely Sean is dead and gone, shot down in Talbot Street.

The gunfight took place in a shop at 94 Talbot Street, Dublin (then a gent's outfitters and a popular republican haunt, now a ladies' hairdressers). Treacy killed two British soldiers, Sergeant Christian and Lieutenant Price, before he himself was hit. Two civilians, caught in the crossfire, also died. With the wonderful asset of hindsight it's hard to imagine why Treacy, one of the most wanted men in Ireland, ever ventured anywhere near 94 Talbot Street. He must surely have known that the shop, owned by senior IRA officer Peadar Clancy, was under regular, if not constant surveillance.

Today Talbot Street, near O'Connell Street, is a busy shopping area and as tourists hunt for souvenirs few notice the small commemorative bronze plaque to a man cut down in his prime there over eighty years ago.

> In Memory of Vice Brigadier Sean Treacy
> 3rd (South) Tipperary Brigade
> Killed in action by British forces outside this house
> 14th Oct 1920

Sean Hogan survived but was imprisoned by the Free State from 1923 to 1932, when he was released 'looking old but unyielding'. The Soloheadbeg Ambush also provides a link with one of Ireland's best-known patriots, Sir Roger Casement (1864-1916). After the attack Breen and Hogan hid out locally for a few days but then headed for the safe house of Father Dick McCarthy in West Limerick. They were driven by Thomas McInerny, who had been the only survivor when the car he was driving plunged into sixty feet of water at Ballykissane Pier, near Killorglin in April 1916. The men were attempting to rendezvous with Casement after his gunrunning mission in Germany. A witness, Jeremiah Murphy, herding cattle near Barraduff about ten miles east of Killarney recorded, 'It almost ran me over. I was surprised the car got as far as it did, for it was travelling at high speed with dim lights on a dark night. It hit a cow but never slowed down'. At Killorglin Thomas McInerney took a wrong turn, ending up on the wrong side of the tidal River Laune, and in his anxiety to get back on schedule overshot Ballykissane Pier. Those who died were Con Keating of Cahersiveen, Charles Monaghan of Belfast and Donal Sheehan of Newcastlewest.

Casement and the three men drowned are commemorated in the compelling dirge *Banna Strand*.

'Twas on Good Friday morning just at the break of day,
A German ship was lying there at anchor in the baym
She had 20,000 rifles there, all ready for to landm
But no answering signal came from lonely Banna Strand,

A motor car was dashing through the early morning gloom,
A sudden crash and in the sea three brave boys met their doom,
Three Irish boys lay dying there just like their hopes so grand
And could not give the signal now on lonely Banna Strand.

They took Sir Roger prisoner in chains to London town
And in their court they named him a traitor to the Crown,
Said he, 'I am no traitor, not to my native land
And I'd bring more German rifles to lonely Banna Strand'.

The Black and Tans were formed in January 1920 and the Auxiliary Division six months later. Both were additional security personnel recruited in Britain as a result of the inability of the Royal Irish Constabulary (RIC) to contain the IRA. The RIC was not equipped to fight a guerrilla war and its effectiveness was further reduced by IRA attacks, intimidation and boycotting which resulted in a decline in morale, a drop-off in recruitment and an increase in resignations. The Auxiliaries were ex-army officers and paid at twice the rate of the Black and Tans, a generous pound per day.

At their peak these special forces totalled about ten thousand men, the Black and Tans taking their sobriquet from their hurriedly put together mismatched uniform. They quickly gained a reputation for being ruthless, brutal and indiscriminating. They were sent in with a free hand to stamp out the IRA, as the legalised Scarriff murders show. However many Tan atrocities did come in reaction to deadly attacks on them, but while the IRA attacked only the 'security forces' (and their 'collaborators'), the Tans lashed out at the whole community, in the process killing, terrorising and torturing thousands of non-combatants. The vicious cycle of retaliation, reprisal and revenge is well illustrated by the chain of events associated with the 'sack of Balbriggan', a village about twenty miles north of Dublin.

On 20 September 1920 RIC Head Constable Peter Burke from Glenamaddy was having a drink with his brother in a Balbriggan hotel when he was shot dead by the IRA. The Tans reacted by speeding into the village during the night. They shot two people dead, looted and burned four pubs, fired into houses, burned a factory (ironically belonging to an English company), burned nineteen houses and wrecked thirty more. Another rebel song *The Bold Black and Tan* bitterly records the events.

> The town of Balbriggan they burned to the ground,
> While bullets like hailstones were whizzing around,
> Families left homeless by this evil clan.
> He waged war on our children, the bold Black and Tan.

The following day a sixty-strong IRA group attacked a Tan convoy at Dineen in County Clare and killed six of them. 'The dead were a gruesome and bloody sight,' said one of the attackers later. 'The Black and Tans then ran riot in Lahinch and neighbouring Ennistymon, killing three, including an old man and a twelve year old boy... a few days later the IRA destroyed Trim police barracks... immediately over two hundred Tans and Auxiliaries looted and burned Trim...'

Regular dramatic and emotional incidents kept levels of tension and expectancy high. On 25 October 1920 Terence MacSwiney, Commander of Cork No. 1 IRA Brigade (and Lord Mayor of Cork), died in prison in London after seventy-four days on hunger strike. (The well-known song *Shall My Soul Pass Through Old Ireland* deals with MacSwiney's final hours.) On 1 November eighteen-year-old medical student Kevin Barry was executed for his part in the death of a soldier. On 21 November, the original Irish Bloody Sunday, just four days after the deaths of *The Scarriff Martyrs*, the IRA killed fourteen British intelligence officers in a ruthless but expertly co-ordinated action in Dublin. The identity of the IRA men involved remains shadowy but one is thought to have been Sean Lemass

(1899-1971) who succeeded De Valera as Taoiseach in 1959. The 'enigmatic patriot' never publicly confirmed or denied his participation saying only 'execution squads don't have reunions'. Sean Russell, head of the IRA in the 30s, is also thought to have been involved. That afternoon the Black and Tans took revenge against a soft target when they killed eleven spectators and one player with indiscriminate fire at the Dublin - Cork football match at Croke Park, Dublin. Later that day the Auxiliaries murdered three prisoners being held in Dublin Castle, IRA officers Dick McKee and Peadar Clancy who with Michael Collins had planned the Bloody Sunday assassinations. Also killed was Conor Clune, often now regarded as innocent, caught in the wrong place at the wrong time. Like the Scarriff victims all three were shot 'while trying to escape'.

The following Sunday the IRA, commanded by twenty-two year old Tom Barry, killed seventeen of an eighteen-strong Auxiliary patrol at a bend in the road two miles south of Kilmichael in Cork. The republican success is commemorated in the triumphalist ballad *The Boys of Kilmichael*, written within weeks of the 'battle', possibly by local teacher Jeremiah O'Mahony. The song is based on William Rooney's *The Men of the West* (1902). The tune is traditional, best known as *Rosin the Bow*.

While we honour in song and in story, the memory of Pearse and McBride
Whose names are illumined in glory, brave martyrs for Ireland they died,
Forget not the boys of Kilmichael, who feared not the might of the foe,
The day that they marched into battle, they laid all the Black and Tans low.

Chorus
So here's to the boys of Kilmichael, those brave men so gallant and true,
They fought for the green flag of Erin and conquered the red, white and blue.

Their wages are twice that of Tommy [Atkins, the regular soldier] and
   twice Tommy's killing they do ,
They're burning up women and children and they boast of the prisoners slew.
But ten times their pay and fancies went out on the lonely hillside,
For the Irish Republican Army, they scattered the Tans far and wide.

On the 28th day of November outside of the town of Macroom
The Tans in their big Crossley tenders went hurtling on to their doom,
For the boys of the column were waiting as any proud rebel can tell
And the Irish Republican Army blew all their battalions to hell.

That brave noble band of coercion with terror and villainy proved
That whatever Lloyd George's assertion the rebels would never be moved,
For up in the hills we were waiting with hand grenade, nitro and shot
And the Irish Republican Army wiped all of them out on the spot.

The sun in the west it was sinking, 'twas the eve of a cold winter's day
When the Tans we were wearily waiting, drove up the spot where we lay.
Then over the hills came the echo, the peal of the rifle and gun
And the flames of the tenders sent tidings that the boys of Kilmichael had won.

The lorries were ours before twilight and high over Dunmanway town
Our banners in triumph were waving to show that the Tans had gone down,
So we gathered our rifles and bayonets and then left the glen so secure,
We never drew rein till we halted at the faraway camp of Granure.

The Auxiliaries are more sympathetically commemorated with a bronze plaque in Macroom, recording the name and rank of twenty-nine government victims of the conflict, including those killed at Kilmichael. The IRA also lost three men in the encounter: Jim O'Sullivan, Michael McCarthy, who had reconnoitred the scene with Barry, and sixteen-year-old Michael Deasy (a brother of Liam Deasy, commander of the West Cork IRA), who ignored warnings to stay clear of the area. 'The faraway camp' was an isolated cottage in the townland of Granure (or Garranure), eleven miles south of Kilmichael, across the Bandon River near Ballincarriga.

The 'boys' of Kilmichael comprised thirty-seven local men aged between sixteen and thirty-five. In the next couple of years most of them would be imprisoned, wounded or killed. The majority remained republican rather than Free State and a number took part in the ambush that killed fellow Cork man Michael Collins at Beal na mBlath, ten miles east of Kilmichael, near Crookstown. 'Whatever Lloyd George's assertion' is a direct riposte to the claim by British Prime Minister David Lloyd George (1863-1945) that 'we have murder by the throat'. It wasn't so much his statement that the security forces were gaining the upper hand that angered the IRA but his assertion that they were engaged in 'murder' rather than 'war'.

Shortly after Kilmichael martial law was declared in Cork, Kerry, Limerick and Tipperary. Crown forces immediately 'celebrated' by burning large parts of Cork City to the ground, causing millions of pounds worth of damage. A couple of months later on 28 February 1921, also in Cork, six IRA prisoners were shot dead. The IRA immediately retaliated by killing six British soldiers. By now martial law had been extended to Clare, Kilkenny, Waterford and Wexford. The war continued relentlessly with neither side having a monopoly on blame or shame.

For many, the police had long been seen as symbols and upholders of British rule, takers of the King's shilling. The ordinary members though, were in the main just raw country youths, strictly disciplined, poorly educated and badly paid, often isolated in barracks far away from their own areas: an attempt to make them less amenable to local 'persuasion'.

Most were simply trying to earn a living but were caught between two political stools and as a result suffered badly both physically and socially. The RIC, based on the Robert Peel's 'Peelers' of 1814, had been founded as a paramilitary force in the politically charged climate of 1867, mainly to maintain civil law but also to combat the threat posed by the Fenians. In the more settled later years of the century, with Home Rule rather than republicanism dominant, they had become better accepted.

However with the outbreak of the War of Independence the police were again thrust back into the political arena as the first line of defence against the most determined, and probably the rebels with the most popular support, that the authorities had ever confronted: the IRA. During the gradually escalating violence they lost about three hundred and fifty men in just over eighteen months and a total of 549 between 1916 and 1922.

Many of the names on the RIC death list are among the most quintessentially Irish imaginable: Boylan, Brady, Brennan, Conlon, Coughlan, Cronin, Delaney, Doyle, Duffy, Fallon, Finegan, Fitzgerald, Flaherty, Flynn, Healy, Higgins, Hughes, Hurley, Keane, Kelly, Kinsella, Lynch, McDonagh, McKenna, Maguire, Malone, Mulrooney, Murphy, O'Brien, O'Connor, O' Hanlon, O' Leary, Quinn, Reilly, Roche, Ryan, Shannon, Sweeny, Tobin and Walsh. Eamonn Ceannt was the son of an RIC man, as was Tom Barry. The 'Anglo-Irish' War was therefore also a civil war and the conflict is indeed more accurately described as The War of Independence as the IRA waged war against anyone, British or Irish, Catholic or Protestant who opposed their ideal of an independent thirty-two county republic.

After an agonisingly drawn out period of anticipation, rumour and behind-the-scenes political activity the War ended with a Truce on 9 July 1921 and the Anglo-Irish Treaty was signed on 6 December. As a result the 'Twenty-Six Counties' gained eventual republican status. The remaining six counties of Antrim, Armagh, Derry, Down, Fermanagh and Tyrone formed the 'statelet' of Northern Ireland and remained within the United Kingdom. The Irish signatories of the Treaty were Robert Barton, Michael Collins, Eamonn Duggan, George Gavan Duffy, a grandson of Young Irelander Charles Gavan Duffy, and Arthur Griffith. After an acrimonious debate on 7 January 1922 the Dáil ratified the Treaty by sixty-four votes to fifty-seven. Disagreement over its acceptance resulted in the Irish Civil War, in the continued intermittent IRA campaign of the 30s, 40s, 50s and 60s and in the last thirty years of 'Troubles' in Northern Ireland.

The geography of *The Scarriff Martyrs* is dominated by the River Shannon (*Sionainn*), 'ancient goddess' or 'old one', the longest river in Ireland or Britain. It begins its journey on a remote hillside near Dowra in north-west Cavan, flows through the major Loughs of Allen, Ree and Derg before joining the Atlantic some two hundred and thirty miles later beyond Limerick.

Scarriff (*An Scairbh*), 'rocky ford', a small town about ten miles north of Killaloe is set just back from the Lough in hilly farm country. Ogonnoloe (*Ó gConaile*), '[territory] of the Ui Chonaile', is a village a few miles south of Scarriff. Four horse-drawn hearses carried the men's bodies home to Scarriff 'through Ballyvanna to the top of Ogonnolle Hill, through the winding turns of Raheen to Scarriff's bridge where Father John Clancy was waiting'.

Killaloe (*Cill Dalua*), 'church of Dalua', at the southern end of Lough Derg, is a major crossing point of the Shannon as it narrows and is spanned by the thirteen-arch bridge where the four subjects of the ballad met their tragic fate. A monument on the north side of the bridge marks the precise spot, identified by the bloodstains. Although the inscription is now faded and almost illegible, it nevertheless still stands as a poignant reminder. Two other monuments also commemorate the events, at Tuamgraney just south of Scarriff and in the graveyard of Scarriff Chapel where the men were buried on Saturday 20 November 1920.

The area has many major historical associations. A thousand years ago Brian Boru's fabled 'Royal Kincora' stood a mile upriver from Killaloe. In 1691 Patrick Sarsfield forded the Shannon at the same point as he set out to raid the Williamite arms train at Ballyneety. In 1920 four 'ordinary' young men of the district also did what they believed to be best for Ireland and it cost them their lives. Though their names will never be compared with Brian Boru and Patrick Sarsfield, they will always be remembered because of a song called *The Scarriff Martyrs*.

IRA in County Donegal during the War of Independence

20.

The Drumboe Martyrs

'Twas the feast of St Patrick by the dawn of the day,
The hills of Tirconnaill stood sombre and gray,
When the first light of morning illumined the sky,
Four brave Irish soldiers were led forth to die.

Three left their loved homes in Kerry's green vale
And one came from Derry to fight for the Gael,
But instead of true friends they met traitors and foe
And uncoffined were laid in the woods of Drumboe.

They were Enright, O'Sullivan, and Daly by name,
From the counties of Kerry and Derry they came,
And gallant Sean Larkin from the banks of the Roe
Completes the four martyrs shot dead at Drumboe.

Four republican soldiers were dragged from their cells
Where for months they suffered wild torments like hell.
No mercy they asked from their pitiless foe
And no mercy was shown by the thugs at Drumboe.

The church bells rang out in the clear morning air
To summon the faithful to penance and prayer
When a crash from the woodlands struck terror and woe
'Twas the death knell of Daly, shot dead at Drumboe.

Let Tirconaill n'er boast of her honour and fame,
All the waters of Finn could not wash out her shame.
While the Foyle and the Swilly continue to flow
That stain will remain on the woods of Drumboe.

The Drumboe Martyrs
The Civil War, Death in Donegal

This little known and seldom performed song deals with a terrible 'incident' in 1923 during the Irish Civil War when four young Republicans were executed by the recently established Free State government at Stranorlar in Donegal. The incident was too common to rate more than a footnote in a few specialist history books and only a grim song serves as a grim reminder. Without it, the memory of the Drumboe Martyrs would have faded into oblivion, like the deaths of so many others.

The ballad was written by Michael (Mick) McGinley (1852-1940), from the townland of Breenagh, about ten miles west of Letterkenny. During the course of my research I had the pleasure of speaking with Mick McGinley's ninety-seven-year-old son Anthony (Tony), born in February 1905. A little hard of hearing but speaking of the events as if they were yesterday, proudly and loudly he told me that his father 'was a Fenian and an IRB man' and that 'he wrote a poem' about the executions at Drumboe. Tony, who had just turned eighteen at the time, remembered the events of that morning clearly: 'My mother, always an early riser, came running into the house saying she heard shots. My father said quietly, that'll be the firing squad at Drumboe'.

Mick McGinley's other well-known song is *The Hills of Glenswilly*, written in 1878 on board ship for New Zealand and suffering from homesickness. Two years later he returned to Ireland and worked on the family farm for many years. In 1914 he sold it and bought a pub in Market Street, Strabane. The pub never had an official name but was known locally as 'The Irish Pub', an indication of its owner's life-long political convictions.

The Drumboe Martyrs has captured well the feel of the traditional ballad, simple, direct and passionate. It is an angry, sombre, terse and bitter lament, using strong, uncompromising language like 'traitor', 'merciless' and 'thugs', for it deals with the real deaths of real people. Allied with the beautiful melody, accompanied by traditional instruments and in the hands of a good vocalist the final package makes a fitting tribute to the memory of four young men who died before their time. Nowhere however does the ballad say that the events occurred during the Civil War and the reader or listener could easily be forgiven for mistakenly assuming that they were the result of British action.

The Irish Civil War saw Irishman pitted against Irishman, 'green against green' and it produced ruthlessness and rivalries on a par with anything seen in the War of Independence. Former friends and fellow fighters became bitter and deadly enemies as communities and even families were split. A week before Drumboe eight men died at Ballyseedy, just south of Tralee, when they were used as human shields and blown up by their fellow countrymen and erstwhile brothers-in-arms. It was the third such incident in the area within five days in which a total of seventeen men died. An estimated total of a thousand people lost their lives in the conflict.

The Anglo-Irish Treaty of 1921 created a fundamental split in the Republican Movement, one that persists to the present day. An important element of the Treaty, a re-examination of the border under the Boundary Commission, was allowed to drift by the British government under pressure and non-co-operation from unionists. The supporters of the Treaty had hoped that those parts of the North with nationalist majorities like areas of Armagh, Fermanagh, Tyrone and the City of Derry would be ceded to the Free State. This would have left the remainder of Northern Ireland, already just about 18 per cent of the total area of Ireland, as an economically and politically non-viable rump, which would then be reunited with the rest of the country. It is sometimes argued that the distraction of the Civil War allowed the British to sideline the Commission. Ironically therefore the anti-Treatyites, including *The Drumboe Martyrs*, could be seen as having unwittingly contributed to the failure of their own cause.

In 1922 those who accepted the Treaty as the best deal with the British then available became known as 'Free Staters' and they formed a big majority in the country as a whole. However within the active Republican Movement the anti-Treaty faction was in a majority. These fundamentalists contained many senior IRA men, some of whom had carved out reputations as national heroes in the War of Independence. The result was a kind of national schizophrenia. The Civil War is usually regarded as lasting from June 1922 to May 1923 but there were victims well into the next few years as no formal peace settlement was ever agreed. Despite winning the war, the Free Staters lost more men than the republicans.

A general election in the Twenty-Six Counties on 16 June 1922 had left the Sinn Féin pro-Treaty faction as the largest party by a considerable margin, with over 60 per cent more seats than the anti-Treaty faction. However some republicans argued, probably with some justification, that the election campaign had been less than democratic. Subsequently the simmering frustrations, uncertainties and resentments of the previous six months began to take the form of military action.

On 17 June, republicans in search of arms raided Kildare police barracks. Five days later in London republicans assassinated Field Marshall Sir Henry Wilson (1864-1922), Unionist MP for North Down and military adviser to the Northern Ireland government. Wilson had long been a republican bogeyman, for many reasons: the Curragh Mutiny in March 1914, the founding of the Ulster Special Constabulary, his personal attacks on Michael Collins and his perceived role in the Belfast pogroms of the early 1920s. Two IRA men, Reginald Dunne, one of Michael Collins' 'top men', and Joseph O'Sullivan, who had lost a leg during the First World War, were hanged for his murder on 10 August 1922. Whether they had acted independently as 'dissidents' or with official IRA sanction is unclear. Historian Robert Kee however has no doubts, stating plainly, 'The killing had been carried out on the order of [Michael] Collins'. IRA historian Uinseann MacEoin also states that the Field Marshall was killed 'on an order, delayed, from Michael Collins'. Dunne and O'Sullivan's remains were reburied at an IRA funeral in Dublin in 1967.

After the assassination the British demanded action to curb the violence. Open warfare broke out on 28 June when Free State troops attacked and captured the republicans' HQ, the Four Courts in Dublin, after an ultimatum to surrender had been ignored. It was at this point (not in 1916) that many irreplaceable documents in the Public Records Office went up in smoke.

The anti-Treaty faction was effectively defeated within a couple of months but under their irreconcilable Chief of Staff Liam Lynch (1890-1923) persisted with the unequal struggle, employing the guerrilla tactics used during the War of Independence. Michael Collins (born 1890), the 'Big Fella' of the struggle against the British and one of the chief signatories of the Treaty, was himself killed in an ambush at Bealnablath, near Macroom on 22 August.

Of all the major rebel leaders, Collins is one of the least known in song, though many songs have been written about him. These include *The Laughing Boy* by Brendan Behan, *Michael* by Johnny McEvoy, and *The Ballad of Michael Collins* by Donagh MacDonagh, son of the executed leader of 1916. The political dilemma of the Treaty is a difficult subject to deal with in song but a couple of ballads have succeeded reasonably well. *Mournful Lines on the Death of General Michael Collins*, includes the verse:

> For the Treaty he wrung from Lloyd George and his train
> He steadfastly pleaded in the Dail but in vain.
> De Valera and his diehards they forced the Civil War
> And Mick Collins was ambushed in lone *Beal na mBlath*.

The final verse of another ballad, *Michael Collins*, is:

Returning then to London town
Who will take the blame?
The Treaty lies before him,
Michael Collins adds his name.
There's a darker time upon the land,
Who will bear the load?
An awkward hero in an armoured car,
On an Irish country road.

The first civil war executions took place on 17 November 1922, a month after the Free State government introduced a Public Safety Bill allowing for internment and execution for possession of arms. The four victims, all young Dubliners who had been caught with guns, were made an example of. They were Peter Cassidy, James Fisher (age 18), John Gaffney and Richard Twohig, all shot in the yard in Kilmainham Gaol where the British had executed the leaders of the 1916 Rebellion.

Liam Lynch now issued an instruction to his men to shoot on sight all those who had voted for the introduction of the legislation. The events that followed illustrate well the particularly bitter nature of civil war. On 7 December 1922 Sean Hales, TD, who hadn't in fact voted for the legislation, was shot dead by republican gunmen. The following night, four senior republican prisoners, Rory O'Connor and Liam Mellows, commanders of the Four Courts garrison, were, along with Joseph McKelvey and Richard Barrett, taken from their cells and shot without trial by order of men who only a few months previously had been their friends and allies. One of the leading proponents of this hard-line policy was Kevin O'Higgins, the strong man of the Provisional Government. In happier times Rory O'Connor had been best man at his wedding. O'Higgins himself was to be murdered by republicans in 1927 as he walked to Mass one Sunday morning. Perhaps an even better example of the 'split' was within the Hales family itself. Tom Hales commanded the republican squad that killed Michael Collins while his brother Sean had commanded the Freestaters who had welcomed Collins to Bandon just an hour earlier.

Liam Lynch fought on until 10 April 1923, when he was killed in a gunfight with government forces in the Knockmealdown Mountains in County Tipperary. The Free Staters' iron fist policy proved highly effective and the anti-Treatyite militants, 'the IRA', shrank drastically and went underground. Lynch's successor, Frank Aiken (1898-1983) was more of a pragmatist and faced with the impossibility of achieving military victory, ordered his men to dump arms until a more opportune time. There had been over eighty executions during the period, including the four men commemorated as *The Drumboe Martyrs*.

These were Charles Daly (age 26), Daniel Enright, and Timothy O'
Sullivan (age 22) who were all from County Kerry and Sean Larkin (age 26)
from near Magherafelt in County Derry. The four republicans had found
themselves isolated in Free State County Donegal and paid dearly for their
continued resistance. The charge against them was possession of arms
and ammunition. The weaponry that was to cost them their lives consisted
of three rifles, one revolver, one 'German egg bomb', 300 rounds of .303
ammunition and 6 rounds of .45 ammunition.

The men had been arrested on 2 November 1922 at Dunlewy, between
Errigal Mountain and the fabled Poisoned Glen. The men were taken south
over the hills and held at Drumboe Castle, Stranorlar, HQ of the Free Staters
in the north-west. The site is signposted 'Drumboe Martyrs Site 1923' on
Drumboe Avenue on the right hand side of Stranorlar's main street if
approaching from Lifford /Strabane. It is less than a mile up this little road on
the right hand side, about a mile north east of where Drumboe Castle, once
stood. The castle belonged to the Hayes family, Anglo-Irish landowners. It
was demolished in 1945, when it became too expensive to maintain.

The men had been tried and sentenced to death on 18 January 1923 but
there was reluctance to proceed with the executions. They finally went
ahead, almost eight weeks later, after a Free State officer, twenty-four year
old Captain Bernard Cannon of Lettermacaward, west Donegal was killed at
Creeslough Barracks in north Donegal. On 12 March *The Derry Journal*
reported, 'on Saturday night a small party of Irregulars attacked the barracks
occupied by National troops and during the firing an officer of the National
Army was shot dead'. Others however claimed that the death was not
politically motivated but came about as the result of a 'drunken quarrel'.
Whatever the truth of the matter, in its wake the Drumboe executions went
ahead. There was also another related death. Hugh Gallagher, also captured
at Dunlewy, was shot dead in December 1922 when attempting to escape.

Charlie Daly was the senior figure of the Drumboe Martyrs, leader of
four brigades in Derry and Tyrone. He was an intelligent and articulate
man who in different circumstances would probably have achieved much.
A farmer's son, Daly was born into a staunch republican family in the
townland of Knockaneacoolten, in the parish of Kiltallagh, eight miles
south-east of Tralee. He was educated first at the local national school,
Ballyfinnane, and then with the Christian Brothers in Tralee, cycling there
and back every day.

He started out then as an idealistic and naïve young rebel, joining the
Irish Volunteers in 1914, aged seventeen. In 1916 he was standing by,
proudly clutching a Lee Enfield rifle, but like most volunteers outside of
Dublin, the Kerrymen obeyed Eoin MacNeill's countermanding order. In
1917 he was arrested by the RIC, beaten up and sentenced to two years

hard labour. In prison he was elected to Kerry County Council. For much of the time he was kept in solitary confinement and his eyesight and general health suffered. Gradually though he made a good recovery and in September 1920 the IRA sent him north to organise County Tyrone. By now he was on the run, widely recognised as a willing, able and trusted rebel with leadership qualities. The Black and Tans proclaimed that 'anybody sheltering Charlie Daly will have their houses burned and themselves hanged by the neck'. He was briefly interned and on his release again made his way north to take up where he had left off. On 9 May 1921 the Black and Tans carried out their threat and burned his family home 'as an act of reprisal'.

'After Truce and Treaty at the parting of the ways' his many letters home reveal 'what a heartbreak the Treaty and Split were'. Although Daly strongly opposed the Treaty and 'nothing but the international recognition of the Republic would satisfy him' he was surprisingly generous in his attitude to the Freestaters for he recognised their dilemma. Two weeks after the Treaty had been signed he wrote of Michael Collins 'tis a great pity that Mick Collins should be in such a position. He, nor the others, can be blamed for what they did, for the position they found themselves in was a dreadful one. If Mick only considered himself he would have no hesitation in refusing'.

Charlie Daly's final letters to his family and friends in the days and hours before his death show a man very much in control of himself with no regrets and no bitterness. Just a few hours before he died he wrote, 'I won't say much about worldly affairs, they look very insignificant now. My last message to you and all at home is not to worry about my death or its circumstances. Forget all about its physical and worldly aspect and look at it only from the spiritual and religious point of view. I am now within a few short hours of death and writing to you with perfect calmness. All I think of is Eternity and am ready to go out at 7 o'clock and face the firing squad with confidence and hope in God's great mercy for the salvation of my soul... I think that I will have the pleasure of answering Mass as I used, long ago in Kiltallagh... goodbye for a while'.

Like Charlie Daly, Sean Larkin, the son of a Magistrate and Justice of the Peace in Magherafelt, was born in 1896 and had a remarkably similar career. He too was a farmer's son, from the townland of Belagherty, in the parish of Ballinderry, in the south-east corner of County Derry, just a few miles from where Roddy McCorley was born. Then there was membership of the Irish Volunteers, stand-by duty in 1916, IRA membership, imprisonment, hunger strike and firm opposition to the Treaty. In November 1920 his father was arrested in error due to having the same name as his son. He expected to be released as soon as the mistake was discovered, but was instead held for four months. The prison experience was too much for the sixty-three year old and he died in April 1921.

Sean Larkin's final letters also show a man in a state of calm resignation to his fate. On reading them I was struck with the resemblance to the thinking of Thomas Russell in Downpatrick Jail 120 years earlier. Larkin wrote, 'I have nothing but praise for our treatment here from both officers and men and especially from the policemen who are in charge of us... I am happy and resigned to the Holy Will of God... dear mother, I will be praying for you that Almighty God may bring you all through this vale of tears and that we will all meet in the land that knows not care or sorrow... and there to sing the praises of Almighty God for all eternity... mother I die for a great and noble cause'.

The short life of Timothy O'Sullivan of Listowel also followed a similar pattern. He too joined the Volunteers and the IRA and spent time on the run. Once, he was badly beaten by Black and Tans named Raymond and Cahill, 'two names that need no introduction to the people of Listowel'.

The day before his death he wrote to a friend, 'Don't be a bit troubled about us as we couldn't be happier, our case is just and tomorrow morning we will meet our doom like men'. The same day he had written to his mother, 'We will have Mass on the morning and will receive Holy Communion... we will go to another land where trouble is unknown. God will judge us according to our works... everyone here is very kind to us and I forgive everyone that has anything to do with our execution'.

Daniel Enright wrote to his mother, 'Myself and Tim are in the best of form, also Charlie Daly and John Larkin... mother let you be brave and trust in God... I have five more hours to spend on old Ireland... we were never so happy... I will look down and pray for you and the lads'. To his brother he wrote, 'Well now my dear Jack, I have only a few more hours to stay. I will be in God's Kingdom at eight in the morning and praying for you and all my pals and for my poor country'.

The executions were by firing squad, by order of a Free State military court under General Joseph Sweeney, commander of the pro-Treaty forces in the area. Earlier in the year Sweeney had arranged a meeting with Daly in an attempt to avoid more bloodshed. According to Michael Hopkinson in his *Green Against Green*, 'Sweeney proposed that the southerners in Donegal should be allowed to leave with their arms, but Daly would not agree to prohibiting his men from serving in other parts of the Twenty-Six counties'. Even the fact that Charlie Daly's brother Tom was a member of the IRA's twenty-two man ruling body was not enough to save him.

The executions were carried out at dawn on 14 March 1923, three days prior to the 'Feast of St Patrick' stated in the song and created a terrible sense of shock in Donegal. Although the majority had not supported the republican cause, local people nevertheless felt guilt and responsibility. The deaths were seen, as the ballad puts it, as a 'stain on Tirconaill', and there was some violent local reaction. An arson attack destroyed Bonnyglen House at Inver, near Donegal Town. This belonged to the British Consulate General in Philadelphia. There were also attacks on the homes of a number of Free State supporters. The following year the men's bodies were disinterred and reburied close to their respective homes. The ceremony in Stranorlar was presided over by Mick McGinley.

Two monuments commemorate the victims of Drumboe, both traditional-style Irish crosses. The first is the Memorial Cross at the burial site, already referred to. The second is on Main Street, Stranorlar, at the entrance to Drumboe Avenue, where the inscription is in Irish only. The first inscription reads:

> In proud and glorious memory of the Drumboe martyrs
> Comdt. Gen. Charles Daly, Brig.-Comdt. Sean Larkin,
> Lieut. Daniel Enright and Lieut. Timothy O'Sullivan
> Who gave their lives in the defence of the Irish Republic
> At this spot on the 14th March 1923

The executions are still commemorated every Easter. Over the decades the main speakers have included such well-known republicans as Peadar O'Donnell (1926), Sean Russell (1933), Maurice Twomey (1934), Brian O'Higgins (1936 – 'shots fired by C.I.D. over crowd at gates'), Maud Gonne (1939), Hugh McAteer (1951), Eamon MacThomas (1963), Martin Meehan (1972) and David O'Connell (1976). In 1937, 1963 and 1964 it was recorded, 'Easter lilies seized by police'.

To mark the 50th Anniversary in 1973 Eamonn Monaghan of Mountcharles composed a second commemorative song, *The Green Woods of Drumboe*, the first verse of which is as follows:

> Near the town of old Stranorlar
> Where the quiet Finn does flow
> There's a lonely grave still open
> In the green woods of Drumboe
> And there each Easter Sunday
> They gather proud and sad
> Where four faithful Irish soldiers
> Fell before the firing squad.

Recently as I stood in the field where these four men were prepared to lay down their lives for a cause, I found the experience to be an eerie and emotional one. Of all the historical sites that I visited this one made the greatest impression on me. I was born only a few miles away and I wondered if I had been born fifty years earlier might my own name have been carved on that cross. Normal country life continued all around, oblivious to the fact that something terrible had once happened here. It is indeed a truism that no death ever stopped the world.

The place name of Drumboe is derived from *druim both*, 'ridge of the hut'. Drumboe Upper and Drumboe Lower are both townlands, just north of Stranorlar. Tirconaill or Tyrconnell (*Tír Chonnaill*), 'Conall's land' is the ancient Irish name for Donegal and has long since fallen into disuse. The origin of the name 'Foyle' is uncertain, but is thought to mean either 'the lip' – from the mouth of Lough Foyle at Magilligan Point – or from the personal name *Feabhal*, one of the *Tuatha de Danaan* people. Swilly (*Suileach*), 'clear seeing' or 'of the eye' is probably another river/lough name with supernatural connotations. Locally however, it's usually called 'the lake of shadows'.

Loughs Foyle and Swilly surround Inishowen, the 'great peninsula of the north'. Most of the Peninsula is in County Donegal and the Republic but a small part, from Derry to the Border at Bridge End and Muff, is in County Derry and Great Britain. The River Finn flows through Stranorlar to meet with the 'sweet Mourne waters' at Lifford/Strabane. The origin of Finn is thought to derive from *An Fhinn*, the name of the goddess believed to inhabit the River in mythical times. This is also the setting for that light-hearted old rebel song *Johnson's Motor Car*: 'you could hear the din going through Glen Finn of Johnson's motor car'. The Finn and the Mourne combine to form the River Foyle, which continues rolling through countryside for fourteen miles to Derry, forming the border as it goes. The River Roe flows off the Sperrin Mountains past Dungiven and into Lough Foyle beyond Limavady.

A few miles away in Inishowen stands the three thousand-year-old fort, the *Grianan of Aileach*, where the preaching of Saint Patrick sowed the seeds of the faith, a version of which was to sustain the Drumboe Martyrs some fifteen hundred years later. From here the ancient High Kings reigned over Ulster.

It seems that in Ireland history never rests and its evidence is never very far away. Around every bend in the road are its reminders, ancient and modern, great and small. In this remote part of Donegal one such reminder stands on one green hill, where the ultimate sacrifice of four young men made a small contribution to the troubled history of the small island where they were born.

21.

Sean South of Garryowen

It was on a dreary New Year's eve as the shades of night came down,
A lorry load of volunteers approached a Border town.
There were men from Dublin and from Cork, Fermanagh and Tyrone,
But the leader was a Limerick man, Sean South of Garryowen.

And as they moved along the street up to the barracks door,
They scorned the dangers they would meet, the fate that lay in store.
They were fighting for old Ireland's cause, to claim their very own
And the foremost of that gallant band, Sean South of Garryowen.

But the sergeant spoiled their daring plan, he spied them through the door,
Then the sten guns and the rifles soon, a hail of death did pour
And when that awful night was past, two men lay cold as stone,
One from near the Border and one from Garryowen.

No more he'll hear the seagulls cry o'er the murmuring Shannon tide
For he fell beneath a Northern sky, O'Hanlon by his side.
He had gone to join that gallant band of Plunkett, Pearse and Tone,
A martyr for old Ireland, Sean South of Garryowen.

Sean South (1928-1957)

Courtesy Mainchín Seoighe

Sean South of Garryowen
The Shades of Night Came Down

This powerful and emotional ballad tells the story of the death of IRA volunteer Sean South, a committed young 'patriot' from Limerick City. South was steeped in the gospel of romantic republicanism, which led him to his fate during an attack on a police station in Brookeborough, County Fermanagh on New Year's Day 1957. *Sean South* has proved itself by becoming established as one of the most popular in the whole nationalist canon of song. No one with any hue of nationalism in his or her veins can fail to be moved by it. The song has made Sean South, the man, one of the best known republicans since the 1920s and Sean South, the symbol, comparable with the republican heroes of the final verse, 'that gallant band of Plunkett, Pearse and Tone'.

The song is set to the same melody as *Roddy McCorley,* and it would seem likely that the composer had *Roddy* very much in mind when he wrote *Sean South,* for many lines from the two songs could almost be interchangeable.

The ballad must have been composed almost as soon as the Brookeborough raid hit the headlines as it appeared in the *Irish Catholic* on 10 January 1957. Little is known publicly about the composer other than his name, Sean Costello, that he also came from Limerick and that he died in 1991. It is unlikely that as he hurriedly scribbled down the lyrics, he could ever have imagined that he would achieve such success. Ironically, as the song is seldom credited to him, it is unlikely that he would have received much income from the dozens of recordings and thousands of performances of his anonymous hit, past, present and to come.

Sean South presses many of the most emotional buttons in the nationalist psyche. The very crux of the perceived problem, 'the Border' is introduced in the second line. In addition we have drama, disaster and death all served with pathos piled on by the use of phrases like 'hail of death', 'awful night', 'cold as stone' and almost the whole of the last verse. The repeated use of the evocative names 'Sean South' and 'Garryowen' also make a powerful contribution to the impact of the song. (Strangely though the name 'South' is a very uncommon one in Ireland. Only six are listed in the phone book for the whole country).

Sean South has also been the subject of a number of other songs. Probably the best known is *Sean South of Limerick* by Dominic Behan, the final verse of which is:

> Was it in vain his life blood drained
> Far from his hills and valleys
> No! we cry, he didn't die,
> But lives for all eternity.

In addition, an interesting 'final verse' for Costello's song was written by Pat McManus, a volunteer who also participated in the IRA campaign which cost Sean South his life. The verse takes on extra poignancy as McManus died in a premature explosion in County Cavan in 1958.

> May God be with those noble hearts,
> May Heaven be their home.
> They never feared the RUC
> Or B-Specials on patrol.
>
> In Brookeborough town they were shot down,
> In a cabin they lay cold,
> O'Hanlon from old Monaghan town,
> Sean South of Garryowen.

The historical characters referred to in *Sean South* – Plunkett, Pearse and Tone – are all republican icons, with the latter two probably jointly topping the all-time list of the 'patriot dead'. Joseph Mary Plunkett (1887-1916) was a poet who became a leading figure in the Easter Rebellion of 1916. As a key member of the Irish Volunteers he had accompanied Sir Roger Casement to Germany in 1915 in search of revolutionary arms. He was a signatory of the Proclamation of the Irish Republic and was executed by a British firing squad. About four hours previously he had married his fiancée Grace Gifford in Kilmainham Jail, inspiring Sean O'Meara's popular ballad *Grace* (1985).

Patrick Henry Pearse (1879-1916), the official commander of the 1916 Rising, was also a poet and also a signatory, and the chief composer, of the Proclamation. Pearse is widely regarded as the most mystical of all the republicans. He was steeped in ancient Irish literature and imagery, his philosophy succinctly summarized by a verse from 16th century poet Aonghus mac Dáire Ó Dalaigh, which Pearse translated,

> Better to be on the mountain tops, keeping watch, short of sleep yet glad,
> urging fight against the foreign soldiery that hold our fathers land.

Pearse's motto, taken from Ulster mythology, was 'I care not were I to live but one day and one night, if only my name and my deeds live after me'. He had the courage of his convictions and lived out his philosophy to the end, for though he was executed by the British, his name and deeds will live for as long as Ireland. Today opinion on Pearse is divided and he tends to be viewed either as a dangerous 'blood sacrifice' fanatic or as a noble, cultured, tolerant and sensitive man who became the ultimate patriot.

Theobald Wolfe Tone (1763-98) is widely regarded as the 'father' of Irish republicanism. He was the outspoken Protestant champion of Catholic civil and political rights and occupies a special place in republican history and mythology. He did not participate directly in the 1798 Uprising as he had been banished to America in 1795. After his arrest on his return to Ireland in September 1798, he committed suicide in prison by cutting his throat after being refused what he saw as an honourable soldier's death by firing squad. His brother Matthew was also executed for his part in the rebellion.

Sean South outlines in reasonably accurate detail the abortive attack on Brookeborough Royal Ulster Constabulary barracks on the evening of New Year's Day 1957 during which another IRA man, Feargal O'Hanlon, was also killed. The raid was part of the IRA's border campaign or *Operation Harvest,* which lasted intermittently from 1956 to 1962. Although there were hundreds of incidents and eighteen deaths, twelve republican and six RUC, the campaign achieved little militarily or politically. It had little public support and the volunteers who took part, though self-sacrificing as individuals, had little experience, few military skills and very little political education or experience.

Where did these young men spring from who were prepared to risk everything and to kill or be killed for a political ideal? Quite simply they were the product of that deep-rooted, fanatically determined, uncompromising strand in the Irish character, created by history and culture, and which exists on both sides of the political, religious and cultural divide. The adherents of this philosophy see politics in terms of black and white, right and wrong, us and them, all or nothing. They subscribe to the 'if you're not with us you're against us' school of thought.

By the time that those involved in the Brookeborough raid took up arms the IRA had been inactive and almost defunct for over a decade. After their defeat in the Civil War the IRA never recognised the legality of the Free State government, at least theoretically. They tried to continue the struggle as best they could and though they were reduced to virtual impotence, they convinced themselves that eventually their day would come. They saw themselves as the true conscience of the Irish people, the only legitimate, non-traitorous heirs to the heroes of the Easter Rising. Regarding partition, a question they often asked was, 'Is this what they fought and died for?'

In 1936 the IRA was declared illegal in the Free State. In the North, the

Special Powers Act was made permanent. With the outbreak of the Second World War the Free State faced the possibility of invasion by both Britain and Germany and the last thing it needed was an internal threat from the IRA. The decision was therefore taken to clamp down hard and draconian legislation, including internment, was introduced on 4 January 1940.

Two leading IRA men of the period were Frank Ryan (1902-44) and Sean Russell (1893-1940). Seeing little opportunity at home Ryan, from Knocklong, led over two hundred Irish volunteers in the Spanish Civil War (1936-39). In 1938 he was captured by the fascists and sentenced to death. After a plea from the Irish government the sentence was commuted to thirty years imprisonment. Ironically the man who had gone to Europe to fight fascism was eventually freed into German custody in 1940 and died of tuberculosis in Dresden in 1944 never having seen Ireland again. Many years later his remains were repatriated and interred in Glasnevin Cemetery, Dublin.

Sean Russell, from Fairview in Dublin, was a cradle-to-grave republican who had fought in the 1916 Rising and was a member of Collins squad in 1920. By the late 30s he was IRA Chief of Staff and a vigorous proponent of a bombing campaign in Britain. The campaign, from 1939 through 1940, was to achieve nothing tangible, though inevitably it would have helped the IRA keep its ideals on the political agenda. It cost seven innocent people their lives, with the worst outrage in Coventry on 25 August 1939 when five people, including an eighty-one year old man and a fifteen year old boy, died in an explosion. Two IRA men, Peter Barnes of Banagher and James McCormick (alias Frank Richards) of Mullingar were executed on 7 February 1940 for their part in the attack. The bomb either exploded prematurely or was a deliberate attempt to kill and maim by a 'psychopath' who was still alive in the 1980s. Whatever the truth of the matter it was no consolation to those killed and injured in the blast. Barnes and McCormick were not the actual bombers and their execution caused considerable disquiet in Ireland. They faced their own deaths with courage and dignity, with McCormick stating simply 'I am a soldier of the Irish Republican Army'. Both men are commemorated in the angry republican ballad *Tribute to Barnes and McCormick*, also in *England's Gallows Tree* by Brian O'Higgins. Sean Russell died on board a German submarine on his way back to Ireland in 1940. Initially it was accepted that he had died of natural causes but many now suspect that he was poisoned, either by the Nazis or by a rival faction with the IRA itself.

In 1942 two related incidents, one in Belfast, one in Dublin, typified the sort of hit and run tactics employed by the IRA. They resulted in the deaths of two policemen, the hanging of two IRA men, the writing of yet more republican songs and in a controversy that was not finally laid to rest until 19 January 2000.

In Belfast Thomas Joseph Williams became the only republican of modern times to be executed in the North. It all started fairly innocently, if that can ever be said of anyone who goes out with a gun in his hand. The IRA had been banned from commemorating the Easter Rising and Tom Williams and five others, one of whom was Joe Cahill, volunteered to stage a diversion. In Kashmir Road they fired a couple of shots over the top of a police car and then intended to disappear into the side streets. However the RUC weren't in on the plan. They returned fire, a gunfight developed and Constable Patrick Murphy was killed, leaving behind a widow and nine children. The wounded Tom Williams was captured, hanged on 2 September 1942 and buried within the grounds of Crumlin Road prison. His family conducted a long-running campaign to have his body returned to them. They were finally successful when his remains were exhumed in August 1999. On 18 January 2000 they were taken to a service in Saint Paul's church and, in a grave long reserved for them, reburied the following day in Milltown Cemetery.

Tom Williams was aged eighteen at the time of the incident, nineteen when executed. Appropriately one of the commemorative songs is entitled *A Boy Called Williams.*

> Tommy Williams, we salute you and we never will forget
> Those who planned your brutal murder, we will make them yet regret
> That sad September morn when Ireland's cross was proudly borne
> By a lad who lies in a Belfast prison grave.

Two days before Tom Williams' execution, the IRA suffered another blow when nineteen-year-old Gerard O'Callaghan was shot dead by police at an arms dump in a disused quarry at Hannahstown, in the hills outside Andersonstown in Belfast. It's thought that the weaponry there was being moved in readiness for use in a revenge attack for Williams' death.

Reacting to Williams's execution, the IRA ordered twenty-five year-old Maurice O'Neill, Officer in Charge in Cahersiveen, County Kerry, to move north to take part in a retaliatory strike on the border. However before he could act he was disturbed by the Special Branch, along with the legendary Harry White, a plumber from Belfast, the real quarry, at a 'safe' house in Holly Road, North Dublin. On a trip to Dublin earlier this year I went to have a look at the scene and managed to speak to a neighbour, now an elderly woman, who has lived in the street all her life. She clearly remembered the incident, the shooting, the police cars, the sirens, etc saying that the owners of the house 'had a lot of bother at the time' and moved away shortly afterwards. She then offered to give me the family's new address so that I could go and speak to them! However researching IRA history, even after sixty years, remains sensitive and I politely declined.

When shots were fired, Detective George Mordant, 'a Free State man from 1922', fell dead in Oak Road. The wounded White somehow managed to escape through back gardens and lanes, survive a sixteen foot drop over a wall aand remain hidden in railway embankment undergrowth for two days before making it safely to the city centre on a corporation bus. He was to spend the next three and a half years on the run, staying in safe houses north and south of the Border, earning a few pounds playing banjo with the Magnet Dance Band, before finally being re-arrested in Derry in October 1945. The RUC, aware that he was wanted for the Mordant death, handed him over to Dublin where he was sentenced to death. However in the changing post-war political climate, and with skilful defence by Sean MacBride, the sentence was commuted to twelve years imprisonment. Ironically his trial and appeal provided the by now almost-moribund IRA with some badly needed public profile. White was released in 1948 when MacBride's new republican party Clann na Poblachta became part of a coalition government.

Maurice O'Neill had been arrested at Holly Road and was hanged on 12 November 1942. The balance of opinion is that O'Neill didn't fire the fatal shot, it being either White or the Special Branch themselves, who had not adhered to their own code of conduct regarding warnings. However in the political atmosphere of the times such mere legal quibbling carried no weight and the IRA had another martyr, and another ballad, *Maurice O'Neill*, written by Brian O'Higgins.

> It rings through the mountains of Kerry, from Tarbert to Cahirsiveen
> And awakens proud memories of valour, in the fights of the days that have been
> And now through the green fields of Ireland it sweeps with a loud welling peal,
> A cry full of anger and sorrow, 'They have murdered young Maurice O'Neill'.

Both Williams and O'Neill went to their deaths philosophically and without regrets, Tom Williams saying: 'I am quite resigned if it is God's Holy Will and if it is done for Ireland', and Maurice O'Neill writing: 'It is the full penalty for me... well, such are the fortunes of war'.

Other IRA casualties in this era included Tony Darcy, from Headford, Galway and Sean McNeela, from Ballycroy, Mayo, both of whom died on hunger strike in Dublin in 1940. Following a shoot-out in Rathgar Road, Dublin, Thomas Harte of Lurgan and Paddy McGrath of Dublin were executed in Mountjoy Jail, also in 1940. In Port Laoise Jail, Richard Goss of Dundalk was executed for armed robbery in 1941. In 1942 George Plant of Tipperary was executed for his alleged part in the death of an informer. In Belfast, Seamus 'Rocky' Burns died in a gun battle with the RUC in February 1944. On 1 December 1944 Charlie Kerins of Tralee became the 33rd and final IRA victim of the period when he was hanged in Dublin. As IRA historian J. Bowyer Bell has written, 'for the first time in generations the line had been broken. There was no longer a Chief of Staff or a GHQ or an Army Council or even an IRA... [it] had become an anachronism for most Irishmen.'

The most striking thing about these men, all practising Catholics (with the exception of George Plant, who was a Protestant) and otherwise law-abiding and decent citizens, was their absolute, unquestioning belief in the legitimacy of their cause. They felt justified and indeed duty-bound to take up arms and to subordinate everything else in their lives 'for Granuaile', Ireland. By the end of the Second World War the IRA may have looked spent as an active force. However as before, a new generation of young men emerged ready to do or die for a thirty-two county republic. Among the new volunteers were Sean South and Feargal O'Hanlon.

The raid on unionist Brookeborough was in fact led by Sean Garland (Dublin), not as in the ballad and as reported in the Limerick press by Sean South. Second in command was David O'Connell (Cork) who was to achieve national prominence in the 1970s as one of the IRA leaders involved in negotiations with British Prime Minister Harold Wilson and Secretary of State William Whitelaw.

The 'lorry load of volunteers' comprised twelve men, most of whom were in the rear of a quarry truck which had been 'liberated' earlier. The names of the participants have been published in *Saoirse*, the organ of Republican Sinn Féin. In addition to South, O'Hanlon, Garland and O'Connell, the group, known as the Padraig Pearse Flying Column, was completed by Vince Conlon (Armagh), Pat Connolly (Fermanagh), Phil Danagher (Dublin), Harry Gonagh (Wexford), Michael Kelly (Galway), Liam Nolan (Dublin), Paddy O'Regan (Dublin), Sean Scott (Galway) and Pat Tierney (Fermanagh). It is interesting to note that, geographically, the group had representatives from all four provinces. At the beginning of 2001 they were all were still alive except for Gonagh and O'Connell.

Their gunfire aimed at the barracks had little impact, two mines that they placed failed to explode, and a home-made grenade rebounded and rolled under the lorry. A few minutes later it exploded, blowing the lorry's occupants onto the street. Meanwhile from an upstairs window RUC Sergeant Kenneth Cordner was raking the truck with Bren gun fire, wounding at least six of the attackers. With any hopes of gaining entry to the building now gone and the lorry, their only means of escape, rapidly being immobilised, its tyres shot out and its oil pipe and windscreen shattered, they decided to retreat as best they could.

The driver, Vince Conlon, who had returned from America to take part in the campaign, couldn't see where he was going. The windscreen was smashed with a rifle butt and the truck limped south towards the border on a minor road in the direction of Roslea, around ten miles away. About half way there it was decided to abandon the crippled vehicle as it presented an exposed target for the RUC men who were giving chase some ten minutes behind. South and O'Hanlon were seriously wounded and had lost consciousness, so the agonising decision was taken to leave them behind. The lorry halted at a roadside farmhouse, which proved to be empty. Time was of the essence and the two dying men were left in an adjacent barn, which at least provided basic shelter in the dead of winter. Neighbours were told to get a doctor and a priest. The wounded Sean Garland volunteered to stay with his dying comrades and create a delaying diversion to give the others a better chance of reaching the border. Eventually he was dissuaded from this and took to the hills with his men. The highest point in the area is Doocarn Mountain, which rises to 1034 feet.

The fugitives managed to elude massive security for about five hours to make it across the border somewhere between Clones and Monaghan town, where they sheltered for a while in a friendly house. The wounded continued to a Dublin hospital from which they managed to 'escape' after treatment. According to J. Bowyer Bell, each of the Brookeborough survivors was later imprisoned in Dublin for six months for refusing to account for their movements during the period of the raid. South and O'Hanlon died of their wounds shortly afterwards. Initially, it was suspected that they had been killed by the RUC as they lay wounded but this theory is now usually discounted on technical grounds.

Although the ballad describes Sean South as being from Garryowen (*Garrai Eoghain*), 'Owen's Garden', a district of Limerick City, he was in fact born and raised at 47 Henry Street in the city centre. In many ways he was an admirable young man, a musician, an artist, a writer and an orator. One obituary described him as 'shy, gentle-natured, even-tempered, a man above the ordinary, possessing fine qualities of mind, and character'. However as his letters to his local newspaper in 1949 reveal, he was also an 'old fashioned', narrow-minded McCarthyite, who railed against 'reds', 'atheists' and 'Judaeo-Masonic controlled sources'. South was far from being unique in these views, which largely reflected the Ireland of the 1930s in which he grew up: conservative, insular, poorly educated and heavily censored.

South was a member of the Gaelic League and when possible always spoke and wrote in Irish. The month before he died he had written, 'the time for talk is over'. He was born on 8 February 1928 and was therefore twenty-eight when he died. He had worked in the office of a local timber company and was planning the announcement of his engagement to a local girl, a teacher in Limerick. After his death South's widowed mother revealed that he often disappeared for weeks at a time. He had been a member of the IRA since 1954 and had left on his final mission 'a month before Christmas', with his family knowing nothing of his whereabouts until contacted by the police. His two brothers went north to bring the body home.

Feargal O'Hanlon, from nearby Monaghan, had written in his diary the previous Easter, 'I know no way by which freedom can be obtained... except by armed men' (a quote from Patrick Pearse). His beliefs were to cost him his life and a career full of talent and promise. Although aged only twenty, he had already played senior football for County Monaghan. However the strongest influence in his life was his inherited republicanism and having made the same choice as his mentor Pearse he was to meet a similar fate and to achieve a similar, though lesser, 'immortality'. 'Brave O'Hanlon' is featured in Dominic Behan's classic song *The Patriot Game*. He is also commemorated in a less well-known song *Feargal O'Hanlon*.

> Oh hark to the tale of young Feargal O'Hanlon
> Who died in Brookeborough to make Ireland free,
> For his heart he had pledged to the cause of his country
> And he took to the hills like a bold rapparee.

In military terms the Brookeborough raid had been a complete failure yet it enjoys a hallowed place in the republican imagination and mythology with both the young men who died in it becoming overnight heroes. Thousands followed Sean South's cortege on its long journey home through Dundalk, Dublin, Port Laoise and Roscrea. Thousands more lined the streets of Limerick as offices, shops and factories closed as a mark of respect. The *Limerick Chronicle* reported 'a scene quite without parallel was witnessed in Limerick last night when the remains of Sean South... reached the City after a journey from Dublin which lasted nine and a half hours'. Another reported under the headline 'The Passing of an Intensely Patriotic Limerick Man'. An estimated fifty thousand people lined the streets. The cortege stretched for five miles. To this day an annual commemorative service is held at the Republican Plot in Mount St Lawrence Cemetery in Limerick where Sean South is buried.

Today the barn in Fermanagh where he and Feargal O'Hanlon died has disappeared. However one Sunday morning in Brookeborough I was given directions to the location near the crossroads in the townland of Altawark. Over the years, the spot became a place of pilgrimage and a small shrine was erected. However, according to *Saoirse*, this was 'levelled by the British Army during the 1980s'. On the 40th anniversary, a much grander monument was constructed, built from the stones of the barn where the men died. It is inscribed:

This monument was erected in memory of
Volunteer Feargal O'Hanlon (Monaghan)
And
Volunteer Sean South (Limerick)
Who died at this spot on 1 January 1957
After an engagement with British forces at
Brookeborough County Fermanagh

I stood in contemplation for a few moments, for on this little country road lay more than the ghosts of two 20th century rapparees. This was as close as it was now possible to get to a man and a song that I had first encountered as a boy in the 1950s, to the sad reality of two young men who became ensnared in and destroyed by the complexities of Irish history. I didn't therefore see the monument as the republican shrine it was intended to be. For me it was a memorial to *all* those who have suffered and died in the various Troubles, on both sides, before, since and yet to come.

It was raining heavily. Hurriedly I took a few photographs and drove off through the morning mist.

A Select Bibliography

Bardon, Jonathan. *A History of Ulster*, Blackstaff Press, 1992.

Bartlett, Thomas (Editor). *Life of Theobald Wolfe Tone, Compiled and arranged by William Theobald Wolfe Tone*, Lilliput Press, 1998.

Barton, Brian. *From Behind a Closed Door: secret court martial records of the 1916 Easter Rising*, Blackstaff Press, 2002.

Behan, Dominic. *Ireland Sings: an anthology of modern and ancient Irish songs and ballads*, Essex Music, 1965.

Bell, J. Bowyer. *The Secret Army: the IRA*, Poolbeg Press, 3rd edition, 1997.

Bennett, Richard. *The Black and Tans*, Barnes and Noble, 1959.

Binions, Gloria Hurley (Compiler). *Rathnure and Killanne: A Local History*, 1997.

Byrne, Miles. *Memoirs*, 3 volumes, 1863.

Carroll, Denis. *The Man From God Knows Where: Thomas Russell 1767-1803*, Gartan, 1995.

Cashman, Denis B. *Fenian Diary: Denis B. Cashman on board the Hougoumont*, Edited by C.W. Sullivan III, Wolfhound Press, 2001.

Clarke, Austin (Editor). *The Poems of Joseph Campbell*, Allen Figgis, 1963.

Clarke, Kathleen. *Revolutionary Woman: My Fight for Ireland's Freedom*, O'Brien, 1991.

Colman, Anne Ulry. *Dictionary of Nineteenth-Century Irish Women Poets*, Kenny's Bookshop, Galway, 1996.

Connolly, S.J. (Editor). *The Oxford Companion to Irish History*, Oxford University Press, 1998.

Coogan, Tim Pat. *The IRA*, Harper Collins, 1995.

Devlin, Cronan, (Editor). *1798: A Union of Wills? Proceedings of Scoil Shliabh gCuillinn 1997*, Ti Chulainn [Mullaghbawn], 1998.

Dickson, Charles. *Revolt in the North: Antrim and Down in 1798*, Constable, 1997. (First published 1960.)

Dickson, Charles. *The Wexford Rising in 1798: its Causes and its Course*, Constable, 1997. (First published 1955.)

Dillon, Martin. *25 years of Terror: The IRA's War Against the British*, Bantam, 1996.

Doherty, Richard. *The Williamite War in Ireland, 1688-1691*, Four Courts Press, 1998.

Dorian, Hugh. *The Outer Edge of Ulster: a memoir of social life in nineteenth-century Donegal*, Lilliput Press, 2000.

Doyle, Geraldine and others. *Boolavogue 1798-1998: A Compilation of Articles Relating to the United Irishmen's Rebellion of 1798 and the Commemoration of that Event Down Through the Years*, Tobin Printers (Enniscorthy), 1998.

Dunford, Stephen. *The Irish Highwaymen*, Merlin, 2000.

Edwards, Ruth Dudley. *James Connolly*, Gill and Macmillan, 1998.

Edwards, Ruth Dudley. *Patrick Pearse: the Triumph of Failure*, Gollancz, 1977.

Fay, Anne. *Roddy McCorley: a study of evidence*, NEELB [Ballymena] [1989]

Flanagan, Deirdre and Laurence. *Irish Place Names*, Gill and Macmillan, 1994.

Foy, Michael and Barton, Brian. *The Easter Rising*, Sutton Publishing, 1999.

French, Noel E. *Battle of the Boyne 1690*, Trymme Press, 1989.

Furlong, Nicholas. *Fr. John Murphy of Boolavogue 1753-1798*, Geography Publications, 1991.

Gahan, Daniel. *The People's Rising: Wexford, 1798*, Gill and Macmillan, 1995.

Galvin, Patrick. *Irish Songs of Resistance (1169-1923)*, Oak Publications, (N.Y.), 1962.

Golway, Terry. *Irish Rebel: John Devoy and America's Fight for Irish Freedom*, St. Martin's Griffin, (New York), 1998.

Graney, Brian. 'East Clare's Calvary [the story of the "Scarriff Martyrs"]'. In *Vexilla Regis — the Annual of the Maynooth Laymen*, edited by Henry O'Mara. Dublin. 1953.

Greaves, C. Desmond. *The Life and Times of James Connolly*, Lawrence and Wishart, 1961.

Haddick-Flynn, Kevin. *Orangeism: The Making of a Tradition*, Wolfhound Press, 1999.

Hammond, David. *Songs of Belfast*, Mercier Press, 1978.

Hanvey, Bobbie (Editor). *Lilliburlero! And More Songs of the Orange Tradition*, The Ulster Society (Lurgan), Volume 2, 1988.

Hanvey, Bobbie (Editor). *The Orange Lark and Other Songs of the Orange Tradition*, The Ulster Society (Lurgan), 2nd Edition, 1985.

Harnden, Toby. *'Bandit Country': the IRA and South Armagh*, Hodder and Stoughton, 1999.

Hart, Peter. *The I.R.A. and Its Enemies: Violence and Community in Cork, 1916-23*, Clarendon Press, 1998.

Herlihy, Jim. *The Royal Irish Constabulary: A Short History and Genealogical Guide: with a select list of medal awards and casualties*, Four Courts Press, 1997.

Hill, Myrtle and others (Editors). *1798 Rebellion in County Down*, Colourpoint, (Newtonards), 1998.

Hopkinson, Michael. *Green Against Green: The Irish Civil War*, Gill and Macmillan, 1988.

Hughes, Herbert [Padraig mac Aodh o Neill] and Joseph Campbell [Seosamh mac Cathmhaoil]. *Songs of Uladh*, Belfast, 1904. (The book was published only under the Irish forms of both authors' names. However the English forms are probably more accessible for readers today.)

Hyde, Douglas. *A Literary History of Ireland: from earliest times to the present day*, Ernest Benn, 1967 (First published 1899).

Kee, Robert. *The Green Flag; a History of Irish Nationalism*, Penguin, 1972.

Kemmy, Jim (Editor). *The Limerick Anthology*, Gill and Macmillan, 1996.

Keneally, Thomas. *The Great Shame: A Story of the Irish in the Old World and the New*, Chatto and Windus, 1998.

Kennelly, Brendan (Editor). *The Penguin Book of Irish Verse*, Penguin, 2nd edition, 1981.

Kenny, Michael. *The Fenians: photographs and memorabilia from the National Museum of Ireland*, The National Museum of Ireland, 1994.

Kinsella, Thomas (Editor and Translator). *The New Oxford Book of Irish Verse*, Oxford University Press, 1986.

Latimer, W.T. *Ulster Biographies Relating to the Rebellion of 1798*, Presbyterian Historical Society of Ireland (Belfast), 1897.

Lyttle, W.G. *Betsy Gray, or, Hearts of Down — With other stories and pictures of '98 as collected and published by the "Mourne Observer"* [based on the research of Colin Johnston Robb]., Mourne Observer, Newcastle, Co. Down, 1968 (First published 1888).

Macatasney, Gerard. *'This Dreadful Visitation': the Famine in Lurgan/Portadown*, Beyond the Pale Publications, 1997.

McCoy, Jack. *Ulster's Joan of Arc: An Examination of the Betsy Gray Story*, North Down Borough Council Heritage Centre, Bangor, 1987.

McDermott, Jim. *Northern Divisions: the Old IRA and the Belfast Pogroms, 1920-22*, Beyond the Pale Publications, 2001.

McDonald, Henry. *Trimble*, Bloomsbury, 2000.

MacEoin, Uinseann. *The IRA in the Twilight Years, 1923-48*, Argenta Publications, 1997.

McFarland, Jim and Jimmy McBride. *My Parents Reared Me Tenderly and other traditional songs sung in Inishowen*, 1985.

McGuffin, John. *In Praise of Poteen*, Appletree, 1999.

McKay, Patrick. *A Dictionary of Ulster place-names*, Institute of Irish Studies, Queen's University of Belfast, 1999

MacLysaght, Edward. *Irish Families: Their Names, Arms and Origins*, Irish Academic Press, 4th edition, 1985.

MacLysaght, Edward. *The Surnames of Ireland*, Irish Academic Press, 6th edition, 1997.

McNeill, Mary. *The Life and Times of Mary Ann McCracken 1770-1886: A Belfast Panorama*, Blackstaff Press, 1960.

McVeigh, Jim. *Executed: Tom Williams and the IRA*, with foreword by Joe Cahill, Beyond the Pale Publications, 1999.

Madden, R[ichard] R[obert]. *The United Irishmen: Their Lives and Times*, Dublin, 1843-46.

Maguire, W.A. (Editor) *Up in Arms: The 1798 Rebellion in Ireland - A Bicentenary Exhibition*, The Ulster Museum, 1998.

Meehan, Helen. *Ethna Carbery: Anna Johnston McManus* [sic], Donegal Annual, 1994.

Meehan, Helen. *The McManus [sic] Brothers: Patrick, 1864-1929: Seamus, 1868-1960*, Donegal Annual, 1994

Miller, Kerby A. *Emigrants and Exiles: Ireland and the Irish Exodus to North America*, Oxford University Press, 1985.

Murphy, Jeremiah. *When Youth Was Mine: a Memoir of Kerry 1902-1925*, Mentor Press, 1998.

Newmann, Kate. *Dictionary of Ulster Biography*, The Institute of Irish Studies, Queen's University, 1993.

Nolan, William and others (Editors). *Donegal: History and Society*, Geography Publications (Dublin). 1995.

O Corrain, Donnchadh and Maguire, Fidelma. *Irish Names*, Lilliput Press, 1990.

O'Dwyer, Martin. *A Biographical Dictionary of Tipperary*, Folk Village, Cashel, 1999

O'Farrell, Padraic. *Who's Who in the Irish War of Independence and Civil War*, Lilliput Press, 1997.

O Lochlainn, Colm. *The Complete Irish Street Ballads*, Pan Books, 1978.

O Tuama, Sean and Kinsella, Thomas. *An Duanaire 1600-1900: Poems of the Dispossessed*, Dolmen Press, 1981.

Poirteir, Cathal (Editor). *The Great Irish Famine*, Mercier Press, 1995

Porter, Norman. *Rethinking Unionism: An Alternative Vision for Northern Ireland*, Blackstaff Press, 1996.

Room, Adrian. *A Dictionary of Irish Place-Names*, Appletree Press, Revised Edition. 1994.

Ryder, Chris. *The RUC 1922-2000: A Force Under Fire*, Arrow, 2000.

Sands, Bobby. *Prison Poems*, Sinn Féin (Dublin), no date.

Saunders, Norah and Kelly, A. *Joseph Campbell: Poet and Nationalist*, 1988.

Stewart, A.T.Q. *The Summer Soldiers: the 1798 Rebellion in Antrim and Down*, Blackstaff Press, 1995.

Story of the Drumboe Martyrs [Anonymous]. Published in Letterkenny [1958]. (Reference copy available from Donegal County Library.)

Toolis, Kevin. *Rebel Hearts: Journeys Within the IRA's Soul*, Picador ,1995.

Welch, Robert, (Editor). *The Oxford Companion to Irish Literature*, Clarendon Press, 1996.

Wilson, Florence M. *The Coming of the Earls and Other Verse*, The Candle Press, Dublin, 1918.

Wilsdon, Bill. *The Sites of the 1798 Rising in Antrim and Down*, Blackstaff Press, 1997.

Woodham-Smith, Cecil. *The Great Hunger: Ireland 1845-1849*, Penguin, 1962.

Younger, Calton. *Ireland's Civil War*, Frederick Mueller, 1968.

Zimmerman, Georges-Denis. *Songs of Irish Rebellion: Irish Political Street Ballads and Rebel Songs*, Four Courts Press, 2002 (originally published 1967)

A Select 'Discography'

In this section brief details are given of a recorded version of each song quoted in the text. The 'discography' itself forms part of my personal musical 'journey' and all of the albums referred to are from my own collection. I hope therefore that readers will tolerate some personal and even some self-indulgent remarks.

'A Boy Called Williams'. Artist: Anonymous. Album: '26 Irish Rebel Songs Volume 2' (various artists). Label: Derry Records (Belfast), 1997.

Comment: Other relevant songs include 'Brave Tom Williams' (or simply 'Tom Williams'), 'The Ballad of Tom Williams' and 'A Soldier of Ireland' (tune: 'The Blue Hills of Antrim', lyrics by Brian O'Higgins, '*Brian na Banba*', 1882-1949).

'A Nation Once Again'. Artist: The Irish Tenors. Album: 'Ellis Island'. Label: Radius/TV Matters, 2001. (Also available on video.)

Comment: Numerous other recordings available. Nowadays the majority are on 'rebel' compilations and are not difficult to find.

'A Rebel Song'. Artist: Jimmy Kelly. Album: 'Songs of Irish Labour' (various artists). Label: Bread and Roses Productions, 1998. (Recorded at Dublin City University.)

Comment: Lyrics only by James Connolly, music by Gerald Crawford. Album available from Dr. Helena Sheehan, Dublin City University, Dublin 9. E-mail: breadandroses2@eircom.net
Website: http://www.comms.dcu.ie/sheehanh/lsongs.htm

'Bagenal Harvey's Lament'. Artist: Sean Garvey. Album: *'On dTalamh Amach* - Out of the Ground - Songs and Music from the Irish Tradition'. Label: Harry Stottle Records, no date given, c. 2000.
Comment: This is the only recorded version of the song traced. The album contains the definitive version of 'The Boys of Barr na Sraide'. Garvey is a native of Cahersiveen in Kerry, of which 'barr na sraide' was the 'high, or top, street'. He was a personal friend of the song's author, Edward 'Sigerson' Clifford (1913-85).

'Ballad of Redmond O'Hanlon '
Comment: No recording traced. Written by P.J. McCall in 1899. Five verses are on the Internet.

'Ballyneety's Walls'. Artist: Na Casaidigh. Album: '1691'. Label: Gael-Linn, 1992.
Comment: An outstanding album, much of it instrumental, a must for anyone interested in the political song in Irish history.

'Banna Strand'. Artist: The Grehan Sisters. Album: 'Irish Folk Favourites [volume] 4.' (arious artists). Label: Castle Communications, 1991.
Comment: Recorded in the 1960s, as 'Lonely Banna Strand' on the Transatlantic label.

'Bard of Armagh'. Artist: John McCormack. Album: 'John McCormack in Irish Song'. Label: Pavilion Records, 1988.
Comment: Recorded in 1920. Other well-known recordings are those of Joseph Locke, and the Clancy Brothers and Tommy Makem.

'Battle of Ballycohey'
Comment: No recording traced. The song consists of eleven verses from a broadside in Cambridge University Library. Printed by Zimmermann, 1967. See Bibliography for details of this essential book.

'Battle of Garvagh'. Artist: Anonymous. Album: 'No Surrender! – 14 Great Loyalist Songs'. Label: Ulster Records (Belfast), 1995.
Comment: Sixteen verses given in 'Lilliburlero! Volume 2' (see Bibliography).

'Bold Black and Tan'
Comment: No recording traced. Six verses published by Patrick Galvin (see Bibliography).

'Bold Fenian Men'. Artist: Patrick Galvin. Album: 'Irish Songs of Resistance Part II'. Label: Topic, 1960s.
Comment: Considering the quality of this song, it's surprising how recording artists have overlooked it in recent decades. My lyrics are from the 1960s recording by Scottish folksinger Josh McCrae, if memory serves. I prefer his 'field glasses' to Scanlan's original 'blessed steel'. I also recall that the song was then titled 'Song of the Irish Republican Brotherhood' which, if correct, would avoid confusion with Peadar Kearney's 'Bold Fenian Men' (Down by the Glenside). No currently available recording traced, though inevitably there will be one somewhere.

'Boolavogue'
Comment: Numerous recording available. The song has now achieved 'respectability' through the recent version by the Irish Tenors with full orchestral backing.

'Boys of Kilmichael'. Album: The same as 'A Boy Called Williams' above. Learned from an early 1960s LP by Willie Brady, recorded then as 'The Irish Republican Army'.

'Boys of Mullaghbawn'. Artist: Christy Moore. Album: 'Christy Moore'. (Often referred to as 'The Black Album' but not to be confused with Planxty's first album 'Planxty', 1973, also called 'The Black Album'.) Label: Polydor, 1976.

Comment: Another excellent version is by the Alias Acoustic Band on their double album 'Irish Songs of Rebellion, Resistance & Reconciliation 1798-1998' in 1998. This group includes such top folk musicians as Ron Kavana and 'Chopper' of the Oyster Band. Traditional, non-commercial recordings are also held by the *Tí Chulainn* Cultural Activity Centre in Mullaghbawn itself.

'Brennan on the Moor'
Comment: Numerous recordings available, including the 1998 version by the Alias Acoustic Band. First learned in the 1960s from a Clancy Brothers and Tommy Makem LP.

'Come to the Bower'. Artist: The Dubliners. Album: 'The Collection Volume 2'. Label: Castle Communications, 1990.
Comment: Recorded 1966, Luke Kelly on vocals.

'Connolly Was There'. Album: The same as 'A Boy Called Williams' above.

'Derry's Walls'. Album: The same as 'Battle of Garvagh' above.

'Dolly's Brae'. Album: The same as 'Battle of Garvagh' above.

'Dolly's Brae No More'
Comment: No recording traced. Lyrics on the Internet.

'Drumboe Martyrs'. Artist: Wolfhound. Album: '50 Best Irish Rebel Ballads, Volume 1' (various artists). Label. Derry Records, 1998.
Comment: This is the only recorded version that I have found. The lyrics were included, with a couple of factual inaccuracies, in O'Lochlainn, as 'The Woods of Drumboe', also by Galvin as 'Drumboe Castle'. See Bibliography entries for both authors plus under 'Story of the Drumboe Martyrs', which also gives the lyrics. These three titles are out of print but the first two are often available second-hand. A copy of the third is held by Donegal County Libraries.

'Erin Go Bragh'. Artist: Declan Hunt. Album: '50 (Complete) Irish Rebel Ballads, Volume 1' (various artists). Label: Derry Records, 1998.
Comment: Not as widely available as might be imagined.

'Factory Girl'. Artist: Margaret Barry. Album: 'I Sang Through the Fairs'. Label: Rounder Records, 1998.
Comment: Also available on Barry's joint album with Sligo fiddler Michael Gorman, 'Her mantle so Green', recorded 1955, released 1994. Also recorded by Sarah Makem in 1952, re-released on a 1995 compilation 'Traditional Songs of Ireland', 26 tracks, on the Saydisc label, with contributions from numerous traditional artists including the McPeake Family and Seamus Ennis, all recorded by Peter Kennedy, 1952-61.

'Feargal O'Hanlon'. Album: The same as 'A Boy Called Williams' above.

'Fenians of Cahersiveen'. Artist: The Johnstons. Album: 'The Barleycorn'. Label: Transatlantic, 1969. (Re-released on double CD along with the Johnstons' first album 'The Johnstons' (1968).
Comment: Recorded as the 'Fenians from Caherciveen'.

'Gartan Mother's Lullaby'. Artist: Mary O'Hara. Album: 'Down by the Glenside: Songs of Ireland'. Label: Tradition, 1997 (recorded 1960).
Comment: Also recorded by Barbara Mullen (of 'Doctor Finlay's Casebook' fame) in 1941, available on various compilation albums.

'General Monro'. Artist: Declan Hunt. Album: 'Wolfe Tone – Rebel Songs of 1798 Rising' (various artists). Label: Outlet (Belfast), 1998.
Comment: Recorded as 'General Munro'. The definitive version is by Andy Irvine,

included on his collaborative album with Donal Lunny 'The High Kings of Tara' (1980), now difficult if not impossible to obtain. A recent version by Richard Gilpin on his album 'Beautiful Mistake' also comes highly recommended.

'Green Grassy Slopes of the Boyne'. Album: The same as 'Battle of Garvagh' above.
Comment: Included on countless other loyalist compilations.

'The Hackler from Grouse Hall '. Album: 'Christy Moore'.
Comment: The same as 'Boys of Mullaghbawn' above.

'Henry Joy'. Artist: Grehan Sisters. Album: 'The Irish Folk Collection – 60 Favourite Irish Songs (Disc 1)', (3 CD Boxed Set – various artists). Label: Kaz Records, 1995.
Comment: Recorded in the 1960s. There are numerous versions of the song on various 'rebel' compilations.

'Hiring Fairs of Ulster'
Comment: No recording traced. Six verses, words and music, published in O'Lochlainn (see Bibliography).

'Jackson and Jane'. Artist: Five Hand Reel. Album: 'Earl O' Moray'. Label: RCA, 1978.
Comment: The only recording of this excellent traditional ballad traced. No longer available but well worth seeking through second-hand outlets. The album also includes an outstanding version of Hamish Henderson's socialist masterpiece 'Freedom Come All Ye', vocals by Dick Gaughan.

'James Connolly' (1) ('A great crowd had gathered outside of Kilmainham...'). Artist: The Fighting Men of Crossmaglen. Album: '50 Complete Irish Rebel Songs'. Label: Outlet (Belfast), undated, late 1990s.
Comment: Numerous other recordings available.

'James Connolly' (2) ('Where oh where is our James Connolly...?'). Artist: Christy Moore. Album: 'Prosperous'. Label: Tara, 1972.
Comment: In his book *One Voice: My Life in Song* (2000) Moore attributes the song to Patrick Galvin, though Galvin himself makes no claim to it in his own book! Numerous other versions are available.

'James Connolly' (3) ('Marching down O'Connell Street with the starry plough on high...') Artist: Black 47. Album: 'Fire of Freedom'. Label: EMI, 1993.

'John Mitchel'. Artist: Terry O'Neill. Album: 'Festival of Irish Folk Music – A Definitive Collection, Volume 1' (various artists). Label: Outlet 1998.
Comment: Also available on 'A Rebel's Heart' by Terence O'Neill and Cormac O'Moore, an album containing some other seldom-heard 'rebel' songs.

'Kelly the Boy from Killanne'. Artist: The Dubliners. Album: 'Original Dubliners' (Double CD). Label: EMI, 1993.
Comment: Originally released in 1967, Luke Kelly on vocals. Inaccurately spelt as 'Killan'. Numerous other recordings available.

'Lament for Dudley Costello'
Comment: No recording traced. Words and music given by Dunford (see Bibliography). 'Lilliburlero'. Album: The same as 'Ballyneety's Walls' above. Instrumental version only. Also on numerous loyalist compilations. No vocal recording of the song traced.

'Man from God Knows Where'. Artist: Five Hand Reel. Album: 'A Bunch of Fives'. Label: Topic, 1979.
Comment: No longer available and according to the record company, there are no present plans to reissue. Tommy Makem recorded a recitation on his album 'Ancient Pulsing – Poetry with Music', Red Biddy Records, 1996.

'Maurice O'Neill '. Album: The same as 'A Boy Called Williams' above.

Comment: Written by Brian O'Higgins (1882-1949) who gave the air as 'Fineen the Rover'. O'Higgins wrote countless rebel songs, including 'The Soldiers of '22', 'Victoria' and 'The Boy from Tralee' (about Charlie Kerins, executed in Dublin, 1 December 1944).

'Memory of the Dead'. Artist: Dermot O'Brien. Album: The same as 'Drumboe Martyrs' above.

'Michael Collins'. Artist: Anonymous. Album: 'Patriotic Names: Songs of Tribute to Historical Irish Patriots', double CD. Label: Derry Records, 1997
Comment: This is a different song from one of the same name by Derek Warfield. The album includes little-known songs such as 'Michael Davitt', 'John Mitchel', 'O'Donovan Rossa', 'Cathal Brugha', and 'Charlie Cairns', a misspelling of Charlie Kerins – 'The Boy from Tralee.'

'Minstrel Boy'. Artist: John McCormack. Album: 'Prima Voce – Arias – Recitals – Songs'. Label: Nimbus Records, 1993.
Comment: Recorded in 1910. Countless other recordings available. Notable versions include those by James W. Flannery, tenor – accompanied on Irish Harp by Janet Harbison. This is on a double CD of Thomas Moore's best songs and included with the book *Dear Harp of My Country* (1997). Look out also for the Irish Tenors version, and a 'punk' one by Shane MacGowan on his 'That Woman's Got Me Drinking' (1994).

'My Lagan Love'. Artist: John McCormack. Album: The same as 'Bard of Armagh' above.
Comment: Margaret Barry's typically distinctive version is included on her albums 'Her Mantle So Green' and 'I Sang Through the Fairs'.

'Outlaw Rapparee'. Artist: Wolfhound. Album: The same as 'Drumboe Martyrs' above.

'Portadown' ('The Drowning of the Protestants from the Bridge over the Bann')
Comment: No recorded version traced. The full song, seven verses, is given in *Lilliburlero! Volume 2*, edited by Bobbie Hanvey (see Bibliography).

'Rising of the Moon'. Artist: The Dubliners. Album: The same as 'Kelly the Boy from Killanne' above.
Comment: Recorded in 1967, Luke Kelly on vocals. Numerous other recordings are available.

'Roddy McCorley'. Artist: The Dubliners. Album: The same as 'Come to the Bower' above.
Comment: Recorded in 1960s, Ciaran Bourke on vocals. Numerous other recordings available notably Shane MacGowan's 'alternative' version on 'That Woman's Got Me Drinking'.

'Rody McCorley'. Comment: No recording traced. Full lyrics given by O'Lochlainn (see Bibliography).

'Scarriff Martyrs'. Artist: Christy Moore. Album: The same as 'Boys of Mullaghbawn' above.
Comment: This is the only recording traced, though others will almost certainly exist.

'Sean South of Garryowen'
Comment: Numerous recordings available on countless 'rebel' compilations. Although now dated stylistically, my favourite version remains the first that I ever heard, by Enoch Kent on the album 'Irish Rebel Songs', Decca – Ace of Clubs, 1963, with Diarmuid O'Neill and Patrick O'Malley. Long since deleted but occasionally available second-hand.

'Sergeant's Lamentation'
Comment: No recorded version traced. Full lyrics given by O'Lochlainn (see Bibliography).

'Siege of Derry'
Comment: No recorded version traced. Lyrics on Internet.

'Skibbereen'. Artist: Joe Heaney (Seosamh Ó hEanai). Album: 'The Road From Connemara - Songs and Stories told and sung to Ewan MacColl and Peggy Seeger' (Double CD). Label: Topic, 2000.
Comment: Heaney's version is quite different from the usual, both lyrically and melodically, but, typically, is quite mesmerising. Numerous other recordings are available. Learned from Bridie Gallagher's 'Old Skibbereen' in 1962.

'Smashing of the Van' (or 'The Manchester Martyrs')
Comment: Learned in the 1960s from the 'Irish Rebel Songs' album (details above under 'Sean South of Garryowen'), sung by Enoch Kent. Also included in Patrick Galvin's *Irish Songs of Resistance*. This album also includes the hauntingly beautiful traditional ballad ' The Fair of Turloughmore', about a fatal incident in 1843. The lyrics of both songs are given by O'Lochlainn, the latter as 'The Sorrowful Lament for Callaghan, Greally and Mullen – Killed at the Fair of Turloughmore' (see Bibliography). In all these years I have found no other recordings of either of these fine traditional songs. Patrick O'Malley's version of 'Roddy McCorley' on the record is, interestingly, spelt and pronounced as 'Rody'.

'Tipperary So Far Away' (or 'Sean Treacy'). Artist: Wolfhound. Album: The same as 'Drumboe Martyrs' above.
Comment: Recorded versions are fairly scarce.

'Watchword of Labour'. Artist: Joe Deasy. Album: The same as for 'A Rebel Song' above.

'West's Awake'. Comment: Numerous recordings available, mostly on 'rebel' compilations.

'Wexford Massacre'. Artist: The Grehan Sisters. Album: 'Irish Folk Favourites, Disc 3' (4 CD Boxed set – various artists). Label: Castle Communications, 1991.
Comment: Recorded in the 1960s, this is the only recording traced but it is enough, powerful and passionate. The lyrics were first published in the *Nation* in the 1840s. They are also given by Galvin (see Bibliography).

'Woodlands of Lough Glynn'. Artist: Brendan Shine. Album: 'I'll Settle for Old Ireland'. Label: Hallmark, 1996.
Comment: Also on some 'rebel' compilations.

Sources of Lyrics

Song enthusiasts are always curious about where the lyrics of published songs originate. Here I give some brief notes on the main sources of the lyrics printed in *One Green Hill*. Details of all books referred to will be found in the Bibliography and this section should therefore be read in conjunction with the Bibliography, and the Discography.

'Outlaw Rapparee' – My lyrics are an amalgam of the Wolfhound recording and as printed in Danny Doyle and Terence Folan's book *The Gold Sun of Irish Freedom: 1798 in song and story* (1998).

'Derry's Walls' – Taken from various Orange songbooks and various recordings, as well from the internet. I have made a few minor edits.

'The Green Grassy Slopes of the Boyne' – Based mainly on Bobbie Hanvey's songbook, The Orange Lark (1987), with some variations from other sources.

'The Bard of Armagh' –An amalgam of various sources, too numerous to list. There is no generally accepted definitive version of the song of which I am aware. The authority for the song being based on the life of Doctor Patrick Donnelly was initially Bardon's *A History of Ulster*. Since then I have seen further local references to this in County Armagh itself.

'**The Boys of Mullaghbawn**' – Again, a mixture of numerous sources, though I have stayed fairly true to the first version of the song that I ever heard, the recording by Christy Moore (1976). It is also given in O'Lochlainn's *More Irish Street Ballads*. I have also heard a traditional version of the song sung in Mullaghbawn itself, which refers to the local place name of 'Killeavy', rather than 'Erin', and I have opted for this as it is more interesting and more likely to be the original.

'**Kelly the Boy from Killanne**' – This is the standard, popular version, culled from numerous sources. I have been very careful to spell the place name as 'Killanne' (not 'Killan') as this is the form used in Killanne itself and in County Wexford generally.

'**Henry Joy**' – Although there are countless versions of this song, the variations are all fairly negligible. I have made a few minor edits.

'**General Monro**' – This too is an amalgam from numerous sources, mainly Oxford University's Bodleian Library via the internet and the very interesting version published in the 19th century by Robert M. Young in *Ulster in '98: Episodes and Anecdotes*. Young took this version from 'a collection of printed ballads by Dr. R.R. Madden'. See the main text for details of Colin Johnston Robb's version of the lyrics and his remarks regarding authorship of the song.

'**Roddy McCorley**' – This is Ethna Carbery's original version from 1902, taken from *The Four Winds of Eirinn*. I have however opted for the modern spelling 'Roddy' rather than the original 'Rody'.

'**The Man from God Knows Where**' – This is Florence Wilson's original from 1918, taken from her poetry collection *The Return of the Earls*.

'**The West's Awake**' – This is the evolved popular, modern version, culled from various sources.

'**Dolly's Brae**' – A selection of verses from Bobbie Hanvey's published version.

'**Skibbereen**' – This is mostly the standard popular version. I have made a few minor edits.

'**The Bold Fenian Men**' – Based on Patrick Galvin's published version.

'**The Hackler from Grouse Hall**' – Taken mainly from the version in O'Lochlainn's *Irish Street Ballads*. His note states that he got the song from John Smith, Stravicnabo, Ballyjamesduff.

'**My Lagan Love**' – This is Joseph Campbell's original version from 1904, including the now seldom sung second and forth verses.

'**James Connolly**' – A distillation from sources too numerous to list.

'**The Scarriff Martyrs**' – My starting point was the 1976 recording by Christy Moore. I have since checked that version against printed ones held by libraries in County Clare. I found no major variations but I have made some minor edits.

'**The Drumboe Martyrs**' – This version is taken from *The Story of the Drumboe Martyrs* and is almost certainly the definitive one.

'**Sean South of Garryowen**' – This is the original version. It is taken from Jim Kemmy's published version, taken in turn from the *Irish Catholic* 10 January 1957, where and when the song was first published.